The Last Days
of the Romanovs

H. I. M. NICHOLAS II, EMPEROR OF RUSSIA

The Last Days of the Romanovs
The Murder of the Tsar & the Russian Royal Family, 1918

George Gustav Telberg and Robert Wilton

LEONAUR

The Last Days of the Romanovs
The Murder of the Tsar & the Russian Royal Family, 1918
by George Gustav Telberg and Robert Wilton

First published under the title
The Last Days of the Romanovs

Leonaur is an imprint of Oakpast Ltd

ISBN: 978-1-78282-080-2 (hardcover)
ISBN: 978-1-78282-081-9 (softcover)

http://www.leonaur.com

Publisher's Notes

Contents

Publisher's Note

During the night between the 16th and 17th of July, 1918, the former Russian Emperor Nicholas II, his family, as well as all the persons attached to it, were murdered by the order of the Yekaterinburg Soviet of workmen's deputies. The news of this crime broke through the closed ring that surrounded Bolshevist Russia and spread over the entire world.

At the end of July, 1918, the town of Yekaterinburg was taken from the Bolsheviks by the forces of the Siberian Government. Shortly after their occupation of the district an investigation was ordered to be made of the circumstances attendant on the murder. A judicial examination therefore took place of the witnesses connected with the life of the imperial family at Czarskoe-Selo, Tobolsk and Yekaterinburg by N. A. Sokoloff, the Investigating Magistrate for cases of Special Importance of the Omsk Tribunal.

Upon the fall of the Kolchak *régime*, copies of the depositions were taken from the archives by M. George Gustav Telberg, Professor of Law at the University of Saratov and Minister of Justice at Omsk, when he fled with the other ministers of the Omsk government. These combined statements reconstruct the life-story of the imperial family from the time of the emperor's abdication until the murder of himself, his wife, his children, including the *czarevitch*, and their few faithful servants in Ipatieff's house at Yekaterinburg,

The translator has endeavoured to preserve the original simplicity, and in some cases the crudeness and lack of education apparent in the witnesses. Colonel Kobylinsky, M, Gilliard and Mr. Gibbes are educated men who apparently gave their evidence without displaying any outward emotion, but, though they did not exaggerate the sufferings of the imperial family, they were not eyewitnesses of the final hours of their captivity.

The testimony of the soldiers strikes a more sinister note. Two of them witnessed most of the daily happenings at Ipatieff's house, but they display certain evidences of pity and of having been well-disposed towards the prisoners whose murder they condemned. Indeed these men are most insistent that the crime was committed by the "Letts." The third soldier (Medvedeff) took an active part in the murder.

The narrative of Mr. Robert Wilton which supplements the translations of the official records is, we think, a document of incalculable value. Written by a man who for sixteen years was correspondent for the London *Times* in Russia, and who not only speaks Russian but was present throughout the investigation of the scene of the murder and during the search for the relics, his story has a poignancy and an intrinsic value that cannot be overestimated.

It is proper here to explain to the reader that the contents of this volume as represented by the Official Depositions in part 1 and Mr. Robert Wilton's narrative in Part 2 came into existence quite independently and without the design, originally, of publishing them together. Mr. Wilton, who escaped from Siberia after the fall of the Kolchak Government, took with him one of three copies of the *dossier* of the official investigation. Upon this original source he based his story, adding to it certain facts which he had personally gathered. By a most fortunate circumstance, George H. Doran Company, who were preparing for the press the depositions secured by M. George Gustav Telberg, learned of Mr. Wilton's narrative, and arrangements were immediately made to combine the records in one volume.

As the two parts of the book are from different sources, no effort has been made to secure uniformity in certain minor variations in the spellings of proper names. The index in Part 3 adopts the spelling used by Mr. Wilton, but the reader will readily recognize the same persons and places in Mr. Telberg's translation in Part 1.

It will be seen by comparing the two parts that, so far as the depositions here published go, they entirely bear out and give, so to speak, chapter and verse for Mr. Wilton's narrative; and we have every reason for stating that, if and when the rest of the *dossier* becomes public, similar affirmation will be given to the whole of his thrilling story, which presents clearly, succinctly, a full and absolutely authentic account of this great human tragedy—the greatest perhaps of all time.

Depositions of Eyewitnesses

1
EXAMINATION OF M. GILLIARD

(*M. Gilliard was attached to the imperial household in the capacity of French tutor to the grand duchesses and the czarevitch. He was with the family at Czarskoe-Selo at the outbreak of the revolution, and like most of the other members of the household, he elected to remain under arrest. M. Gilliard especially mentions the emperor's love for his country and his bitterness of heart after the Treaty of Brest-Litovsk, and he insists that the attitude of the emperor and the empress towards Germany was one of hatred and contempt.*

M. Gilliard's deposition is important inasmuch as it includes a conversation which he had with Tchemodouroff in the latter part of August, 1918. Tchemodouroff then believed that the imperial family had not been murdered, but had been removed to an unknown destination. M. Gilliard did not, however, place much reliance in this statement. He describes his visit to Ipatieff's house and relates a curious superstition of the empress, who seems to have placed credence in the efficacy of two Egyptian symbols as luck-bringers.—Original editor's note.)

On March 5, 1919, the Investigating Magistrate for cases of special importance of the Omsk District Court, in conformity with Paragraph 443 of the Criminal Code Procedure, questioned the man named below in the capacity of a witness, notifying him that during the investigation he might be interrogated under oath.

Replying to the questions that were put to him, the witness gave his name as: Peter Andreievitch Gilliard, and said:

Since 1905 I have been giving French lessons to the daughters of his majesty. From 1912 I began to teach French to the Grand Duke Alexis. I started my instructions in Spala, but very shortly afterwards they were interrupted, as the grand duke met with an accident. I heard about it from other people who were attached to the emperor's family.

I heard that the Grand Duke Alexis, while swimming in a pool, fell and hurt his stomach. The result of this accident caused his foot to be temporarily paralysed. He was ill a very long time, consequently all studies were interrupted. They were, however, resumed in 1913, at the time when I became assistant tutor to the grand duke.

After that I moved to the palace, where I occupied the rooms next to the *czarevitch*. In 1913 we went to Crimea and later came to Czarskoe-Selo. In the spring of 1913 we went to Crimea, Constance and Finland. From Finland we returned to Peterhoff, in order to meet the President of France, M. Poincaré. It was in Peterhoff that the imperial family resided at the beginning of the war.

In 1915 we lived at Czarskoe-Selo up to the time when the emperor assumed supreme command of the army. During this time I often went with the *czarevitch* to the *Stavka* (general army headquarters), to the front, and generally to every place that the emperor took his son.

At the outbreak of the revolution the emperor was at the Stavka and his family lived in Czarskoe-Selo. The imperial family passed through many alarming moments during this period. All the children had the measles. At first the *czarevitch* got it and later all the grand duchesses in succession. Everybody was worried by the uncertainty of the situation and ignorance of the fate of the emperor. There was unrest amongst the Guards Rifles quartered in Czarskoe-Selo. One night was particularly alarming. Fortunately the commotion amongst the soldiers was calmed down by the officers.

The emperor's abdication in behalf of the *czarevitch* was learned of by the imperial family from the general in command of the Svodny guard regiment. Later the Grand Duke Dmitry Pavlovitch came to the palace and officially announced to her majesty the news of the abdication of the emperor.

General Korniloff also came to the palace and informed the empress that she must consider herself under arrest. After General Korniloff's arrival her majesty instructed me to say that everyone must leave the palace except those who would like to stay of their own free will, and who would consequently have to submit to the routine of those who were arrested. Nearly everybody elected to stay in the palace, and so did I. During this time the Grand Duchess Maria Nicholaevna was taken ill with inflammation of the lungs. After some time the emperor arrived at Czarskoe-Selo.

The restrictions imposed upon the imperial family consisted of a certain limitation of their freedom. The palace was surrounded by sentries. They were allowed to leave the palace to walk in the park only during a fixed time and always accompanied by a sentry. All the mail went through the hands of the commandant of the palace. Kotsebue was the first commandant. He was replaced by Korovitchenko and the latter was replaced by Kobylinsky who was formerly in command of the garrison.

Kerensky came to Czarskoe-Selo on several occasions. He visited us in the capacity of the head of the new government to observe the conditions of our life. His manners and attitude towards the emperor were cold and official. His behaviour towards him gave me the impression of the treatment of the accused by a judge who is convinced of his guilt. It looked as if Kerensky believed the emperor was guilty of something and therefore treated him coldly. Nevertheless, I must state that Kerensky was always perfectly correct in his manner. When addressing the emperor he called him His Majesty, Nicholas Alexandrovitch. At the same time I must say that during this period Kerensky, as well as everybody else, avoided calling the emperor by his name, as though it were embarrassing to them to address him as Nicholas Alexandrovitch.

On one occasion Kerensky arrived at the palace in the company of Korovitchenko and Kobylinsky and confiscated all the emperor's private papers. It seemed to me that after Kerensky was through with those papers, he understood that the emperor had done no wrong to his country and he immediately changed his attitude and manners towards him.

During the stay of the imperial family in Czarskoe-Selo several disagreeable incidents took place. The first was the confiscation of a toy rifle from the *czarevitch*, which was done on the request of the soldiers. The second incident was the refusal of the soldiers to answer the emperor's greeting. The emperor always addressed the soldiers with words of greeting. After the abdication the soldiers used to answer: "*Sdrávstvouyte Gospodín Polkóvnik*" (Good-day, Colonel). On one occasion, after being addressed by the emperor, the soldiers remained silent. It appears, however, that this took place not on account of their own decision but by orders of some assistant commandant of the palace, whose name I do not remember.

There were days when the imperial family had to wait a considerable time in the semicircular hall where everybody used to assemble before taking the walk in the park. It was always the guards who were late and who kept everybody else waiting.

However, all these incidents were mere trifles in comparison to the sufferings that were later inflicted on the imperial family.

In the middle of July it became known, I cannot tell how, that the emperor and imperial family had to change their residence from Czarskoe-Selo to some other place. At first it was rumoured that it was to be a voyage to the south, but later it transpired that we were to proceed to Tobolsk.

The reason that we had to move was due to the fears of the government for the safety of the imperial family. During this time the government intended to take a firm course in handling the affairs of the nation. At the same time it feared that such a policy would create some outburst amongst the population which would have to be checked by armed force. Thinking that in the course of the struggle we might also be injured, the government made up its mind to send the imperial family to a quieter place than the vicinity of Petrograd. All this I relate to you from the words of her majesty, who was informed through Kerensky, as to the decision of the government.

I remember that the following persons moved to Tobolsk with the imperial family: Prince Dolgoruky, M. Tatischeff, Dr. Botkin, Miss Schneider and myself. Later we were joined in Tobolsk by Derevenko, Mr Gibbes and Baroness Buxhoevden, who volunteered to stay with the imperial family.

The imperial family was placed in Tobolsk in the house of the governor. I lived with the imperial family. All the other people were placed in a house belonging to M. Korniloff, opposite the governor's house. The life in Tobolsk was very much as it had been in Czarskoe-Selo. The same restrictions were imposed.

Our guards were composed of soldiers who were formerly in the Czarskoe-Selo sharpshooter regiments. Kobylinsky was, as previously, the *commandant* of the house. We were accompanied during our journey to Tobolsk by representatives of the government, Makaroff and Vershinin (the latter being a member of the *Duma*). They spent a few days in Tobolsk and then departed. Their attitude towards the imperial family was quite correct, and even kindly disposed—this was particularly true of Makaroff, and especially so in his manner towards the children.

In the middle of October there arrived one Pankratoff, a commissar of the government, accompanied by his assistant, Nikolsky. They were to supervise our life and Kobylinsky was subordinate to them.

These two men did not wilfully interfere with the welfare of the imperial family, but a great deal of harm was done by them unknowingly by their behaviour towards the guards and they demoralised the morale of the soldiers.

As far as we could judge, being prisoners, the inhabitants of Tobolsk were well disposed towards the imperial family. Now and then they sent us *bon bons*, cakes and various sweets. When they passed by the house and noticed any members of the imperial family, they bowed.

The Rifles, who composed our guards, were *en masse* rather benevolent. There were some good men among the soldiers, but some of them were very bad. Until the Bolshevist revolution the latter kept quiet.

The Bolsheviki brought misfortune to the imperial family as well as to the whole of Russia. The Bolshevist revolution immediately reflected on the minds of the soldiers and those that were bad and evilly disposed became rough in their ways.

On January 25th the soldiers turned out Pankratoff and Nikolsky and made up their minds to ask for a Bolshevik *commissar* from Moscow. The soldiers forbade the Baroness Buxhoevden to live in Korniloff's house.

The worst came after the Brest-Litovsk treaty. The soldiers began to behave in a disgraceful manner. On one occasion the *czarevitch* noticed on the board of the swing on which the grand duchesses liked to pass the time, some inscriptions. He did not have time to read them. When the emperor noticed them he asked Dolgoruky to remove the board. Vulgar, disgraceful, cynical and stupid words were cut on this board by soldiers' bayonets.

The imperial family was forbidden by the soldiers to visit church. They were allowed to go to church only on *Dvounadesiaty* holidays (very important feast-days in the Orthodox religion) . The soldiers insisted that the emperor should remove the shoulder straps from his uniform. Twice he refused, but finally, after Kobylinsky informed the emperor that his refusal might result in serious trouble for himself and his family, the emperor had to submit to this demand.

A little hill was made in the garden for the amusement of the children. Once the emperor and the empress viewed from the top of this small hill the departure of a large number of the soldiers (at that time many soldiers left on account of the demobilisation of the army); but afterward the remaining soldiers levelled the hill to the ground.

Things became worse and worse. It was especially severe after all sources of revenue were confiscated from the imperial family. This occurred on February 12th. That day a wire from Moscow was received. I cannot tell you who sent it. In this wire a new order of life for the imperial family was prescribed. Up to this time the imperial family had been maintained by the government treasury. Their life was quite appropriate and fitting for them and ran along in the same way that the former emperor and his family had been accustomed to.

By the order of the Bolshevist authorities, lodging, heating and lighting were to be provided for the imperial family, everything else had to be obtained at the expense of the family or of those persons connected with them. We were also restricted in earning of money. I wanted to earn some by giving private lessons in the town, but the soldiers would not allow me to do so, and told me I was to leave the house altogether in the event that I could not adapt myself to conditions as they were.

By Bolshevist orders the imperial family could not spend for themselves and their servants more than four thousand, two hundred *roubles* per month. This state of affairs affected life very detrimentally. Coffee, butter and cream disappeared from the table. Scarcity of sugar was felt very seriously, as sugar was distributed in the quantity of half a pound per person for each month. Dinner consisted of two courses, and for those who were accustomed from the time of their birth to entirely different conditions of life, it was far more difficult to bear the situation than it was for those who were not familiar with the luxuries that the imperial family had always enjoyed.

The lack of resources and the necessity of economising made it impossible to continue to pay the church chorus for their singing during the divine services held at home. The church choristers volunteered to sing free of charge. After that a small fee was still paid to them.

The number of servants was considerably reduced and ten of their staff were discharged.

Finally the attitude of the soldiers became so menacing that Kobylinsky, after losing all hope of retaining or regaining control, declared to the emperor that he desired to resign from his present position. The emperor asked him to stay, and Kobylinsky yielded to his request.

In order to make life a little more cheerful, playlets were staged, in which the children took an active part. The emperor tried to find forgetfulness in physical labour. He sawed wood with Tatischeff and Dolgoruky, the daughters or myself. He also attended to the lessons of the *czarevitch* and personally instructed him in history and geography.

But all the efforts made by the emperor to conceal his feelings could not hide from any observant person his terrible sufferings. Especially after the Brest-Litovsk peace treaty a very marked change was noticed in him that indicated his mood and mental suffering. I could say that his majesty was affected by this treaty with an overwhelming grief.

During this time the emperor on several occasions spoke of politics to me—a thing he had never allowed himself to do before. It seemed as if his soul was yearning for the companionship of another soul, hoping by such companionship to find relief from the intensity of his grief. I could not relate everything he told me, but the central idea of his words and thoughts was that up to the moment of the Brest-Litovsk treaty he believed in the future prosperity of Russia—after that treaty he lost all faith.

During this time he criticised Kerensky and Goutchkoff in sharp terms, considering them to be the most guilty for the collapse of the army. The emperor thought that by their weakness and incapacity the army disintegrated, and the result was that it opened the way for the Germans to corrupt Russia. He regarded the Treaty of Brest-Litovsk as a disgrace and as treason on the part of Russia towards her Allies. He said: "And those who dared to accuse her majesty of treason have in the end turned out to be the real traitors."

The emperor looked upon Lenin and Trotzky, the leaders of the Bolshevist movement, as German agents who had sold Russia for a large sum of money.

After the Brest-Litovsk treaty a profound disdain was felt by the emperor and empress towards the German Government and Emperor Wilhelm. They both felt deeply that the German Government and Emperor Wilhelm had lowered themselves by dealing with the Bolsheviki and by resorting to such outrageous methods of warfare.

Such was the tenor of our life during February and March. On March 30th a delegate, previously sent to Moscow by the committee of our soldiers, returned to Tobolsk. He brought a written order to Kobylinsky which stated that our life from this time on must be more severely supervised. We were all to live in the governor's house and a new plenipotentiary *commissar* had been ordered to Tobolsk for the purpose of enforcing new restrictions. On April 9th this *commissar* arrived. His name was Iakovleff. On April 10th he came to our house for the first time and was received by the emperor. On the same day he visited the *czarevitch* who at that time was sick. He returned shortly after his departure with an assistant (whose name I do not remember). They both visited the *czarevitch*. On the same day Iakovleff was received by the empress. Iakovleff made quite a favourable impression on the emperor, who told me that he though Iakovleff not so bad, and that he believed him to be quite straight.

The reason for Iakovleff's arrival was quite a puzzle to us. This puzzle was solved on April 12th. On that date Iakovleff went to the emperor and announced that he had orders to take him away from Tobolsk. The emperor replied that he would not leave Tobolsk, as he could not be separated from his son who was so ill (the *czarevitch* during this period suffered from the same affliction he had in Spala in 1912, with the difference that this time the bruise involved paralysis of the right foot), and that he did not intend to leave his family. Iakovleff answered that he was merely fulfilling his instructions, and as the emperor refused to leave Tobolsk, a choice of two decisions had to be made: Either Iakovleff must refuse to obey the orders, in which case another commissar with fewer scruples would be sent; or he must employ force in imposing the order. At the same time Iakovleff told the emperor that he might be accompanied by any other persons he desired. The only thing that could be done was for the emperor to submit to Iakovleff's demands. Everything that I have told in this connection I know from the words of her majesty.

Nobody knew where the emperor was to be taken. His majesty inquired of Iakovleff in advance, but the latter answered iii a way that did not make the matter clean Kobylinsky told us that Iakovleff at first informed him the destination was to be Moscow, but that he later said he did not know where the emperor was going to be taken.

All this sort of thing was intensely painful and humiliating for the imperial family, all of whom suffered most acutely. Her majesty was greatly tortured by having to decide whether to accompany the emperor or stay with the *czarevitch*.

She made up her mind that she would go with the emperor and it was decided that the Grand Duchess Maria Nicholaevna should accompany them. The rest of the family was to stay in Tobolsk until the recovery of the *czarevitch*.

Iakovleff fixed the time of departure for four o'clock in the morning of April 13th. The evening before we all had tea together. The emperor and empress wished us farewell and thanked us all for our services.

At three o'clock in the morning the carts arrived at the door. They were wretched looking vehicles with plated bodies and had no seats and no springs. One had to sit on the bottom, stretching out the feet. Only one *telega* (peasant cart) had a "*capot*" (hood). In this cart we decided to place her majesty. There was hardly anything on the bottom of the carriages. We went to the courtyard where an *employé* by the name of Kirpitchnikoff kept his pigs. There was some straw in stock. This straw we used for covering the bottom of the cart that was supplied with a hood and, I think, we put some straw also on the bottoms of some other carts. In the covered cart we also put a mattress. The emperor desired to go with her majesty and Maria Nicholaevna. Iakovleff insisted that the emperor should ride in the same cart as he did. They all left on April 13th shortly after four o'clock in the morning.

At this time the following persons departed from Tobolsk: The emperor and empress, Grand Duchess Maria Nicholaevna, Botkin, Dolgoruky, Tchemodouroff, Sedneff and Demidova. They were accompanied by six Rifles men and two officers—Matveieff and Nabokoff, as well as by soldiers of Iakovleff's detachment.

Sometime after the departure one of the coachmen brought us a short note from Maria Nicholaevna. She said in her note that the conditions of travelling were extremely hard, that the road was bad and the carriage was awful.

Later Kobylinsky received a wire from Nabokoff announcing the arrival of the party at Tumen. Greatly to the surprise of everybody Kobylinsky suddenly received a telegram from Matveieff stating that the emperor and all the persons in his party were held up in Yekaterinburg. This was quite unexpected, as we all thought that the emperor was to be taken to Moscow.

On April 24th a letter came from the empress. She wrote that they had all been placed in two rooms of the Ipatieff house, that they felt very much crowded, and that the only place where they could walk was a small garden that was very dusty. She wrote also that all their belongings had been searched, even "medicines." In the same letter in very discreet language she made us understand that we should take from Tobolsk all our precious things. As previously agreed, she used in her letter the word "medicines" instead of "jewels." Later Tegleva received a letter from Demidova, undoubtedly written by order of her majesty. In this letter we were instructed how to deal with jewels, instead of which she used the expression "Sedneff's belongings."

On April 25th two officers, .as well as five soldiers who escorted the emperor, returned to Tobolsk and told us the following story: Iakovleff took the emperor to Omsk. About one hundred *versts* before arriving at Omsk he took the train and proceeded to Omsk alone. After that he came back and turned the train towards Yekaterinburg. The *commissars* in Yekaterinburg held up the train. Dolgoruky was arrested and taken to prison directly from the station. All the officers and men were also put under arrest in some cellar, where they were kept for two days, and let free only on the third day and after some protest was made. The general idea to be gathered from their narrative was that the detention of the train and the party was unexpected by Iakovleff. They told us that he was hustling around all over the place, but was unable to accomplish anything. It was also told us that later, Iakovleff proceeded independently from Moscow and wired to Kobylinsky and Hohriakoff (the Chairman of the Tobolsk Soviet), that he resigned from his mission of *commissar* to the imperial family.

We started with the preparations for our trip. On April 25th the chairman of the local soviet, Hohriakoff, visited our house for the first time. After that he called on us frequently, urging us and hurrying our departure. I remember that on May 6th, the birthday of the emperor, the grand duchesses wanted to have divine service. Hohriakoff forbade it, saying that no time should be wasted. On May 7th, at eleven o'clock in the morning, we moved to the steamer *Russ* and about three or four o'clock that day departed from Tobolsk. We were escorted by a detachment commanded by Rodionoff, which was composed chiefly of Letts. Rodionoff did not behave well; he locked the cabin door, in which were the *czarevitch* and Nagorny. All the other cabins, including those of the grand duchesses, were locked also, by his order.

On May 9th we reached Tumen and the same day took a train. We arrived at Yekaterinburg on May 10th at two a. m. During the whole night we were switching from one station to another and being transferred from one track to another. Approximately at nine o'clock the train was stopped between two stations. It was muddy and there was a continuous drizzling rain. Five *isvostchiks* (cabs) were awaiting us at the station. Rodionoff, with some *commissars*, approached the car where the children were placed. The grand duchesses walked out of the car. Tatiana Nicholaevna carried in one hand her pet dog and in the other a hand bag, the latter with great difficulty, dragging it on the pavement.

Nagorny wanted to help her, but was roughly pushed aside. I noticed that Nagorny went in the same cab as the *czarevitch*. I remember

18

that in every one of the other cabs there was a *commissar* or some other Bolshevik agent. I wanted to leave the car and wish them goodbye, but I was held up by a sentry. I never thought at that moment that I was seeing all of them for the last time; and I did not even know that I was then already discharged from the service of the imperial family.

At last our train came into the station. About three hours later I saw Tatischeff, Hendrikova and Schneider being taken out of the train and escorted by soldiers. A little later Haritonoff, the little Sedneff, Volkoff and Troupp were also taken away. I had almost forgotten to say that the children were accompanied by Dr. Derevenko. In a little while Rodionoff came and announced to us that: we "were not wanted," and that we were "free." The Baroness Buxhoevden was then transferred to our car.

In about three days we received an order from the Soviet to leave the Perm district and return to Tobolsk. We could not fulfil the order as the way was cut off by the advancing Czechs, so we stayed in Yekaterinburg. During this time I visited the town and had a look at the Ipatieff house.

On the 14th or 15th of May I witnessed the following: I was walking on the streets of Yekaterinburg with Derevenko and Mr. Gibbes. While we were passing Ipatieff's house we noticed that Sedneff was sitting in a cab surrounded by soldiers who carried rifles with fixed bayonets; in another cab Nagorny was seated. When the latter looked up he saw us and looked at us for quite a long time but did not make a single movement that could betray to the people surrounding him that he knew us.

The cabs, surrounded by horsemen, quickly drove to the centre of the town. We followed them as fast as we could and finally saw them disappearing in the direction of the prison.

Our party consisted of eighteen persons and we proceeded to Tumen. At Kamishlov the soviet did not allow us to go any further. We stayed there for ten days. It was dirty and the whole place was infected by disease. Finally we were attached to a train full of Serbs and we arrived at Tumen.

We suffered very severely, but at present I do not want to speak about my personal suffering.

In the latter part of August I was visited by Tchemodouroff. His first words were: "Thank God, the emperor, her majesty and the children are alive—all the others are killed." He told me also that he was in the rooms of the Ipatieff's house where "Botkin and others" were shot. He told me that he had seen the bodies of Sedneff and Nagorny, whom he recognised by their clothes and that their bodies were put in a coffin and buried. He told me that all the others were obliged to dress themselves in soldiers' uniforms and had been taken away. It was difficult for me to understand Tchemodouroff, as he talked very wildly,

Tchemodouroff also told me that the life of the imperial family in Yekaterinburg was terrible, that all of them were very badly treated and that they had their meals together with the servants. The commandant, Avdeieff, had his meals also with the imperial family; he was often drunk and sometimes came into the room where the imperial family was without his tunic.

Tchemodouroff also told me that Avdeieff often behaved towards the emperor in an indecent and insulting manner. For example, during the meals, when he wanted to help himself from the dish, he stretched his hands before the emperor and her majesty and in doing so touched the emperor's face with his elbow.

The grand duchesses after their arrival at Yekaterinburg slept on the floor. The Bolsheviki took away from her majesty a little bag which she used to hold in her hand, and also a gold chain that supported the holy images by the *czarevitch's* bed.

After Tchemodouroff's arrival Mr. Gibbes and myself went to Yekaterinburg for the purpose of giving assistance to Sergeeff, a member of the court. Tchemodouroff told us that Sergeeff was in charge of the investigation of the fate of the imperial family. Together with Sergeeff we visited the Ipatieff house and inspected the room that had the bullet holes on the wall and on the floor. In this house I found two "Egyptian signs" which the empress had the habit of drawing on various things for good luck. One of these signs I noticed on the wall paper of her majesty's room, the other on the side of the window in a room where, under the Egyptian sign, the date was written in pencil: 17/30 April—the date of the arrival of her majesty in Yekaterinburg. My attention was also attracted to the stoves; they were all full of various burned articles. I recognised a considerable number of burned things such as tooth-and hair-brushes, pins and a number of small things bearing the initials: "A. F." (Alexandra Feodorovna.)

I got the impression that if the imperial family had been taken away from Yekaterinburg, they must have been taken as they were, without any of their belongings. All the things they might have taken with them were burned. Nevertheless, at the time I left the house I could not believe that the imperial family had perished. It seemed to me that there was such a small number of bullet holes in the room I had inspected that everybody could not have been executed. When, a considerable time later, I returned from Yekaterinburg to Tumen, Volkoff called on me. I did not recognise him at first, as I had read in the newspapers that after the attempt on the life of Lenin, Hendrikova, Schneider and Volkoff were shot.

Volkoff told me that he was taken directly from the train and put in the Yekaterinburg prison. From this prison he, Hendrikova and Schneider were transferred to a prison at Perm. Tatischeff was also in prison in Yekaterinburg. He was once taken out of prison but was never put back. I could hardly understand from Volkoff's words what happened to Tatischeff. Volkoff told me that he had seen in Tatischeff's hands a written Bolshevik order commanding him to leave the Perm district. In the prison Volkoff was put in the same cell with the valet of the Grand Duke Michael Alexandrovitch. The valet said that when the grand duke resided in Perm, four armed men called on him late at night. One of them aimed his pistol at the valet and ordered him to stand still. The others told the grand duke that he had to follow them. The grand duke refused to obey their orders unless he were asked to do so by a member of the soviet personally known to him. In reply one of the armed men went up to the grand duke, took him by the collar and grumbled: "Here is one more of the Romanoffs."

On one occasion Volkoff, Hendrikova, Schneider and some other people were taken out of prison to the woods, Volkoff understood they were all going to be shot, so he started running. After he got out of danger and stopped, he heard the sounds of volleys from the place where the others had been left. He believes that Hendrikova and the rest were murdered. He thinks that the Bolsheviki considered him dead, because they were firing at him when he was running, and when he accidentally fell, he heard a voice say: "He's done for."

About the fate of the Grand Duke Michael, Volkoff related the following: The grand duke had to submit to force and followed the armed men. One of these men remained with the valet to prevent him from calling for help. When this man left the valet ran to the soviet and told everything that had happened. A tumult started in the soviet, but nevertheless, the members of the soviet were in no hurry to start a pursuit. About an hour later they began looking for the grand duke. It was very hard to get any definite information from Volkoff about the fate of the Grand Duke Michael.

I recall another detail of Volkoff's narrative: When the grand duke followed the strangers the valet said to him: "Your highness, don't forget to take your medicine from the stove shelf."

I have nothing more to declare. My statement has been read to me and it is correctly written.

(Signed) Gilliard,
" N. Sokoloff.

2

EXAMINATION OF MR. GIBBES

(The deposition of Mr. Gibbes should prove interesting to the public as being that of an Englishman who was wholly and unselfishly devoted to the imperial family, Sidney Gibbes acted as tutor to the czarevitch, and after the arrest of the emperor and his family, he followed them to Tobolsk without a thought for his own safety.

Mr. Gibbes knew the emperor and the empress intimately during these days of sorrow, and his deposition shows that the czar was genuinely affected by the Treaty of Brest-Litovsk and the subsequent Red ruin of Russia. These recollections are absolutely unbiased, and there is no reason to doubt their accuracy.—Original editor's note.)

On July 1, 1919, the Investigating Magistrate for Cases of Special Importance of the Omsk Tribunal, N. A. Sokoloff, questioned in Yekaterinburg the man named below in conformity with Paragraph 443 of the Code of Criminal Procedure, in the capacity of a witness, and the witness stated, in reply to questions:

My name is Sidney Ivanovitch Gibbes. Up to the year 1916 I was a visiting teacher of the English language to the grand duchesses and the *czarevitch*. I started my lessons with the Grand Duchesses Olga Nicholaevna, Tatiana Nicholaevna and Maria Nicholaevna in 1908. When Anastasia grew up I began to give her lessons also. I started to give instructions to the *czarevitch* in 1914. In 1916 I was appointed tutor to the *czarevitch*. The same year I moved to the Yekaterinensky Palace. In 1917 the duties of tutor to the *czarevitch* were performed partly by myself and partly by Gilliard.

During the early part of the revolution the imperial family resided in Czarskoe-Selo. The empress and all the children were there. The emperor was at the Stavka. At the beginning of the revolution all the children were taken ill with the measles. The first to be attacked by that disease was the *czarevitch* and after him, all the daughters in succession.

Personally I did not observe how the news of the revolution was

22

taken by the empress. I heard from someone who was near to her that she wept. As far as I know the empress, my conviction is that she did not expect the revolution. It seemed to me that the empress thought that only a few concessions ought to have been made. The revolution was a blow to her and therefore she suffered, but being a firm character she did not cry very much.

The empress and the imperial family were arrested by General Korniloff. I was not present at the palace during the time of the arrest. I cannot tell how it happened. I know that Korniloff was received by her majesty and that he announced to her that she was under arrest. The empress told me about that. She did not give me any details; she just related all that in a general way and, at the same time, added that she was very cold towards Korniloff and did not give him her hand. After Korniloff's announcement of the arrest I was not allowed into the palace. My request for admittance met with a negative response. The provisional government would not allow me to stay with the imperial family. I remember this fact distinctly. I saw the letter which stated so. It bore the signature of five ministers. At the present time I do not remember their names, but I have it plainly in my memory that there were the signatures of five ministers. It was stated in my application that I was giving lessons to the children. I cannot tell whether the answer also carried the signature of the minister of public education. Being an Englishman I considered all this very funny.

Such is the reason why I was not allowed to be with the imperial family during the time of their stay in Czarskoe-Selo, and consequently, I did not see anything of their life during that period of time.

Later I heard in Tobolsk that some soldiers and officers in Czarskoe-Selo behaved roughly towards the imperial family. The emperor himself told me in Tobolsk that on one occasion an officer refused to shake hands with him, explaining to him that he was on duty, and, therefore, had no right to shake hands. The emperor also spoke to me a little about Kerensky. He said that Kerensky was very nervous when he spoke with him. In fact, once he was so nervous that he grabbed an ivory knife from the wall and nervously began bending it so badly that the emperor was afraid he would break the knife, and so he took it away from him. The emperor also told me that Kerensky believed that he (the emperor) wanted to make a separate peace with Germany. The emperor denied that this was so. Kerensky insisted, and got nervous. I cannot tell whether the private papers of the emperor were searched by Kerensky or not; but the emperor told me that Kerensky believed he had some papers that indicated his desire of making peace with Germany. I knew the emperor well and I understood the feeling of disdain he had towards Kerensky, when he spoke to me on those subjects.

Kerensky was very nervous, the day of the departure of the imperial family from Czarskoe-Selo. During the night he telephoned to the minister of communication, insisting upon his coming at once to Czarskoe-Selo. The minister of communication was in bed at this time, but that fact did not deter Kerensky.

I cannot tell anything else about the life of the imperial family in Czarskoe-Selo. I was devoted to the family and I wanted to be near them. I went to Tobolsk of my own free will. I arrived in Tobolsk in the beginning of October. From Tumen I travelled with Klavdia Michaelovna Bitner.

For two days I lived in Korniloff's house. On the third day, at one p. m. I was called by the emperor. He received me in his workroom. The empress and the *czarevitch* were also present. I was very glad to see them and they were very glad to see me. At this time the empress began to realise that not all the people who had been devoted to her were unfaithful.

Our stay in Tobolsk was altogether very agreeable. I did not see anything very objectionable in the conditions of our life. Certainly there were some disadvantages as compared to what it had previously been; there were lots of trifles that created friction, but one could get used to them.

We all used to work very hard. The empress was teaching theology to the children (all the children took lessons except Olga Nicholaevna who had completed her course of studies in 1914). She also taught a little German to Tatiana Nicholaevna. The emperor personally gave lessons in history to the *czarevitch*. Klavdia Michaelovna Bitner was giving instruction in mathematics and the Russian language to the Grand Duchesses Maria, Anastasia and the *czarevitch*. Hendrikova gave lessons in history to Tatiana Nicholaevna. I was instructor in English.

The lessons started at nine a. m. and continued up to eleven o'clock. From eleven till twelve o'clock the children were free to take a walk. Studies were resumed at twelve and continued for an hour. At one p. m. lunch was served, and after that coffee was drunk. According to the doctor's advice the *czarevitch* had to rest a little on the sofa after lunch. During his rest Gilliard or myself used to read to him aloud. After that

24

Nagorny dressed the *czarevitch* and we went out for a walk till about four or five o'clock. After we returned the emperor gave a lesson in history to the *czarevitch*. After the lesson the *czarevitch* liked very much to play a game called: "The slower you ride the farther you go." We divided into two parties: The *czarevitch*, Gilliard or myself were one party; Dolgoruky and Schneider the other. The *czarevitch* used to be extremely fond of that game. Schneider also used to put her heart into the game and fussed a little with Dolgoruky over it. This was quite funny. We played the game nearly every day and Schneider always used to say that she would never play the game again.

From six to seven p. m. the *czarevitch* took lessons with me or with Gilliard. From seven to eight p. m. he prepared his lessons for the next day. Dinner was served at eight p. m. After dinner the family assembled upstairs. Sometimes we played cards. I played double patience with Schneider. Tatischeff, Olga Nicholaevna, Botkin, Schneider, Gilliard and Dolgoruky played bridge. The children and the emperor occasionally played bezique. At times the emperor read aloud.

Sometimes the Grand Duchesses Olga, Maria, and Anastasia would go up to Demidova's room where Toutelberg, Ersberg and Tegleva had their meals. Occasionally Gilliard, Dolgoruky, the *czarevitch* or myself used to accompany them. We stayed some time in this room and had plenty of jokes and laughter.

The emperor got up early. At nine a. m. he always had tea in his workroom and read till eleven a. m. He then had a walk in the garden and during the walk always took some physical exercise. In Tobolsk he frequently used to saw logs. With some assistance the emperor built up a platform on the roof of the orangery. A staircase which was constructed by our combined efforts led to the platform. The emperor liked very much to sit on this platform when the weather was stormy. Up till noon the emperor took his exercises, after which he always used to go to his daughters' room where sandwiches were served. Later he retired to his quarters and worked till lunch time. After lunch the emperor took a walk or worked in the garden till dusk. At five p.m. the family had tea, after which the emperor used to read till supper time.

The empress got up at different times, sometimes much later than others. Sometimes she was ready with everybody else, but she was never seen by strangers in the morning. There were times when the empress came out only for lunch. In the morning she occupied herself with her children or worked at something. She preferred fancy work:

embroidery or painting. When there was nobody in the house, and she was left all by herself, she played the piano.

The lunch and dinner were good. At lunch we used to have soup, fish, meat and dessert. Coffee was served upstairs. The dinner was similar to the lunch, with the difference that some fruits were served.

If the empress was present at dinner we used to sit in the following order: The emperor in the middle of the table; opposite him, the empress. To the right of the emperor, Hendrikova, and next to her the Grand Duchess Maria. To the left of the emperor, Schneider and Dolgoruky. To the empress's right, the *czarevitch*; to her left, Tatischeff and the Grand Duchess Tatiana. Gilliard was seated at the end of the table and opposite to him were the Grand Duchess Anastasia and myself. If the empress dined upstairs her place was taken by the Grand Duchess Olga.

Botkin always dined with the imperial family, but had his lunch with his own family. He was seated with the Grand Duchess Olga and the *czarevitch*. Sometimes on holy days Dr. Derevenko and his son Kolia were invited to dinner. Dinner was cooked by Haritonoff. The food was good and there was plenty of everything.

Besides dinner and lunch, tea was served twice daily. In the morning the emperor had tea with the Grand Duchess Olga in his workroom. Tea in the evening was always served in the emperor's workroom and only the family was present.

At the time of my arrival in Tobolsk two *commissars*, Pankratoff and Nikolsky, stayed there. Pankratoff was not a bad sort of a fellow, but showed weakness, and was influenced by Nikolsky. Pankratoff did not cause us any uneasiness. The emperor used to talk to him and Pankratoff told him many interesting things about Siberia, where he used to live in exile. The emperor spoke in a rather sarcastic way about Pankratoff calling him, "the little man"—he was rather small in stature. Nikolsky was rough and the family did not like him. I do not remember if Nikolsky ever made us feel uncomfortable or if ever the *czarevitch* cried on account of his rudeness. During the Bolshevik period no *commissars* were allowed in our house. It seems to me that some *commissars* arrived in Tobolsk, but were not recognised by the soldiers. The first *commissar* that ever entered the house was Iakovleff.

The Bolshevist revolution at first paid no attention to us and it looked as if we were completely forgotten. However, finally the Bolsheviki remembered us, and our money allowance was stopped short. We were given a soldier's ration and were ordered to limit our necessities to 150 *roubles* per week. Several servants were discharged, and we began to get very inferior food. Only two courses were served—soup and meat.

I did not speak to the emperor about the Brest-Litovsk Treaty but I noticed that the emperor suffered greatly after the Bolshevist revolution. The emperor abdicated because he thought it would be better for Russia. It turned out to be worse. He did not expect that and suffered dreadful remorse. After we received the news that the state of affairs in Russia was very bad, I twice saw the emperor looking very much upset, remaining silent for a long time. His personal situation did not grieve him and he endured it without repining.

Iakovleff arrived in Tobolsk in the beginning of April, at the time when the *czarevitch* was sick. I was sitting by the *czarevitch's* bed. The emperor, accompanied by Iakovleff and another man, who seemed to be his assistant, entered the room. Iakovleff looked at the *czarevitch*. The emperor said: "My son and his tutor."

Iakovleff did not appear to me to be a man of culture. He looked more like a clever sailor. I do not remember the appearance of the other man. Iakovleff gazed attentively at the *czarevitch*, after which they departed. Later the emperor and Iakovleff returned to the room, but without the third man. They looked at the *czarevitch* and kept silent. A few days later I was again in the *czarevitch's* bedroom. He was very ill and, suffered greatly. The empress promised to see him after lunch. He waited and waited, but no one came. All the time he called: "Mamma, mamma." I went out of the room and looked down the hall. I noticed the emperor, the empress and Iakovleff standing in the middle of the hall. I did not hear what they were talking about. I returned to the *czarevitch's* room. He began to cry and asked: "Where is Mamma?"

Once more I left the room. Somebody told me that the empress was anxious about something and this was the reason why she had not come to see the *czarevitch*. I was told that she was alarmed because the emperor had to be taken away from Tobolsk. I returned to the room. Between four and five o'clock the empress came. She was quite calm, but her face showed traces of tears. Being afraid to disturb the *czarevitch* she began to tell me in an undertone that the emperor must leave Tobolsk, and that she and the Grand Duchess Maria were to go with him, and that as soon as the *czarevitch* was well the others would all follow them. The *czarevitch* overheard her but did not ask her to tell us where we were going, and wishing to avoid embarrassment, I did not ask her either. Soon after that I left the room. 1 thought that during the time they were preparing themselves for the journey, they probably would not like anyone to be present. They dined alone upstairs.

In the evening we were all invited to the empress's *boudoir* (the green room), where the tea was served. Conversation ran on travelling. We spoke mostly of luggage. At two o'clock the coaches arrived, one of them had a hood. I wished them goodbye in the lobby. The emperor took a place with Iakovleff, the empress with the Grand Duchess Maria, and they departed. They were accompanied by Botkin, Tchemodouroff, Dolgoruky, Demidova and Sedneff. We did not know the place of their destination. Not one of us had any idea that they were to be taken to Yekaterinburg. We all thought they were going to Moscow or to the east. The children were of the same opinion. We were all very anxious. We did not know what was going to happen to them. Of the persons left behind Tatischeff was the senior; and of the remaining part of the imperial family, Tatiana was considered senior in the place of the Grand Duchess Olga.

The *czarevitch* was gradually recovering, though very slowly. The first news we received was brought by an *isvostchik* who drove one of the coaches used by the family.

We heard that the family reached Tumen safely. Later, somebody sent a wire that they were "held up" at Yekaterinburg. We were badly stricken by this news.

Iakovleff told us nothing of Yekaterinburg and I heard someone saying that Iakovleff himself was sent from Moscow and not from Yekaterinburg, and I don't think there is any doubt about this.

Sometime after that Hohriakoff came to our house. It turned out that previously to that time this man had spent quite a considerable time in Tobolsk, but we had never seen him in the house before. It was thought that he was sent by Iakovleff. When he came he wanted to see the *czarevitch*. Possibly he did not believe in his illness as, after he left him, he immediately returned expecting that the *czarevitch* would get right up. About three days before our departure our guards were replaced by a detachment of Reds. This detachment was under the command of a certain Rodionoff. This man did not make a very bad impression on me. We were all very much interested in him. Tatischeff had known him before, but could not remember who he was nor where he had seen him. Hendrikova also knew him. Tatischeff thought he had seen Rodionoff in Berlin; and Hendrikova believed she had seen him in Verjbolovo.

Tatischeff was formerly attached to the Emperor Wilhelm, and he thought he had seen Rodionoff in the Russian Embassy in Berlin. Tatischeff asked him what he did before. Rodionoff, not wishing to give a reply, answered: "I have forgotten." We were very much interested in all that. When speaking about Rodionoff, Tatischeff used good-naturedly the expression: "My acquaintance." Personally, I remember the following: In 1916 I was in Petrograd, where I visited an acquaintance of mine by the name of Ditveiler. I believe he was a Jew and a Russian subject. He used to work in a rope concern. During our conversation I asked him where he had been. He answered that he spent his time with so and so (I have forgotten the name at present). I asked Ditveiler who the man was and Ditveiler answered: "Probably a German spy," and he added that an officer by the name of Rodionoff was present at one of their meetings.

Rodionoff did not allow us to lock the doors of our bedrooms at night.

We left for Tumen on a steamer. A few days before our departure Hohriakoff told us that he did not know whether we were going. to be allowed to stay in the house which was occupied by the emperor, the empress and the Grand Duchess Maria in Yekaterinburg or not. Rodionoff told us that from now on things were going to be much worse for us than they had been. In Tumen the children, Hendrikova, Schneider, Tatischeff, Buxheovden, Nagorny and Volkoff were placed in a passenger wagon, the rest of us were placed in a box car (*teploushka*). We arrived at Yekaterinburg during the night of May 9th. It was cold. The whole night we were moving and changing tracks. At seven a. m. our cars were taken out of town.

Some *isvostchiks* were waiting, and I watched through the window the departure of the children. I was not allowed to wish them goodbye. At ten o'clock we were moved to a station platform and Tatischeff and Schneider were taken out of the train. I cannot tell anything about Hendrikova. After that Rodionoff came and announced that little Sedneff and Troupp must proceed to the house. Later Nagorny came and took with him some of the luggage as well as the children's beds. The beds were all alike, made of nickeled iron similar to the bed the Emperor Alexander II had used during the Turkish war. The beds were comfortable and not heavy. After Nagorny's departure, Rodionoff said to us: "You are free and you can go wherever you like."

I stayed in Yekaterinburg. Two or three days later I was walking with Derevenko and Gilliard on the Vosnesensky Prospect and suddenly noticed that Nagorny and Sedneff, surrounded by soldiers, were leaving Ipatieff's house, on two *isvotschiks*. We followed them and saw that they were taken to prison.

A considerable amount of time elapsed when the former Prime Minister Prince George Eugenievitch Lvoff, who was in prison in Yekaterinburg together with Nagorny, told me that Nagorny often had disputes with the Bolsheviki on account of their bad treatment of the *czarevitch*. The Bolsheviki left for the *czarevitch* only one pair of boots. Nagorny insisted upon two pairs of shoes being left, telling the Bolsheviki that the boy was of delicate health and, in case he got his feet wet, he would very badly need another pair of shoes. Sometime later the Bolsheviki took from the *czarevitch* a long gold chain which supported the holy images which hung by his bed. Nagorny had several arguments with the Bolsheviki: "So finally I understood why he was shot," added Prince Lvoff.

After the Bolsheviki left Yekaterinburg I met Tchemodouroff, who came to see me. His words were: "Thank God, the children are saved." I understood him badly. In the course of his conversation he suddenly asked me: "Do you think they are saved?" About ten days before his death he sent me a letter asking if there was any hope of their being alive.

Tchemodouroff told me that the conditions of their life in Yekaterinburg were bad. For example: at Easter they had cakes. The *commissar* came and cut himself big lumps. In general he spoke about rough treatment, but it was very hard for me to understand him. He told me that the grand duchesses had no beds.

I have visited Ipatieff's house but found nothing out of the ordinary. The house was battered. The stoves were full of burned objects, and I saw many remainders of burned objects, such as portrait frames, all sorts of brushes and a little basket in which the *czarevitch* used to keep his brushes. A few things were just scattered around, but I did not see much of their personal belongings.

The emperor used to wear uniform trousers and high boots, which had been often patched, and a soldier's shirt. The *czarevitch* wore khaki trousers, high boots and a soldier's shirt.

In regard to the rubies you have shown me, I can state that the imperial family had quite a number of them in their various articles of jewellery. The Grand Duchess Olga had a brooch with similar rubies, which was given to her by Queen Victoria. The sapphires looked very much like fragments of the stone that the emperor had in his ring It was shaped the same way, and I think there is a complete resemblance between them. The emperor wore the ring on the same finger with his wedding ring, and he told me that he could not take it off.

My personal impressions of the imperial family are as follows:

The Grand Duchess Olga Nicholaevna was about twenty-three years old, she was fair and had the lightest hair in the family. After her illness she got much thinner. She had beautiful blue eyes. All her personality was seen in her eyes. She was straight, just, honest, simple, sincere and kind. She was easily irritated and her manners were a little harsh. She was a good musician. She had a talent for music. She composed, though I do not think she wrote poetry. I believe that Hendrikova wrote some poetry, as she was well able to do. The Grand Duchess Olga was very modest. She liked simplicity and did not pay much attention to dress. Her morals reminded me of those of her father. She was very religious and it seems to me that she loved her father more than anybody else.

The Grand Duchess Tatiana Nicholaevna was very thin. You could hardly imagine anybody as thin as she was. She was twenty-one years of age, was tall, darker than the rest of the family, and elegant. The colour of her eyes was dark grey. Her eyes made her look different from all of her sisters, who showed their souls through their eyes. She was reserved, haughty, and not open hearted, but she was the most positive. She was also religious, but the motive back of her religion was: "It is my duty," while Olga Nicholaevna had it in her heart. She was always preoccupied and pensive and it was impossible to guess her thoughts. She played the piano and played it better than anyone else in the family. However, she had only a better technique and did not show feeling in her music. She painted and embroidered well. She was her mother's favourite and the one in whom, of all the daughters, she confided the most. If any favours were to be obtained they had to be gotten through Tatiana Nicholaevna.

The Grand Duchess Maria Nicholaevna was a young woman of broad build. She was very strong; for example, she could lift me up from the ground. She had lighter hair than Tatiana, but darker than Olga. (Olga Nicholaevna had brown hair, of a golden shade, and Maria Nicholaevna had brown hair with a light shade.) She had very nice, light grey eyes. She was very good looking, but got too thin after her illness. She had a great talent for painting and always liked to exercise it. She played the piano indifferently and was not as capable as Olga or Tatiana. She was modest and simple and probably had the qualities of a good wife and mother. She was fond of children and was inclined to be lazy. She liked Tobolsk and told me that she would be quite happy to stay there. It is quite difficult for me to tell you whom she preferred—her father or her mother.

The Grand Duchess Anastasia Nicholaevna was sixteen or seventeen years old; she was short, stout and was, in my opinion, the only one in the family that appeared to be ungraceful. Her hair was of a lighter colour than that of Maria Nicholaevna. It was not wavy and soft, but lay flat on the forehead. Her eyes were grey and beautiful, her nose straight. If she had grown and got slim she would have been the prettiest in the family. She was refined and very witty. She had the talents of a comic actor, she made everybody laugh, but never laughed herself. It appeared as if her development had stopped and, therefore, her capacity faded a little. She played the piano and painted, but was only in the stage of studying both.

The *czarevitch*, Alexis Nicholaevitch, was not healthy. He was tall for his age and very thin. He suffered much in his childhood. He was sick with a disease inherited from his mother's family. He grew worse in Tobolsk, as there it was very difficult to obtain means to effect a cure. He had a kind heart and was very fond of animals. He could be influenced only by his feelings, and would not yield to authority. He submitted only to the emperor. He was a clever boy but was not fond of books. His mother loved him passionately. She tried, but could not be strict with him, and most of his desires were obtained through his mother. Disagreeable things he bore silently and without grumbling. He was kind-hearted and during the last period of his life he was the only one who liked to give things away. In Tobolsk he had some odd fancies—for example, he collected old nails, saying; "They may be useful."

The grand duchesses spoke English and French well, but German badly. Alexis Nicholaevitch did not speak German at all—he never had German lessons. His father spoke Russian to him, his mother English or French.

The empress formerly used to be very good looking and graceful, though "her feet were large. I was quite surprised when I saw her in Tobolsk. She looked much older and had many grey hairs. She had wonderful, soft, grey eyes. She was clever, but seemed cleverer to the people who knew her least. She was not haughty in the ordinary meaning of the word, but she always realised and did not for one moment forget her position in life. She always looked queenly. I never had a feeling of uneasiness when I was in her presence. I liked very much to be with her. She was kind-hearted and liked to perform kind deeds. She always had something in sight when she worked. She was extremely fond of house secrets, for example: to prepare a present for somebody and keep it a secret until it was ready. I felt a German in her. She was more economical than an English woman. She loved Russia and considered herself Russian. The thing she dreaded most was losing Russia. Though during the reign of the emperor she was a number of times in Germany I never heard a single word from her about the Emperor Wilhelm, She was sincerely religious in the Orthodox way and was a true believer in God. She was most devoted to her family and religion entered into her feelings immediately after the family.

Her feeling of religion was quite normal and was not a product of hysteria. She had a stronger and more aggressive character than the emperor, but she had such a deep feeling of love for the emperor that when she knew beforehand his opinion she always submitted. I never witnessed a single quarrel between them. It was quite obvious that she was very much opposed to his abdication, but she never reproached him. This was very clear to all the persons who were near them. And nobody could ever think of her being untrue to the emperor. They were an ideal couple and never separated. My opinion is that it would be hard to meet, especially in Russia, such a devoted pair who missed each other so much when they were parted. That is the reason why the emperor took Alexis Nicholaevitch with him so frequently on his trips. I suppose the latter in a way served as a substitute for the rest of his family.

The emperor was very well educated. He spoke (and wrote) English and French to perfection. I could not judge of his knowledge of German. He was very orderly and did not like to have anyone touch his things. He had an exceptionally good memory. He did not care much for light reading. He read a great deal on social sciences and studied history. He gave the impression of an extremely honest character. He was very kind and had a compassionate heart. He was modest but reserved, and hated any sort of familiarity. His disposition was gay and he was fond of games. He was fond of conversation and sometimes had a chat with the soldiers in the guardroom. He loved his country devotedly and suffered for it greatly during the revolution. After the Bolshevik revolution it was felt that his sufferings were not due to his situation but that he suffered for Russia.

The emperor was a good hunter and was fond of hunting, though

I could not tell which forms of it he preferred.

In regard to their attitude towards each other, this was an ideal family, very rarely met with. They did not need the presence of other people.

Of the *aides-de-camp*, the most closely attached to the family were Dimitry Pavlovitch (Grand Duke Dimitry), Mordvinoff and Sabline. The nearest to the empress was Anna Alexandrovna Viroubova.

With regard to Rasputin, it seems to me that the empress believed in his holiness, his power of healing, and in the efficacy of his prayers. Rasputin did not visit the house as frequently as reported by gossipers. His visits to the palace, I think, were due to the illness of Alexis. I thought him to be a clever, cunning and good-natured *moujik* (peasant). I have nothing to add to the above statement. My statement has been read to me and it is written correctly. . . . The imperial family used to drink tea three times during the day. The third time at approximately eleven p. m., in the emperor's workroom.

(Signed)   S. I. Gibbes
"   N. Sokoloff.

3

EXAMINATION OF COLONEL KOBYLINSKY

(*The deposition of Colonel Kobylinsky affords complete documentary evidence of the conditions of life experienced by the imperial family from March 1917 until May 1918, during which time they were under his charge. Colonel Kobylinsky appears to have been a brave soldier and a just man who did what he considered to be his duty, but who treated the unfortunate prisoners with humanity and courtesy. His statement will be of enormous value to historians of the future, inasmuch as it reveals a new aspect of the character of the Emperor Nicholas II, and negatives the pro-German tendencies of which both he and the empress have been so persistently accused.—original editor's note.*)

On April 6-10, 1919, the Investigating Magistrate for Cases of Special Importance of the Omsk Tribunal questioned in Yekaterinburg, in conformity with Paragraph 443 of the Penal Law Regulations, the person named below in the capacity of witness. The witness stated:

My name is Eugene Stefanovitch Kobylinsky, age forty years, colonel attached to the commander of the Tumen military district. I belong to the Orthodox Church. At the beginning of the great war I was in command of a company of Petrogradsky Guard Regiment.

On November 8, 1914 I was wounded in my foot by a rifle bullet. In July, 1916, I was severely shell-shocked on the Austrian front during the battles near Gouta-Staraya. The shell-shock was followed by a very severe case of kidney trouble. In September, 1916, I was sent to the hospital in Czarskoe-Selo. From this hospital I was sent to Ialta and on my return to Czarskoe-Selo, after a medical examination, I was reported in 1916 as physically unfit for active service, and was transferred to the reserve battalion of my former regiment. I was in this battalion at the beginning of the revolution.

Late in the evening of March 5th I was told to report to the headquarters of the Petrograd military district. At eleven p. m. I went to the headquarters and was told that I was called by order of General Korniloff (the famous Korniloff, who was at the time commanding the forces of the Petrograd military district).

I was received by Korniloff, who said: "I have assigned you to a very important and responsible position." I asked him what it was. "I will tell you tomorrow," answered the general. I tried to learn from Korniloff why the choice fell on me. "Mind your business and get ready," answered the general. I saluted and left. The next day, March 6th, I received no orders. No orders arrived on March 7th either. I began to think then that my appointment had lapsed, when suddenly I was informed by telephone that Korniloff ordered me to be at Czarskoe-Selo station at eight a. m. on March 8th. I arrived at the station, where I met General Korniloff and his A. D. C. Korniloff said, "When we get into a compartment of the car I will tell you the destination."

We boarded the train, where Korniloff told me: "We are going to Czarskoe-Selo. I am going there to announce to the empress that she is under arrest. You are going to be in command of the Czarskoe-Selo garrison. Captain Kotsebue will be *commandant* of the palace, but you will also supervise the palace and Kotsebue will be subordinate to you."

We arrived at the palace. In the waiting-room we were met by the grand marshal of the imperial court, General Benckendorf. Korniloff explained to him that he would like the emperor's suite to be assembled and begged to be received by her majesty. Benckendorf sent a footman to ask everybody down and personally went to present to the empress our plea for an audience. After he returned he told us that the empress would see us in ten minutes. Shortly after this we were told by a footman that her majesty desired to see us. Together with Korniloff we entered the children's room. There was nobody there, but the moment we came in the empress entered from another door. We bowed. She gave her hand to Korniloff and nodded to me.

Korniloff said:

"I have the heavy burden of informing you of the decision of the council of ministers. From this moment you must consider yourself under arrest. If you are in need of anything kindly apply to the new *commandant*." After that, addressing me Korniloff said: "Colonel, leave us together and take a position by the door." I retired. About five minutes later Korniloff called me in and when I entered the empress held out her hand to me. We bowed and went downstairs. In the waiting-room some of the emperor's suite were assembled, Korniloff announced to them:

> Gentlemen, this is the new *commandant*; from this time on the empress is under arrest. If anybody desires to share the fate of the family he may stay with them, but make up your minds at once, as later I will not let anyone enter the palace.

At this time the guard was kept by His Majesty's Svodny Guard Regiment commanded by Major General Ressin. The major general declared that he wanted to leave. The grand marshal of the imperial court, Count Benckendorf and Count Apraksin, who was in charge of the empress's personal affairs, announced that they would remain with the empress.

On the same day Korniloff confirmed the instructions regarding the status of the arrested persons and the restrictions imposed upon them. The guards of this Svodny regiment were relieved by the First Rifles regiment. Korniloff left Czarskoe-Selo and I remained there as *commandant*.

Before the change of the guards Colonel Lazareff asked my permission to say goodbye to the empress. I allowed him to do so. He saw the empress and wept bitterly. He also wept another time when he saw the colours of the Svodny regiment being taken out of the waiting-room. Some days later, I do not remember the date, I was notified by telephone of the arrival of the emperor. I went to the station. After the arrival of the train the emperor left his car and walked very quickly through the station without throwing a single glance at anybody, and took his seat in an automobile. He was accompanied by a marshal of the court, Count Vasily Alexandrovitch Dolgoruky. Together with Dolgoruky the emperor seated himself in the automobile.

Two men dressed in plain clothes came towards me; one of them was Vershinin, a member of the *Duma*. They told me that their mission was ended and that from this time on the emperor was to be under

THE MARTYRED FAMILY

In this group, photographed four years before their death, the Tsar Nicholas II, the Tsaritsa Alexandra Feodorovna, and their youngest daughter, the Grand Duchess Anastasia, are seated in the centre; behind them stand (from left to right) the Grand Duchesses Maria, Tatiana and Olga. The Tsarevich Alexis, then ten years old, wears a sailor suit. Nicholas II is in the uniform of the Fusilier Guards. The Mother and Daughters have on some of the matchless pearls afterwards stolen from their dead bodies by the murderers.

Что завтра? ты наш
руководитель боже
сколько въ жизни
путей тернистыхъ.

RASPUTIN—WOUNDED AT HIS VILLAGE HOME
Just before the outbreak of hostilities in 1914 the "saint" had been
stabbed by a peasant girl whom he had wronged, and was being nursed
by his wife and daughters at Pokrovskoe (Tobolsk province). Here
he received the only letter that he ever had from Nicholas II, and
here he boasted that if he had been in Petrograd at the time, he
would have stopped the war. Nicholas and Alexandra had no suspicion that "Grishka" was a German agent. On this portrait, the
"saint" has inscribed some of his pious reflections, translated as follows: "What of tomorrow? Thou art our Guide, O God. How many
Thorny paths in this Life?"

ALEXANDRA'S DESPAIR OVER RASPUTIN'S DEATH

Facsimile of a letter in which the Empress for once betrays her feelings. The closing sentence, written disjointedly, refers to his "murder" which occurred a week before, and her anxiety for the safety of the Tsar, showing that she knew of a plot against his life. "Besides everything, try for a moment to realise what it is to know a friend in daily, hourly danger of also being foully murdered. But God is all mercy."

EMPRESS ALEXANDRA FEODOROVNA
AND THE TSAREVICH ALEXIS
NIKOLAEVICH IN LIVADIA
(CRIMEA)

THE TSAREVICH ALEXIS AND
HIS SPANIEL JOY, IN THE
PARK AT TSARSKOE

my guard.

I cannot forget a certain circumstance I witnessed at that time. There were quite a number of persons who had been in the emperor's train. When the emperor left the train these people crowded out to the station platform and quickly dispersed, throwing frightened looks in all directions. It appears that they were very much afraid of being recognised. All this looked rather disgusting.

I accompanied the emperor to the palace. He immediately went upstairs to see his children who were sick.

Shortly afterwards the emperor's baggage was brought from the station.

The life of the imperial family during their stay in Czarskoe-Selo was in keeping in every way with the conditions that the imperial family had the right to expect. The instructions limited the connections of the imperial family with the outer world, and, of course, brought some restrictions in their interior life. The mail always went through the hands of the commandant of the palace. It was allowed to leave the palace only through the park. The palace and the park were always surrounded by sentinels. Walking in the park was allowed only from morning till dark.

These were the only restrictions, and the government by no means interfered in the intimate life of the family. Except the above-mentioned limitations as to the time of walking in the park, the government imposed no hardships.

During the first days in Czarskoe-Selo the children were sick with measles; Maria Nicholaevna and, I think, Olga Nicholaevna had also inflammation of the lungs. Very soon they all recovered.

Usually the day was spent in the following manner: The family got up early, with the exception of the empress. Indeed she also occasionally would get up early but she usually stayed a long time in bed. At eight a. m. the emperor always had a walk in the company of Dolgoruky. They walked for about an hour and a half, taking also some physical exercise. At one o'clock the family had lunch. After lunch until three o'clock the family used to work in the garden. After that the children took lessons. Tea was served at four p. m. Sometimes after tea the family went out to the park. Dinner was served at seven o'clock.

During the stay in Czarskoe-Selo, some incidents took place to which I would like to draw your attention: A few days after the arrest of the imperial family a disagreeable incident took place in regard to

41

the body of Rasputin. His corpse was in Czarskoe-Selo. A church was being built and he was buried in one of its sections. After that became known to the soldiers they dug up the grave, removed the cover of the coffin and began to examine the body. They found a holy image in the coffin that bore the signatures of Alexandra, Olga, Tatiana, Maria, Anastasia and Ania. This image was placed by his right cheek.

In some way all this became known to the commander of an anti-aircraft battery and he took the image away from the soldiers. I saw it personally. I think the image represented the holy virgin. I reported by telephone all these facts to the district headquarters. I was instructed to take the body of Rasputin to the station and to ship it to Sredniaya-Rogatka, where it was to be interred. I was told to do this in secret. Obviously it was impossible to carry out this order without the soldiers and the populace learning of it. Later I was told to take the body to Czarskoe-Selo station; I did this and put it in a box car. In another car I placed some soldiers without explaining to them what they had to guard.

The next day a *commissar* by the name of Kouptchinsky (who was also in charge of automobiles) forwarded me a written order signed by the chair-man of the council of ministers. The order stated that I was to transmit the body of Rasputin (the name was written as "Novykh"), to Kouptchinsky so that he might deliver it on a truck to the place of its destination. We could not do all that in Czarskoe-Selo, so we moved the car with the corpse to the station Pavlovsk Second. In that station we found an old case and put in this case the coffin containing Rasputin's body. All this was covered with mats and old empty bags. Kouptchinsky went with the body to Petrograd, but on the way the secret became known to the mob which threatened to snatch away the body so Kouptchinsky had to burn it on the way.

The other incident in our peaceful life was the sudden arrival of a stranger. This stranger came to me, presented himself as Maslovsky and handed me a letter from, the executive committee of the soviet of the workmen and soldiers' deputies. This man wore the uniform of a colonel. I do not remember his features. The letter contained a demand that I assist the bearer in the execution of his orders. I remember very well that the letter was signed by Tscheidze, a member of the *duma*. It also bore a proper seal. This man who called himself Maslovsky told me that he had the order of the executive committee to take the emperor to the St. Peter and Paul fortress. I told Maslovsky firmly that I would not let him do it.

"Well, colonel, understand that the blood that will be shed will be on your conscience," answered Maslovsky. I said that I could not help it, and he retired. I thought he had left for good but it appeared that he went to the palace, where he was met by the commander of the first regiment. Captain Aksiouta. He showed him the letter and told him that he wanted to see the emperor. After searching Maslovsky's pockets, Aksiouta showed him the emperor in such a way that the emperor did not notice it. I reported this event to headquarters, where my actions were approved.

Kotsebue did not occupy the position of *commandant* of the palace for a very long time. He was dismissed on account of the following: There lived in the palace a maid of honour to the empress, Viroubova, and with her stayed a lady by the name of Den, who wore a Red Cross uniform.

The soldiers learned through the servants that Kotsebue often stayed for quite a long time with Viroubova and spoke English with her. After I heard it I verified this rumour. The footman (I do not remember his name), who told the story to the soldiers, confirmed to me the fact that Kotsebue was often seen with Viroubova. Fearing agitation amongst the men I reported it to Korniloff. Korniloff called for Kotsebue, forbade him to enter the palace, and ordered me temporarily to fulfil the duties of *commandant* of the palace.

I was not on my new post more than a week when Paul Alexandrovitch Korovitchenko was appointed to be *commandant* of the palace. Korovitchenko was a colonel in one of the regiments which was stationed in Finland. He was graduated from the military law academy, after which he stayed some time on active service. He was called back into active service at the beginning of the war. He had some private connection with Kerensky, who at this period succeeded Prince Lvoff, leaving his position of minister of justice to Pereverseff. Korovitchenko was also on good terms with the latter.

Kerensky came to Czarskoe-Selo several times. The first time he arrived when Korovitchenko was there. I cannot tell you anything about his behaviour towards the emperor, as I was never present at their conversations. I cannot tell you anything about it from Korovitchenko's words either. As far as I can remember Tegleva told me that Kerensky always behaved to the emperor in a very correct manner. During one of the visits of Kerensky Viroubova was arrested.

This took place while I was present. Together with Korovitchenko we entered her room. Korovitchenko announced to her that she had to be taken to Petrograd. She dressed for the occasion and asked permission to say goodbye to the empress. This was granted. We were both present at their parting, watching it from a certain distance. They both spoke English and cried. Madame Den was taken to Petrograd together with Viroubova.

Korovitchenko was once present at a conversation between Kerensky and the emperor. Kerensky declared to the emperor that he must confiscate some of his private papers and that he had detailed Korovitchenko to do it. I was also told to be present and distinctly remember the scene. It all turned out very unpleasantly. The private papers of the emperor were kept in a special, very large case. There were a large number of papers and they were placed in bundles in very good order. While indicating the papers, the emperor took a letter from the case, saying: "This letter is of a private character." The emperor by no means wanted to keep the letter from being confiscated, but simply took it as it was lying separately from the others and intended to put it back in the case. At the same time Korovitchenko abruptly grabbed the letter and for a moment it seemed that the emperor was holding one end of the letter and Korovitchenko was pulling the other. The emperor looked vexed. He let go his end of the letter with the words: "Well, it looks as if I am not needed any longer; I had better go and have a walk." Saying this he departed.

Korovitchenko took all the papers he considered interesting and delivered them to Kerensky. Kerensky and Pereverseff expected to find in them something that would indicate the treachery of the emperor or empress in favour of the Germans, especially as at this time it was insinuated by all the news-papers. They found nothing that could compromise the emperor or empress. At last they got hold of a telegram that was sent in code from the emperor to the empress. After some hard work in deciphering if they made out a sentence, "Feeling well, kisses."

The family did not like Korovitchenko, but personally I can state that Korovitchenko exerted his best efforts to please the imperial family. For example: he obtained for them permission to work in the garden and go out in rowboats. But the best disposed towards the imperial family were some soldiers and officers of the first regiment.

Following an old custom the officer of the day in the palace used to be given at Easter time a pint of wine. This custom was not changed and after the soldiers learned about it they started fussing and it took fifty bottles of vodka to pacify them.

Once the soldiers accused Ensign Zeleny of kissing the empress's hand.

This last-mentioned incident and the story about the wine made a lot of trouble and an investigation was ordered.

The morale of the soldiers grew worse and worse. They were quite intoxicated by their peculiar understanding of freedom and they began to invent all sorts of crazy demands. The worst in this respect was the second regiment, where not only the soldiers behaved badly, but also the officers.

On one occasion an officer of the second regiment declared: "We must see them ourselves. As they are under guard they have to be seen." It is obvious that only vulgar curiosity or a desire to inflict useless mental sufferings, prompted the officer to make such a demand. My efforts to oppose their desires were fruitless, and my argument that the parents would never desert their sick children had no effect whatever. Fearing that they would be able to accomplish their purpose without my authority I reported this matter to General Polovtseff, who at that time occupied General Korniloff's position. It was decided to do everything in the following manner: When the new captain of the guards came for the relief of the one on duty they were both to be taken to the emperor, with the empress present also. To avoid unnecessary embarrassment we decided to conduct this formality just before lunch—the time when the family was always gathered together.

It was decided that the captain of the guard on duty was to take his leave from the emperor and the new one was to greet the emperor. After all this had been decided upon and carried out for a certain while, a very disagreeable incident took place. When the guards of the first regiment were being relieved by the guards of the second, as usual, both captains went to see the emperor. The emperor wished goodbye to the captain of the departing guard and shook hands with him. When the emperor extended his hand to the new captain it remained stretched out in the air, as the officer stepped backward. Being unpleasantly impressed by this the emperor went towards the officer, put his hands on his shoulder and with tears in his eyes asked him: "Why did you do that?" The officer once more drew backwards and answered: "I was born of common people and when they stretched out their hand to you you did not take it, so now I will not shake hands with you." I relate this story as I heard it from the officer of the first regiment who witnessed this revolting incident

As the revolution proceeded the agitation grew deeper amongst the soldiers. Having no opportunities to find anything wrong in the life of the arrested ones they tried to find new ways of inflicting suffering upon the imperial family. On one occasion they saw the *czarevitch* carrying a small rifle. This rifle was a model of the standard infantry rifle and was presented to the *czarevitch* by some munition works. It was absolutely harmless, as special cartridges had to be used for it and none of those cartridges were available. Of course, the trouble was started by the soldiers of the second regiment All the efforts of the officer (I do not remember his name) to persuade the men that their demand was ridiculous, had no results. In order to avoid violence he took the rifle from the *czarevitch*. After this thing occurred I came to the palace where Gilliard and Tegleva told me the story and added that the *czarevitch* was crying. I ordered that the rifle should be forwarded to me, took it apart, and in this way, smuggled it back to the *czarevitch*.

Finally the soldiers and through them the soviet of Czarskoe-Selo ceased entirely to comply with my orders and appointed Ensign Domodziantz, an Armenian, to act as my assistant. He was a rough man and made the utmost efforts to get into the palace, where I tried my best to prevent him from going. After that he began to pass his time in the park, especially when the family were walking there. Once as the emperor was walking by and held out his hand to him, he refused to shake hands with the emperor, saying he had no right to do it, being an assistant *commandant*.

After this incident was related to Kerensky he came to the palace at Czarskoe-Selo and called for the chairman of the local soviet (he did not come in regard to this incident, but on some other business). The chairman of the soviet said to Kerensky: "I want to let you know, minister, that we elected Ensign Domodziantz to be assistant commandant of the palace." Kerensky answered: "Yes, I know it, but was it so necessary to elect him; couldn't you elect somebody else?" However, no changes were made, as Kerensky himself had no power.

It was Domodziantz who told the soldiers not to answer the emperor's greeting. Of course the soldiers followed his advice, and, of course, it was the soldiers of the second regiment. I had to ask the emperor not to greet the soldiers, as I was losing control over the men, so the emperor refrained from further greetings to them.

At the same time I must state that it was not only the soldiers who were unfair in their attitude towards the imperial family.

People began to get frightened to show their feelings towards the imperial family. The Grand Duchess Olga was very much liked by

Margaret Hitrovo. Often she came to me and asked me to deliver letters to Olga Nicholaevna. She always used to sign her letters: "Margaret Hitrovo." In the same way, all the letters that were brought to me by Olga Kolsakova, bore also her full signature.

But there were some letters brought to me to be delivered that were signed merely: "Lili" (Den) or "Titi" (Velitchkovskaya). I said to Miss Hitrovo: "You always sign your letters with your full name, the same as is done by Olga Kolsakova, but there are others who hide their names. This is not fair. Suppose the mail should be seen by somebody else and I should be asked who are the authors of those letters? My position would be extremely embarrassing. Please inform the writers of those letters that I desire them to call on me. I must know who they are." After that I ceased to receive letters from "Lili" or "Titi."

Count Apraksin very shortly after the arrest made a request to be allowed to resign, as all his business in the palace was finished and his family resided in Petrograd. By order of the minister of justice (the order was given to me through Korniloff) he was allowed to leave the palace.

Now I have related everything that I remember about the state of the imperial family in Czarskoe-Selo.

I can only add that the imperial family received all the newspapers that appeared at this time, as well as English and French magazines. Of the Russian newspapers I can name: "*Russkoe-Slovo,*" "*Russkaia-Volia,*" "*Retch,*" and "*Novoe-Vremia,*" "*Petrogradsky Listok,*" and "*Petrogradskaia-Gaseta.*"

Now I am going to tell you how the imperial family was moved to Tobolsk. This was preceded by the following events:

About a week before the departure of the imperial family, Kerensky arrived at Czarskoe-Selo. He called me up as well as the chairman of the soviet and the chairman of the military section of the Czarskoe-Selo garrison, Ensign Efimoff (Efimoff was an officer of the second regiment). Kerensky said to us: "Before speaking to you I ask your word that everything I say will be kept secret." We gave our word to Kerensky. Then he told us that according to the resolution of the council of ministers, the imperial family were to be taken out of Czarskoe-Selo, but that the government did not consider it a secret from the "democratic organizations." He said also that I had to go with the imperial family. After that I retired but Kerensky continued a conversation with the chairman of the soviet and Efimoff. In about an hour I met Kerensky and asked him where we were going, adding that

I must give notice to the family so that they could prepare themselves for the trip. Kerensky responded that he would do it personally and proceeded to the palace. In the palace he had a personal talk with the emperor, but he did not give any answer to my question as to when and where we were going.

Later I saw Kerensky about two or three times and always asked him where we were going and what things were to be taken by the imperial family. Kerensky did not answer my questions but only replied: "Tell them that they must take plenty of warm things."

About two days before our departure Kerensky called me up and ordered me to form a detachment of men out of the first, second and fourth regiments that would perform guard duty and that I was to appoint officers in the companies. The word: "Appointment" at this time had quite a special meaning. The agitation in the army was so great that we could not make appointments. A commander of a regiment had no influence whatever—his power being in the hands of the soldiers' committee.

Being afraid that in this way it might happen that amongst the officers selected, there would be some unreliable ones, I asked Kerensky for permission to make my own choice of five officers for each company, out of which two (this number of officers had to be in each company, according to military regulations) could be selected by the men. Kerensky agreed to this.

The evening of the same day I called for the commander of the regiment and chairman of the regimental committees. I said: "A very secret and important mission is going to take place. I want every commander of a regiment to choose a company of ninety-six men and two officers." At the same time I forwarded them a list of officers that I named, out of which the selection had to be made. In answer to my words the commanders of the regiments and the chairmen of the committees of the first and fourth regiments answered: "Very well, sir," but the chairman of the second regiment committee, of course a soldier (whose name I don't remember), answered: "We have made our choice already. I know what sort of mission is being prepared."

"How do you know it, when I don't know anything about it myself?" I asked.

He replied: "Certain people told us all about it and we elected Ensign Dekonsky." Previous to that this ensign was dismissed from the fourth regiment by its own officers and men, but was taken into the second regiment. Even at this time Ensign Dekonsky was undoubtedly a Bolshevik.

When I heard about his election I told the chairman of the committee that Dekonsky should not go under any circumstances. The chairman answered: "Yes, he shall." I had to go to Kerensky and tell him that if Dekonsky was to go with the mission, I refused to go, and that Kerensky being Minister of War could easily make things straight. Kerensky came to Czarskoe-Selo, called for the chairman of the committee and some desperate arguing took place. Kerensky insisted on his demands, but the chairman kept on answering: "Dekonsky shall go."

Finally Kerensky got excited and said in a very loud voice: "Such are my orders." The chairman submitted and departed. When the soldiers that were appointed to the departing detachment learned that Dekonsky was not going, they also refused to go. And due to that the company of the second regiment was composed of the worst elements.

On July 29th I called on Kerensky and met there the assistant *commissar* of the ministry of the court, Paul Michaelovitch Makaroff, an engineer by profession. From their conversation for the first time I understood that the imperial family was being transferred to Tobolsk. The same day Makaroff ordered Engineer Ertel, who formerly used to accompany the dowager empress on her trips, to prepare a train for two a. m. on August 1st.

On July 30th I was asked by the members of the imperial family to bring to the palace the Znamensky holy image of the virgin from the Znamensky Church, as they wanted to hold divine service on the birthday of Alexis Nicholaevitch. I remember that during this day as well as the following I had an enormous amount of trouble on account of the state of mind of the soldiers. I had personally to fulfil all the demands of the imperial family. When the question about the holy image was settled and I think, even after divine service, I was visited by the commander of the district forces (at that time Ensign Kousmin), a colonel and some man in plain clothes. The latter, stretching out his hand to me, said: "May I introduce myself? I was in prison in the Kresty." To this moment I still remember his dirty paw.

As if for the inspection of the guards, Kousmin and the colonel hid themselves in a room that had a door leading into the corridor and waited a full hour for the end of the service, on purpose to watch the imperial family walking back from church. The same evening, after the departure of Kousmin and his gang, Makaroff and Eliah Leonidovitch Tatischeff came to see me. Tatischeff told me that the emperor proposed to him, through Kerensky and Makaroff, to share the fate of the family. He told me: "I was rather surprised, as I am not a member of the court, but if it is the desire of the emperor I will not hesitate for a moment, as my duty is to fulfil the desire of my emperor." (I must note that Tatischeff was invited by the emperor instead of Benckendorf.) It was obvious that Benckendorf could not go. He was very old and he had a wife who was also very old and very ill. Benckendorf was married to the Princess Dolgoruky, mother of Vasily Alexandrovitch Dolgoruky, so it turned out that the stepson had to take the stepfather's place. It was for similar reasons that Madame Narishkina, a lady of honour to the empress, could not go with the imperial family, as she was extremely old and had inflammation of the lungs.

The same day Margaret Hitrovo called on me and made a terrible row, accusing me of concealing from her the fate of the imperial family and stating that she heard that the imperial family were going to be imprisoned in a fortress.

In the evening Kerensky telephoned to me that he would come to Czarskoe-Selo at midnight of August 1st and would say a few words to the detachment of soldiers before its departure.

All the day of July 31st I spent in preparation for the departure. As far as I remember nothing important occurred. Kerensky arrived at midnight. The detachment was ready and we went to inspect the first battalion. Kerensky said a few words to the soldiers, the substance of which was: "You kept the guard of the imperial family in Czarskoe-Selo, and you must do the same thing in Tobolsk, whither the imperial family is being moved, according to the resolution of the council of ministers. Remember, don't strike a man when he is down. Don't behave like ruffians, be polite. You will receive allowances as for the Petrograd district, as well as tobacco and soap. You will also receive a daily allowance."

The same was said by Kerensky to the fourth battalion, but he did not visit the second battalion at all. I must draw your attention to the fact that the soldiers of the first and fourth regiments were in quite different conditions from the soldiers of the second regiment. The former were dressed very smartly and had a large stock of clothes. The soldiers of the second regiment had altogether a low morale, were dirty, and had a smaller supply of clothes. This difference, as you will see, had very important results. After Kerensky had said farewell to the soldiers, he said to me: "Well, now go and get Michael Alexandrovitch.

50

He is at present at the Grand Duke Boris Vladimirovitch's." I went for him in a motor car to the place indicated and met Boris Vladimirovitch, an unknown lady, and Michael Alexandrovitch with his wife, and Mr. Johnson, an English secretary.

The three of us, Michael Alexandrovitch, Johnson and myself, proceeded to the Alexandrovsky palace. Johnson remained in the motor car and Michael Alexandrovitch went to the waiting-room, where were Kerensky and the officer of the day. All three of them went to see the emperor in his room. I remained in the waiting-room. Suddenly Alexis Nicholaevitch ran towards me and asked: "Is that Uncle Mimi that has arrived?" I answered that it was he, and Alexis Nicholaevitch asked my permission to hide himself behind the door. "I want to see him when he goes out," said the *czarevitch*. He hid himself behind the door and looked through the slit at Michael Alexandrovitch laughing like a child at his ingenuity. Michael Alexandrovitch spoke with the emperor for about ten minutes and then left.

The imperial family left for the station at five o'clock in the morning. Two trains were prepared. The imperial family, the people with them, some servants and a company of the first regiment took the first train; the remaining servants and companies the second train. The luggage was distributed in both trains. In the first train Vershinin, a member of the *duma*, also took a place, and Engineer Makaroff, and the chairman of the military section, Ensign Efimoff was also sent at the wish of Kerensky, in order that on his return he might report to the soviet the arrival of the imperial family at Tobolsk. The places in the trains were distributed in the following manner: In the first very comfortable car (of the International Company sleeping cars) went the emperor in one compartment, the empress in another, the grand duchesses in the third, Alexis Nicholaevitch and Nagorny in the fourth. Demidova, Tegleva and Ersberg in the fifth, Tchemodouroff and Volkoff in the sixth.

In another car the places were taken by Tatischeff and Dolgoruky in one compartment, Botkin in a small compartment, Schneider with her maids, Katia and Masha, in one compartment, Gilliard in one compartment, Hendrikova with her maid, Mejanz, in a compartment. In the third car places were taken by: Vershinin, Makaroff, myself, my A. D. C, Lieutenant Nicholas Alexandrovitch Mundel, the commander of the First company, Ensign Ivan Trofimovitch Zima, Ensign Vladimir Alexandrovitch (I am not very sure of his name) Mesiankin, and in a separate little compartment. Ensign Efimoff took his place, as nobody desired to travel in his company. The fourth car was a dining car, in which the imperial family used to have their meals, except the empress and Alexis Nicholaevitch who had their meals together in the empress's compartment. The soldiers were placed in three third-class cars. Several baggage cars were also attached to the train. Nothing particular happened until we arrived at Perm. Just before the arrival our train was stopped and a man looking like a minor railroad official, with a big white beard, boarded the car I was in. He introduced himself as the chairman of the railroad workmen and announced that the railroad workmen ("*Tovarischy*," comrades) wanted to know who was in the train and would not allow the train to proceed until their curiosity was gratified. Vershinin and Makaroff showed him the papers with Kerensky's signature on them.

The train continued on its journey. We arrived at Tumen approximately the fourth or fifth of August (of the Old Style). We arrived at Tumen in the evening and on the same day took our places aboard two steamers. The imperial family, the persons with them, and the company of the first regiment took their places on the steamer *Russ*. A part of the servants and the company of the second and fourth regiments— on the steamer *Kormiletz*. The ships were good and comfortable, but the *Kormiletz* was inferior to the *Russ*. We arrived at Tobolsk, as far as I can remember, during the evening of August 6th, about five or six p. m. The house where the imperial family was to take residence was not yet ready, so we spent a few days on the ships.

When we travelled on the train, it did not stop at big stations, but only at the intermediate stations. The emperor and other passengers frequently left the train and proceeded ahead of it, and the train slowly moved after them. When we lived on the steamers, sometimes we put them alongside on the bank, at a distance of about ten *versts* from the towns, where the family could have a walk.

During the time when the family lived on the steamers Engineer Makaroff was putting the house in order. Tatischeff, Hendrikova, Schneider, Toutelberg, Ersberg, Tegleva and Demidova were engaged in arranging the furniture. When the house was ready the family moved into it. For this purpose a good-looking carriage was assigned to the empress. She rode with Tatiana Nicholaevna. All the others walked.

Two houses were assigned for the residence of the imperial family, their suite and servants. One was the governor's house, the other was opposite to the governor's and belonged to Mr. Korniloff.

Not any of the furniture was taken from Czarskoe-Selo. So the furniture of the governor's house was used, but some of the things had to be ordered and bought in Tobolsk.

The only things that were taken from Czarskoe-Selo for the imperial family were camp beds. Later, a number of things were sent from Czarskoe-Selo after the necessity for them was discovered by Makaroff.

The arrangement of the rooms in the governor's house was as follows: The first floor opened into the lobby; from this lobby there ran a corridor that divided the house into two parts. The first room opening out of this lobby on the right-hand side was occupied by the officer of the day. Next to it was the room occupied by Demidova. In this room she had her meals, as well as Tegleva, Toutelberg and Ersberg. The room next to it was occupied by Gilliard, who used to give lessons to Alexis Nicholaevitch, Maria Nicholaevna, and Anastasia Nicholaevna. Next to that was the dining-room of the imperial family. On the left side of the corridor, opposite the room of the officer of the day, was a room occupied by Tchemodouroff, next to it the pantry, next to the pantry a room occupied by Tegleva and Ersberg, next to that a room occupied by Toutelberg.

A staircase above Tchemodouroff's room led to the upper story into the workroom of the emperor. Next to the workroom was a hall. There was also another staircase leading from the hall to the lobby. A corridor leading from the hall divided the upper story into halves. The first room on the right was a drawing-room, next to it was the emperor and empress's bedroom, next to the bedroom was the bedroom of the grand duchesses. Opposite the drawing-room was the room occupied by Alexis Nicholaevitch, next to that was the lavatory, and next to the lavatory was the bathroom.

All the other people of the suite were located in Korniloff's house.

The following persons arrived with the imperial family at Tobolsk: (1) Eliah Leonidovitch Tatischeff, general *aide de camp* to the emperor; (2). Prince Alexander Vasilievitch Dolgoruky; (3) Eugene Sergeevitch Botkin, physician; (4) Countess Anastasia Vasilievna Hendrikova, personal maid of honour to the empress; (5) Baroness Sophie Carlovna Buxhoevden, personal maid of honour to the empress; (6) Katherine Adolfovna Schneider, court lecturer; (7) Peter Andreevitch Gilliard; (8) Alexandra Alexandrovna Tegleva, nurse; (9) Elizabeth Nicholaeyna Ersberg, waiting-maid to the grand duchesses; (10) Maria Goustavovna Toutelberg, waiting-maid of the empress; (11) Anna Stephanovna

Demidova, another waiting-maid of the empress; (12) Victorina Vladi-morovna Nikolaeva, a ward of Hendrikova; (13) Pauline Mejanz, Hendrikova's maid; (14) Katia and Masha (I do not know their sur-names), maids of Miss Schneider; (15) Terenty Ivanovitch Tchemo-douroff, valet of the emperor; (16) Stephan Makaroff, assistant to Tchemodouroff; (17) Alexis Andreevitch Volkoff, servant of the empress; (18) Ivan Dimitrievtch Sedneff, servant of the grand duchesses; (19) Michael Karpoff, grand duchesses' footman; (20) Klementy Gregory-vitch Nagorny, *czarevitch's* footman; (21) Sergius Ivanoff, Gilliard's serv-ant; (22) Tioutin, the waiter of Tatischeff and Dolgoruky; (23) Francis Jouravsky, waiter; (24) Alexis Troupp, footman; (25) Gregory Solo-douhin, footman; (26) Dormidontov, footman; (27) Kisseleff, footman; (28) Ermolay Gouseff, footman; (29) Ivan Michaelovitch Haritonoff, cook; (30) Kokischeff, cook; (31) Ivan, I think, Vereschagin, cook; (32) Leonid Sedneff, assistant cook; (33) Sergius Michailoff, assistant cook; (34) Francis Purkovsky, assistant cook; (35) Terchin, assistant cook; (36) Alexander Kirpitchnikoff, clerk, performing in Tobolsk the duties of janitor; (37) Alexis Nicholaevitch Dimitrieff, barber; (38) Rojkoff, in charge of the wine cellars; after our arrival in Tobolsk we were joined by (39) Vladimir Nicholaevitch Derevenko, physician; (40) Mr. Sidney Ivanovitch Gibbes.

Our life in Tobolsk went on peacefully. The restrictions were the same as in Czarskoe-Selo and all felt even freer than in Czarskoe-Selo.

The officer of the day kept to his room and nobody interfered with the private life of the imperial family. Everybody got up early, except the empress, as I told you when I was describing the life in Czarskoe-Selo. In the morning, after breakfast, the emperor usually took a walk and always had some physical exercise. The children also had their walk. Everybody did what he or she wanted to do. In the morning the emperor used to read and write his diary. The children took lessons. The empress read and embroidered or painted. Lunch was served at eleven o'clock. After lunch the family usually had a walk. Frequently the emperor used to saw logs with Dolgoruky, Tatischeff or Gilliard; sometimes the grand duchesses took a part in this exercise. Tea was served at four o'clock and usually during this time everybody was at the window watching the outside life of the town. Six o'clock was dinner time. After dinner came Tatischeff, Dolgoruky, Botkin and Derevenko. Sometimes they played cards. Of the family the only card players were the emperor and the Grand Duchess Olga. Sometimes in the evening the emperor used to read aloud while everybody listened. Sometimes plays were staged, usually French or English. Tea was served at eight o'clock and a conversation always took place until about eleven but never as late as twelve o'clock. After that everybody retired. The *czarevitch* retired at nine o'clock, or at a time very close to it.

The empress always dined upstairs and sometimes the *czarevitch* dined with her. The rest of the family ate in the dining-room.

All the members of the suite and the servants could go out of the house when and where they wanted to. They were not under any restrictions in this way. The movements of the imperial family were, of course, limited, the same as in Czarskoe-Selo. They could go only to church. Divine service was conducted in the following manner: If it was a late service it took place in the house and was there performed by the clergy of Blagoveschensky church. The priest. Father Vasilieff, officiated. The imperial family went to church only for the early service. For the purpose of going to church they had to go through the garden and across the street. Sentries were placed all the way leading to the church, and there was no admittance to church for strangers.

As far as you could judge, even from the list of the servants attached to the imperial family, the government tried to conserve the condition of life that was appropriate to the position of the imperial family. When we left Czarskoe-Selo I was told by Kerensky: "Don't forget that this is the former emperor and neither he nor his family must be in need of anything." The guard of the house was under my command. After the family arrived at Tobolsk I think they got used to me, and as far as I understand, they did not have any feeling against me. I can state that because before our departure I was received by the empress who gave me a holy picture, with which she blessed me.

This peaceful and quiet life did not continue very long.

I see some resemblance between the first periods of life in Czarskoe-Selo and Tobolsk. The relatively easy conditions of life in Czarskoe-Selo at the beginning gradually got worse. At that time the government was gradually losing ground. At the same time agitation grew amongst the soldiers whose state of mind got worse and worse. Finally, seeing the necessity of fighting for power and at the same time wishing well towards the family, the Kerensky government made up its mind to transfer the imperial family from the centre of the political struggle to a quiet and peaceful place. This turned out to be absolutely right. The population of Tobolsk was very well disposed towards the imperial family. When we were approaching Tobolsk, all the inhabitants turned out on the piers and when the family was proceeding towards the house it was apparent that the population had kindly feelings towards them. At this time the people were afraid to show their sympathies openly, so they tried to show their feelings in a secret way. Many donations were made to the imperial family, mostly food and sweets, though I must say that the imperial family received very little of it, as most of it was eaten on the way by the servants.

Soon the general agitation struck Tobolsk, as special attention was given to this town by all sorts of politicians, solely because of the fact that it was the residence of the imperial family.

I had the command over my men only till September. In September there came a *commissar* of the government by the name of Vasily Semenovitch Pankratoff. This man brought a letter signed by Kerensky which stated that from now on I would have to be subordinate to Pankratoff and therefore obey all his orders. Pankratoff told me himself that when aged eighteen, defending a woman, he killed a *gendarme* in Kiev. For that he was court-martialled and imprisoned in Schüsselburg fortress, where he was placed in solitary confinement for fifteen years. After that he was exiled in the Yakout district, where he lived for twenty-seven years.

His assistant was Ensign Alexander Vladimirovitch Nikolsky, who was also exiled in the Yakout district for being a member of the Social-Revolutionary party. During this time he got friendly with Pankratoff. When Pankratoff was appointed *commissar* to the imperial family he asked Nikolsky to be his assistant.

Pankratoff was a clever man with a well-developed mind, and an extraordinarily mild disposition. Nikolsky was tough; he was graduated from a seminary and had hardly any manners. He was as obstinate as a bull, and the moment he decided anything he went towards his object breaking everything in his way. After they had arrived and seen how things were getting along, Nikolsky immediately announced to me his surprise about the way that "Everybody is so freely coming and going (the suite and servants). It can't be done in such a way. This way they can let in an outsider. Photos have to be taken of everybody." I started to persuade him not to do it, as the sentries knew everybody's appearance very well.

Nikolsky responded: "We were ordered to have our pictures taken in front view and profile, so their pictures should be taken." He ran to the photographer and pictures were taken of a number of people and suitable inscriptions were placed on each photo. Alexis Nicholaevitch, being a very playful and mischievous boy, on one occasion peeped through the fence. After this was learned by Nikolsky he came and made a huge fuss about it. He reprimanded the soldier who was on duty and spoke in a very sharp tone to the *czarevitch*. The boy got offended and protested to me that Nikolsky was shouting at him. The same day I asked Pankratoff to cool down Nikolsky's zeal.

As I stated before, Pankratoff personally would not have done any harm to the imperial family, but nevertheless it turned out that, both being politicians, they were the cause of a lot of trouble. Not understanding life, and being true members of the Social-Revolutionary party, they insisted upon everybody joining the party and began to convert the soldiers to their faith. They started a school where they taught soldiers literature and all sorts of useful knowledge, but after every lesson they talked politics to their pupils, telling them the program of the Social-Revolutionary Party. The soldiers listened and understood it in their own way. The results of these lectures were that the soldiers were converted to Bolshevism. They also wanted to print a newspaper and call it *Zemliai Volia* (Land and Freedom).

There was a man by the name of Pisarevsky who lived during this period in Tobolsk. He was a wild social democrat and therefore an enemy to the S. R.'s. This Pisarevsky started his campaign among the soldiers against Pankratoff and Nikolsky. Pisarevsky was publishing a Bolshevik newspaper called *Rabotchaya-Gazeta* (*Workmen's Newspaper*). Seeing that Pankratoff had a certain influence amongst the soldiers, Pisarevsky began to invite the soldiers to his home and demoralise them. Shortly after the arrival of Pankratoff and Nikolsky our detachment was divided into two groups—the Pankratoff party and the party of Pisarevsky—in other words, Bolsheviks. This Bolshevik party was composed of the soldiers of the second regiment who were the poorest and had a very low morale. A very small number of men formed a third group, I should say, neutral, and most of its members were soldiers that were mobilised in 1906 and 1907.

The result of these political campaigns was the demoralisation of the soldiers, who began to act like ruffians. Formerly they did not want to make trouble for the imperial family. Now they did not know what next they should demand for themselves. They followed only their own interests, but the result of it was always that either a member of the imperial family or some of the persons attached to them had to suffer. At first the soldiers came to me under the influence of the political struggle and said: "We have to sleep in bunks, our food is bad, but '*Nicholashka*' (a slang name for the emperor that was popular during the revolution) who is arrested, has such an amount of food that his cooks throw it in the waste bucket."

At this time life in Tobolsk was not expensive. Though Kerensky had not fulfilled his promise and we received Omsk allowances and not those of the Petrograd district, the allowances were large enough to obtain very good food for the men. For the purpose of avoiding new protests from the soldiers it was necessary to take up money matters with Pignatti, the district *commissar*, and increase the allowance to one thousand *roubles*, substituting the good food of the soldiers for the unnecessary and luxurious.

As I said before, Kerensky promised the soldiers some pay additional to their previous daily allowance. The month of November came and no additional money was forwarded to us. Again the soldiers came to me and said: "They promise us everything and give us nothing. We are going to procure for ourselves the daily pay. We intend to demolish the shops and to obtain daily pay in this manner." Once more I had to visit Pignatti and borrow from him fifteen thousand *roubles*. In this way I distributed to the soldiers daily pay to the amount of fifty *kopeks*, and shut their mouths for a time.

At the same time the soldiers made up their mind to send delegates to Moscow and Petrograd to settle this question of pay. They chose for their mission Matveieff and Lupin. After some time they both returned (Matveieff returned as an officer); they said that they were promised that the money would be forwarded. Again I had to go to Pignatti and beg him once more for fifteen thousand *roubles*, as the soldiers did not believe any more in promises, and being out of my control, could create an unbelievable amount of trouble.

When the soldiers learned from the newspapers that the men called to the colours in 1906-1907 were demobilised, they demanded their demobilisation also. After I got on my side the soldiers who were not to be demobilised the others were persuaded to stay.

Then came the Bolshevist revolution. The wild movement that spread throughout Russia caused us many sufferings. It was about this time that the following incident took place: Father Vasilieff, the clergyman who performed divine service, was not a man of great tact. Although he was very well disposed towards the imperial family, he rendered them very poor service by his behaviour. On October 24th (before the Bolshevist revolution), the day of the anniversary of the

GRAND DUCHESS OLGA

GRAND DUCHESS TATIANA

GRAND DUCHESS MARIA

GRAND DUCHESS ANASTASIA

accession of the emperor to the throne, the imperial family was having its communion. (The day before, during the night service held in the house the imperial family had made their confessions.) Nobody took any particular notice of divine service on this day, but Father Vasilieff permitted a very foolish thing to happen: when the imperial family left the church, the church bells rang continuously until the family entered the house.

At Christmas, on December 25th, the imperial family was present in church during the early service. As was the custom, after the service a thanksgiving prayer took place. On account of the cold weather I relieved the sentries from their posts before the end of the service, leaving only a small number on duty by the church. Some of the remaining soldiers entered the church, the older ones, to pray, but the majority to warm themselves. Usually the total number of soldiers in the church at any one time was very small. On entering the church on this day I noticed that there were more soldiers present than usual. I could not explain how it happened. Maybe the reason was that Christmas was considered a big holiday. When the thanksgiving service was coming to an end I left the church and ordered a soldier to call the guard.

After that I did not enter the church and I did not hear the end of the service. When the imperial family left the church, Pankratoff, who was there too, said to me: "Do you know what the priest has done? He has read the prayer for the prolongation of the life of the emperor, the empress and the whole family, mentioning their names in the prayer. After the soldiers heard it they started grumbling." This useless demonstration of Father Vasilieff resulted in much trouble. The soldiers started an uprising and made up their minds to kill, or at least to arrest the clergyman. It was very difficult to persuade them not to take any aggressive steps and to await the decision of an investigating committee. The bishop, Hermogen, immediately transferred Father Vasilieff to the Abalaksky monastery for the time being, the situation was so strained. I went to the bishop personally and requested that another clergyman be appointed. After that Father Hlynoff performed the services for the imperial family.

The results of these troubles with the clergyman was that the soldiers lost all faith in my word. Their comment was: "When the service takes place in their home, probably a prayer for the prolongation of the life of the imperial family is always made." So the men decided not to allow the imperial family to go to church, and to permit them to pray only in the presence of a soldier. The only thing I could obtain for them was permission for the imperial family to visit church on the "*Dvounadesiaty-Prasdniky*" (very important holy days in the orthodox church). I had to submit to their decision that a soldier should be present at divine service at home. In this way the tactlessness of Father Vasilieff was the reason why the soldiers were permitted to enter the house, which, prior to that time, they were not allowed to do. Another incident happened a little later. A soldier by the name of Rybakoff was present at divine service and heard the clergyman during his prayer using the name of Queen Alexandra (a saint). A new fuss was started. I had to call up Rybakoff, find a calendar, and explain to him that during the prayers they did not speak of the Empress Alexandra Theodorovna, but only of a saint by the name of Queen Alexandra.

When the demobilisation of the army took place my sharpshooters began to take their discharge. Instead of the old soldiers who were departing, some young ones were sent from the reserves of Czarskoe-Selo. And those soldiers that came, having previously been located in the centre of the political struggle, were vicious and corrupt.

The Pisarevsky group increased in number and was strengthened by new Bolsheviki arriving. Finally, Pankratoff, due to the propaganda of Pisarevsky, was declared to be "counter-revolutionary" and expelled by the soldiers. He departed and so did Nikolsky.

The soldiers sent a telegram requesting the presence of a Bolshevik *commissar* in Tobolsk, but for some reason the commissar did not arrive.

Not knowing what other objections could be made, the soldiers decided to forbid the persons of the suite to leave the house. I explained how ridiculous this demand was. They changed their mind and decided to let them go out, but only in the company of a sentry. Finally they got sick of that and changed their minds so as to let everybody out of the house twice a week, and each time for not longer than two hours, but without the company of a sentry.

On one occasion, wishing to say goodbye to a large number of departing soldiers, the emperor and empress ascended a small hill formed of ice for the amusement of the children. The remaining soldiers, feeling very angry about it, levelled the little hill to the ground, saying that somebody might shoot at the imperial family when they were on the top of the hill, and the guard would be responsible for it.

One day the emperor dressed himself in a "*tcherkeska*" (uniform of a tribe) and wore a dagger in his belt. Tumult started amongst the soldiers: "They must be searched, they carry weapons." I made great efforts to persuade them not to make the search. Personally I went to see the emperor and, explaining the situation, asked him to give me the dagger (later it was taken by Rodionoff). Dolgoruky and Gilliard handed me their swords and these were all hung up on the wall of my office.

I have quoted the words of Kerensky spoken before our departure from Czarskoe-Selo. The imperial family was in no need of anything in Tobolsk, but money vanished and no more arrived. We began to live on credit. I wrote about this to Lieutenant General Anitchkoff, who was charged with the intendency of the court, but with no results. Finally, Haritonoff, the cook, told me that he was no longer trusted and that it looked as if they wouldn't give him anything more on credit. I went to the director of the Tobolsk branch of the national bank and he advised me to speak to a merchant X, who was a monarchist, and had some money free in the bank. By virtue of a letter of exchange endorsed by Tatischeff, Dolgoruky and myself, the merchant gave me twenty thousand *roubles*. Of course I asked Tatischeff and Dolgoruky to remain silent about this loan and by no means to mention it to the emperor or any one of the imperial family.

All these events were very trying to me. This was hell and not life. My nerves were strained to the limit of their endurance. It was very hard for me to look for and beg money for the maintenance of the imperial family, so one day when the soldiers made a resolution that the officers should take off their shoulder straps, I could stand no more. I understood that I had lost absolutely all control of the men and realised my impotence. I went to the house and asked Tegleva to report to the emperor that I begged to be received by him. The emperor received me in Tegleva's room and I said to him: "Your majesty, authority is slipping out of my hands. They took off our shoulder straps. I can't be useful to you anymore. I wish to resign, if you will not object to it. My nerves are strained. I am exhausted."

The emperor put his arm over my shoulder, his eyes were filled with tears. He said to me: "I beg of you to remain, Evgenii Stepanovitch, for my sake, for the sake of my wife and for the sake of my children. You must stand it. You see that all of us are suffering."

Then he embraced me and we kissed each other. I resolved to remain.

It happened once that Dorofeef, a soldier of the fourth regiment (the appearance of the detachment changed completely), came and told me that at a meeting of the soldiers' committee it was decided that the emperor must take off his shoulder straps and he was charged to go with me and take them off. I tried to persuade Dorofeef not to do it. He behaved aggressively, calling the emperor "*Nicolashka*" and was extremely angry during the conversation. I pointed out to him that it would be very embarrassing if the emperor were to refuse to do it. The soldier answered: "If he refuses to do it I will tear them off myself."

Then I said: "But suppose he strikes you in the face?"

He replied: "Then I will strike him also."

What more could I do? I tried again to persuade him, saying that things are not always as easy as they look and that the emperor was a cousin of the king of England, and that very serious complications might follow. I advised the soldiers to ask instructions from Moscow. I caught them on that point—they left me and wired to Moscow. Then I went to see Tatischeff, asking him to beg the emperor to refrain from wearing shoulder straps in the presence of the soldiers. After that the emperor wore a black fur Romanoff overcoat that bore no shoulder straps.

Swings were made for the children. The grand duchesses used them. The soldiers of the second regiment while on sentry duty carved out on the board of the swings with their bayonets the most indecent words. The emperor saw them and the board was removed. This was done when Sergeant Shikunoff was the captain of the guard. He was a Bolshevik.

I do not remember what day it was when I received a telegram from Karelin, a *commissar* in charge of the former ministry of the imperial court. It stated that the nation had no more means to maintain the *czar's* family, that they ought to support themselves and the Soviets would give them only a soldier's ration, quarters and heat.

This was one of the worst hardships inflicted by the Bolsheviki on the imperial family. It was also said in the telegram that the family could not spend more than six hundred *roubles* monthly per person. Naturally, after this order, the quality of the food served to the family deteriorated. It acted detrimentally also on the position of the persons belonging to the suite. The imperial family could not any longer maintain the persons belonging to their suite, so those who had no money of their own were obliged to leave. A number of servants were discharged: (1) The waiter, Gregory Ivanoff Solodouhin; (2) The waiter, Ermolai Guseff; (3) Dormidontoff, the waiter; (4) Kisseleff, the waiter; (5) Vereschagin the cook; (6) Semen Michailoff, the cook's assistant; (7) Francis Purkovsky; (8) Stepan Makaroff, Tchemodouroff's assistant; (9) Stupel, the valet (I forgot to mention his name before as having been among the servants); and there were some others.

The soldiers still having their minds occupied with the question of their daily pay sent to Moscow a man by the name of Loupin, a Bolshevik. Having returned, he described the situation in Moscow in rosy hues and brought the very encouraging news to the soldiers that instead of the fifty *kopeks* per day they received at the time of the provisional government, they were to get three *roubles* per day. This news quickly made all the soldiers Bolshevik. "This shows what a good sort *commissars* really are. The provisional government promised us fifty *kopeks* per day, but did not pay it. The *commissars* will give us three *roubles* per day." Joyfully they told this news to one another.

Loupin brought the paper that contained the order to put Tatischeff, Dolgoruky, Hendrikova and Schneider under arrest. He also brought the news that our detachment would soon be relieved and a new commissar sent with a fresh detachment of men. I suppose the soldiers were afraid of the arrival of the new *commissar*. All persons belonging to the suite they decided to transfer to the governor's house and to put them under guard there. All these persons were moved to the house except Gibbes (the Englishman did not like to live with anybody else, so he was allowed to live outside).

New partitions were made in the house, in the entrance room adjoining Tchemodouroff's room, thereby providing space for Demidova, Tegleva and Ersberg. Demidova's room was divided by a curtain, and Tatischeff and Dolgoruky were quartered there. In the room where Ersberg and Tegleva previously lived, Schneider and her two maids were placed. The room previously occupied by Toutelberg was; given to Hendrikova and Nikolaieva. Toutelberg was placed under the main stair-way behind the partition. In such a manner we were able to avoid intruding upon the privacy of the imperial family.

Gibbes was settled in a small house near the kitchen. So all persons, including the servants, were under arrest. Only in cases of the utmost necessity were a few of the servants allowed to go to town.

As I said, Loupin brought news of the coming of a new *commissar*. The *commissar* arrived, but he was not the same man that Loupin had been speaking about. The *commissar* who was sent from Omsk to supervise the life of the imperial family, was a Jew named Dutzman. He took up his quarters in Korniloff's house. He did not play any active part, and never came to the house. Very soon he was elected to be secretary of the district soviet and stayed there permanently.

During this time the leaders of the soviet were: Dutzman, a Jew named Peissel and a Lett named Disler. Zaslavsky also apparently took part in the soviet activities. He was, as I understand, the representative of Yekaterinburg, or, properly speaking, Ural district soviet. The reason for his arrival was not clear to me. It seemed that at this time the Omsk Bolsheviki were quarrelling with those of Yekaterinburg. The Omsk Bolsheviki desired to include Tobolsk under their jurisdiction in Western Siberia; but the Yekaterinburg people wanted to in-elude it in the Ural district. Dutzman was an Omsk Bolsheviki representative, and Zaslavsky was a representative of Yekaterinburg Bolsheviki. I presume that Zaslavsky came to Tobolsk because, even at this time, the Yekaterinburg Bolsheviki intended to move us from Tobolsk to Yekaterinburg. Matveieff, a Bolshevik, whom I have mentioned many times, used to visit the soviet frequently. Once he told me that the soviet asked that two soldiers selected from each company should call on them. Six soldiers were delegated. They informed me that the soviet had decided to transfer all the *czar's* family "To the Hill," which meant prison.

(The Tobolsk prison was situated on a height, so it was called "The Hill"). I pointed out that the *czar's* family were under the authority of the central soviet and not of the local soviet, but this did not help. I advanced another argument, saying that it was impossible to execute their order or demand, as with the imperial family it would be necessary also to transfer to the prison all the soldiers of our detachment— which was not practicable, and that we could not do otherwise, as in case of an attack on the prison there would be no force left to defend it. Our soldiers began to get boisterous, and the soviet was obliged to change their opinion and announced that no decision had yet been arrived at, but that the soviet merely mentioned this suggestion in a tentative way.

All of us were awaiting the arrival of the new *commissar*. It was rumoured that it was Trotzky himself who was coming. Finally the Commissar Iakovleff arrived. He came to Tobolsk in the evening of February 9th and stayed in Korniloff's house. He was accompanied by a certain Avdeieff (I considered him to be Iakovleff's assistant), a telegraph operator, who was transmitting Iakovleff's telegrams to Moscow and to Yekaterinburg, and a young boy.

Iakovleff appeared to be thirty-two or thirty-three. His hair was of jet black colour; he was taller than the average; thin, but strong and muscular, apparently Russian; gave the impression of being very energetic; he was dressed like a sailor; his words were short and abrupt; but his language was suggestive of a good education; his hands were clean and his fingers thin; he gave one the impression of being cultivated and having acquired a training and experience usually associated with those who have lived abroad for a long time. Leaving Gilliard, he said: "*Bon jour, Monsieur.*" (This showed some knowledge of French.) Iakovleff told me that he lived in Finland, where for some reason or other he had been sentenced to be hanged. He succeeded in escaping, and later lived in Switzerland and in Germany. As far as I remember his Christian names were Vasily Vasilievitch, Iakovleff being his surname.

Avdeieff appeared to be about twenty-six or twenty-seven years of age, medium height, rather thin, dirty, uncultivated; he wore soldier's clothes. His face was round but not fat and bore no signs of drunkenness.

Iakovleff said that he was born in Ufa or perhaps somewhere in the Ufa district. A detachment of Reds came with him. They were cavalry and infantry and all young soldiers. Iakovleff's idea was to make us understand that he was quite popular in Ufa, that he knew there quite a large number of people; and for this reason he had organised his detachment there. His men were quartered partly in Korniloff's house and partly in the apartment occupied by my soldiers. On the morning of April 10th Iakovleff came to me together with Matveieff and introduced himself as extraordinary *commissar*. Three documents were in his hands. All these documents bore the imprint of the "*Russian Federated Soviet Republic*," and were signed by: Sverdloff and Ovanesoff (or Avanesoff). The first document was addressed to me and contained an order for me to execute without delay all the requests of the extraordinary *commissar*, Tovarisch (comrade) Iakovleff, who was assigned to perform a mission of great importance.

My refusal or neglect to execute these orders would result in my being killed on the spot. The second document was addressed to the soldiers of our detachment. It contained the same orders as the first, and carried also a threat of the same penalty—court-martial by a revolutionary tribunal and instant death. The third document was an identification of Iakovleff that stated the fact of his having been appointed for an extraordinary mission, but no details of the character of the mission were given. Without explaining to me the reason of his arrival, Iakovleff told me that he wanted to talk to the soldiers.

At eleven o'clock I assembled the men of my detachment. Iakovleff announced to them that their representative "Tovarisch" (comrade) Loupin, had been in Moscow, where he petitioned for an increase in their daily allowance.

Now Iakovleff had brought the money with him. Every soldier was to get three *roubles* per day. After that he exhibited his identification. Matveieff read it aloud. The soldiers started to examine the document. They paid great attention to the seal on it. It appeared as if they did not have very much confidence in Iakovleff. Iakovleff understood this and began speaking about daily allowances, the time for the relief of our detachment, and things of the same sort. Apparently he knew very well how to handle a mob and how to play upon their weak points. He spoke eloquently and earnestly. At the conclusion of his speech he dwelt on the misunderstanding between the soldiers and the local soviet that occurred on account of the Soviet's decision to imprison the imperial family, and he promised to settle this question.

After that he went with me to see the house. He looked first at the exterior view; then he entered the lower floor, and then the upper. As far as I can remember, he saw from a distance the emperor and the grand duchesses, who were at that time in the court. I suppose he did not see the empress, but, as I remember, accompanied by Avdeieff, he visited the *czarevitch*. I had the impression that Iakovleff tried to persuade Avdeieff that the *czarevitch* was ill. I remember that this day the officer on duty was Ensign Semenoff. Avdeieff wished to remain in the room of the officer of the day, but Semenoff protested and succeeded in drawing Avdeieff away. Nothing else happened during this day.

On April 11th Iakovleff again requested that the soldiers be assembled. There came to the meeting with him, Zaslavsky, a representative of the soviet, and Degtiareff, a student. The student was sent from Omsk, so he represented the Siberian interests in the Tobolsk soviet. Zaslavsky represented the interests of the Ural district. The student began to speak to the soldiers. He accused Zaslavsky of upsetting the nerves of the soldiers, of spreading false rumours about the danger threatening the imperial family, and of saying that somebody was digging a tunnel under the house. Such rumours were really afoot, and once we passed a very disturbed night awaiting trouble. These rumours originated in the soviet. I had learned about them when I went to the soviet the time they resolved to imprison the imperial family. At this time the main argument for their decision was the "danger for the imperial family in remaining in the governor's house." Such was the substance of the student's speech. Zaslavsky vainly tried to defend himself. He was hissed and went away. Zaslavsky came to Tobolsk about a week before Iakovleff's arrival and left Tobolsk about six hours before Iakovleff's departure. Later I will tell you the motive of this performance in assembling the soldiers and why Iakovleff had to do it.

The same day at eleven o'clock in the evening, Captain Aksiouta came to me and reported that Iakovleff had assembled the detachment's committee and announced his intention of taking the *czar's* family out of Tobolsk. Iakovleff said that not only the emperor but also the whole family would have to leave. In the morning on the 12th of April Iakovleff came to me and said that according to the decision of "the central executive committee" he must take the family out of Tobolsk. I asked him: "Why?" and "What will you do with the *czarevitch?* He cannot travel as he is sick."

Iakovleff answered me: "This certainly is the trouble. I have talked this matter over through direct wire with the C. E. C. and received the order to leave the family in Tobolsk and to transfer only the emperor." (Usually he called him "the former emperor.") "When could we go to see them? I intend to leave the town tomorrow." I told him he might see the family after lunch—around two o'clock. Then he left me. I went to the house and asked, as far as I remember, Tatischeff, to ask the emperor at what time he could receive Iakovleff and myself. The emperor made an appointment at two o'clock, after lunch was over. At two o'clock Iakovleff and I entered the hall. The emperor and empress stood in the middle of the hall. Iakovleff stopped a little distance from them and bowed. Then he said: "I have to tell you" (he was talking to the emperor only), "that I am the special representative of the Moscow Central Executive Committee, and my mission is to take all your family out of Tobolsk, but, as your son is ill, I have received a second order which says that you alone must leave."

The emperor answered: "I will not go anywhere."

Upon which Iakovleff said: "I beg you not to refuse. I am compelled to execute the order. In case of your refusal I must take you by force or resign. In the latter case they would probably decide to send a less scrupulous sort of man to take my position. Be calm, I am responsible with my life for your security. If you do not want to go alone you could take with you the people you desire. Be ready, we are leaving tomorrow at four o'clock."

Then Iakovleff again bowed to the emperor and the empress and left. At the same time the emperor, who did not reply to Iakovleff's last words, turned abruptly and accompanied by the empress, went out of the hall. Iakovleff went down. I followed him, but when we were going out the emperor made a sign to me to remain. I went down with Iakovleff and after he left, returned upstairs. In the hall I saw the emperor, empress, Tatischeff, and Dolgoruky. They stayed by the round table in the comer. The emperor asked me where they intended to take him. I replied that personally I did not know, but that it was possible to understand from some hints made by Iakovleff that it was intended to take the emperor to Moscow. The following reasons made me think of that: In the morning on the 12th of April, Iakovleff came to me and said that he would go at first with the emperor, then return to get the family. I asked him: "When do you intend to come back?"

Iakovleff answered: "Well, in four or five days we will reach our destination. I will remain there a few days and start back. I will be here again in about ten days or two weeks."

This is the reason why I told the emperor that Iakovleff intended to take him to Moscow. Then the emperor said: "I suppose they want to force me to sign the Brest-Litovsk treaty, but I would rather give my right hand to be cut off than to sign that treaty."

"I shall also go," said the empress giving evidence of deep emotion. "If I am not there they will force him to do something in the same way that it was done before," and added something about Rodzianko. Obviously the empress referred to the emperor's abdication.

Thus ended the conversation and I went to Korniloff's house to see Iakovleff. He asked me who were the persons going. And he repeated (for the second time), that anybody could go with the emperor on condition that he did not take much baggage.

I returned to the house and asked Tatischeff to let me know who were the persons who intended to go. I promised to call in an hour's time for the answer. I came back and Tatischeff said to me that the following persons were leaving Tobolsk: the emperor, the empress, the Grand Duchess Maria, Botkin, Dolgoruky, Tchemodouroff, Sedneff, the waiter, and Demidova, the maid. When I reported the names to Iakovleff he answered: "It's all the same to me." I suppose Iakovleff's only idea was to get the emperor out of Tobolsk as soon as possible. When he noticed the emperor's unwillingness to go alone, Iakovleff thought: "That's all the same to me; let him take whom he likes; but do it quickly." That was the reason why he repeated so often: "That's all the same, let them take anybody they want"—not expressing the second part of this. thought—"Do it quickly." He did not mention it but all his actions indicated that that really was his desire. He was also in a great hurry and for this reason too he gave the order to limit the amount of baggage.

I did not enter the house any more on this day. I thought that they would feel better if they were left to themselves, so I did not go there. The family at this time was making preparations for the departure. As Gilliard told me, the empress was extremely downhearted. Though a very reserved woman, she nevertheless worried much about her decision to go, with the emperor, which involved leaving her beloved son behind. If the empress knew that they were going to take her to Yekaterinburg, why should she have been depressed? Yekaterinburg is not so far from Tobolsk. But she felt from all of Iakovleff's actions, and so did everybody else in the house, that he was not taking them to Yekaterinburg, but to some other distant place, such as Moscow. And that they were not taking them away in order to advance their interests in any way, but for something else, that was connected with the state's interest, and that once in Moscow the emperor would be compelled to make some very serious and responsible decisions. The emperor had the same ideas and apprehensions, He expressed them when he spoke of the Brest-Litovsk treaty.

I did not sleep all that night. According to the order of Iakovleff, in the evening I assembled the soldiers again. Iakovleff explained to the men that he intended to take the emperor out of Tobolsk; he did not name the place he was taking him to, and asked the soldiers to keep the matter secret.

From whom was Iakovleff hiding his intentions? I explain it in this way: In the local soviet (Pessel, Disler, Kagomitzky, Pisarevsky and his wife) there were two factions—the Siberian, that considered Tobolsk in their sphere of influence; and the Uralian, that considered Tobolsk to be in their region. Zaslavsky represented the second. What was the reason for his arrival in Tobolsk? I could not explain that. Many things are still a mystery to me. I don't know whether he came to Tobolsk because we were there or not. It was perfectly clear from Iakovleff's speeches that he, Iakovleff, represented a third power, the central Moscow authorities. After he came to Tobolsk he began to fear an opposition to the removal of the imperial family from the Tobolsk soviet. However, he settled this matter with the Tobolsk soviet.

Zaslavsky was opposed to the removal, so I think that Iakovleff asked the soldiers to keep the departure of the imperial family secret because he feared that the local authorities would interfere. So I felt persuaded that Iakovleff, being a representative of the third power, worked in accordance with its desires, fulfilled the instructions he got from them in Moscow, and that that was the place where the imperial family was to be taken.

It appeared that the soldiers were confused and disturbed by Iakovleff's declarations and by his anxiety for secrecy. I noticed they were afraid for themselves, for fear some evil might befall them in consequence of all this. They said it was necessary for them to go with the emperor, and told Iakovleff this.

Iakovleff at first refused this demand, saying that his own detachment was quite reliable. But finally he made a compromise and a small detachment of six men from our soldiers was selected to escort the emperor.

At four o'clock a. m. the Siberian carriages (Koshevy) were prepared. One carriage had a cover; the seat was made of straw, which was tied with strings to the body of the carriage. The emperor, the empress and all other persons left the house. The emperor embraced and kissed me. The empress gave me her hand. Iakovleff seated himself in the same carriage as the emperor. The empress took her seat with the Grand Duchess Maria; Dolgoruky with Botkin, Tchemodouroff with Sedneff. There were some carriages containing soldiers at the head and some in the rear. The departing detachment was composed partly of our soldiers, but mostly of Iakovleff's. Two machine guns were with the detachment. A number of cavalrymen from Iakovleff's detachment accompanied the party. There were also some carriages with the baggage. They all started on their trip about four o'clock.

After their departure everybody in the house was distressed and sad. I noticed that even the soldiers had the same feeling. They began to behave in a more humane way towards the emperor's children. Later, when I was in Tumen, I was told by one of the coachmen who accompanied the imperial party that as soon as they reached the stage posts, the horses were immediately changed and the journey continued without any delay. Once the horses were changed in the village of Pokrovskoe, where the stage post was situated, opposite to a house formerly belonging to Rasputin. I was told that his wife was standing by the house and his daughter was looking out of the window. Both of them made the sign of the cross to the *czar's* family.

I had asked two soldiers, Lebedeff and Nabokoff (who were a

good sort of men from our detachment), to telegraph to me along the route how things were proceeding. I got a telegram from Lebedeff that was sent from the village Ivlevo. Nabokoff telegraphed me from Pokrovskoe. Both of their telegrams were very brief. "Proceeding safely." One telegram was sent from a railway station: "Proceeding safely. God bless you; how is the little one? Iakovleff." Of course the telegram was written by the emperor or empress, but sent by Iakovleff s permission.

On the 20th of April the committee of our detachment received a telegram from Matveieff who informed them of the arrival at Yekaterinburg, I cannot remember the exact words, but we were all surprised at its contents. We were all thunderstruck, as we were previously convinced that the emperor and empress would be taken to Moscow. We began to await the return of the soldiers from the escorting detachment. After they returned Loupin made a report to our soldiers. He scored the Yekaterinburg Bolsheviki. Labedeff and Nabokoff told me the following: Having arrived at Tumen, the emperor, the empress and the other persons were placed in a passenger car (I cannot tell you anything about the arrangement in the car); this car was guarded by our six soldiers. From Tumen they proceeded in the direction of Yekaterinburg.

In one station they learned that they would not be allowed to proceed beyond Yekaterinburg, where they would be held up. (This was a mistake of Iakovleff's. Zaslavsky left Tobolsk a few hours before him, and I suppose, informed the Yekaterinburg soviet of the departure of the imperial family from Tobolsk.) Having learned this news Iakovleff turned the train back to Omsk, in order to go forward *via* Ufa, Cheliabinsk, etc. As I understood Nabokoff, the train was approaching Omsk, when it was stopped a second time, Iakovleff went out in order to find what was happening. He learned that Yekaterinburg informed Omsk that Iakovleff was declared to be an outlaw on account of his intention to take the *czar's* family to Japan. Iakovleff went to Omsk personally and had a talk with Moscow by a direct wire. After returning he announced: "I have orders to go to Yekaterinburg."

Arriving in Yekaterinburg, the emperor, empress. Grand Duchess Maria, Botkin, Tchemodouroff, Sedneff and Demidova were placed in Ipatieff's house. Dolgoruky was taken to prison. All our soldiers were kept in the car, and later disarmed and arrested. They were kept under arrest for a few days and then released. Each of our arrested soldiers received different treatment. Lebedeff and Nabokoff were treated worse than the others. Matveieff and some of the others a little better. They were released at different times. On one occasion Matveieff went (for what purpose I do not know), to see Goloschekoff and Beloborodoff. When all of them were released and placed in a railway car in order to go back to Tobolsk, Iakovleff came to them and said that he had resigned and was going to Moscow, and that the soldiers should go with him and report about everything that had happened.

It was clear that Iakovleff regarded the stoppage of the train at Yekaterinburg as an act of insubordination of the Yekaterinburg Bolsheviki to the orders of the central authorities. What was the matter? Why could Iakovleff not proceed to Moscow? (The soldiers said that he finally left them and went to Moscow alone.) I explain those events in this way: Yekaterinburg was a centre of widespread Bolshevism. It was the capital of the whole Ural region: "The Red Yekaterinburg." I heard that Moscow reproached the Yekaterinburg Bolsheviki for spending too much money and threatened that they would stop sending them money altogether if they did not expend it more economically in future. Following their local interests, the Yekaterinburg Bolsheviki detained the imperial family in Yekaterinburg as hostages, in order to converse with Moscow in a freer manner and make Moscow more amenable to their demands. Possibly I am mistaken, but that is my idea.

Further, the telegraph operator who remained after Iakovleff's departure received a telegram that read as follows:

"Take the detachment with you and depart. I have resigned and am not responsible for the consequences."

A part of Iakovleff's detachment was still remaining in Tobolsk; and that is why Iakovleff sent the telegram. The telegraph operator, a very young man, and the soldiers of the detachment departed. I don't know where they were going. Avdeieff left Tobolsk before Iakovleff, as he was sent by Iakovleff in order to prepare a train for the imperial family.

Some time elapsed when our detachment committee received a telegram from Moscow (I don't know from whom it came. It announced that Iakovleff was replaced by Hohriakoff. About the appearance of Hohriakoff in Tobolsk I will tell the following: There were no real Bolsheviki in the Tobolsk soviet. The leaders were mostly social revolutionists. So it was even at the time when almost everywhere the Soviets consisted of communists. There was a time when even Nikolsky was temporary chairman of the soviet. Later, Dimitrieff an extraordinary "*Commissar,*" came from Omsk to Tobolsk. His intention was to organise the Bolshevik power. A special detachment of soldiers arrived with him from Omsk. At the same time Yekaterinburg claimed that Tobolsk was in their jurisdiction, so another detachment arrived from Tumen. But Dimitrieff, as representative of Siberian opinion, had the upper hand and the Tumen detachment left. Having organised the Bolshevik power, Dimitrieff returned to Omsk.

During this period of organisation of the soviet rule in Tobolsk Hohriakoff was the first chairman of the soviet. In those days various Bolshevik detachments arrived from different places at Tobolsk. A detachment of Letts was also formed there. Long before the imperial family had all left Tobolsk, the Letts were already there, and created considerable disorder, as for example, when they searched Baroness Buxhoevden. I do not know who was their commander, but he apparently did not please Hohriakoff, and was relieved by Rodionoff who came from Yekaterinburg. A short time after Hohriakoff took his appointment, replacing Iakovleff as *commissar,* he received a telegram from someone in Moscow that instructed him to remove all the remaining members of the family to Yekaterinburg.

I must not forget to mention that Hohriakoff after being appointed *commissar,* ordered Rodionoff to come from Yekaterinburg to Tobolsk. When asking for Rodionoff from Yekaterinburg, Hohriakoff had in mind that he would be in charge of the imperial family, but not of the Tobolsk district. Hohriakoff did not act as the chairman of the district soviet, but in the capacity of an extraordinary *commissar* having supervision of the imperial family. Sometime after he was appointed *commissar,* however, before our detachment was relieved by Letts, I went to the house. Our soldiers were on sentry duty. They did not allow me to enter, saying that that was Hohriakoff's orders. I applied to Hohriakoff. "They did not understand me," he answered.

For several days after this incident took place I continued to visit the house. But shortly after Rodionoff arrived our guards were relieved by the Letts, who occupied all the sentry posts simultaneously and I was not allowed to enter the house. It was just a few days before the family left. How things went after this I can tell you, as I heard from people who remained in Tobolsk. I remember also that Rodionoff on his arrival, came to the house, assembled the members of the family, and made a regular roll call. This surprised me very much. Shortly afterwards, unexpectedly for me, the Letts assumed the sentry duties and I was not allowed to enter the house. I was told that the

Letts behaved in the following fashion.

Once divine service took place in the house. The Letts searched the priest. They searched the nuns in a very indecent manner and touched everything in the sanctuary. Rodionoff placed a Lett by the sanctuary in order to supervise the priest. It created such an unhappy effect that the Grand Duchess Olga wept, and said that if she had known beforehand that conditions were to have been like this she would never have made a request for divine service.

After I was not allowed to enter the house any more, my nerves gave way, I became ill and had to remain in bed. The family left Tobolsk on the 7th of May. I was unable to leave my bed and could not bid them "Farewell." The following persons went to Yekaterinburg: (1) Tatischeff; (2) Derevenko; (3) Hendrikova; (4) Buxhoevden; (5) Schneider; (6) Gilliard; (7) Gibbes; (8) Tegleva; (9) Ersberg; (10) Toutelberg; (11) Mejantz; (12) Katia; (13) Masha; (14) Volkoff; (15) Nagorny; (16) Ivanoff; (17) Tutin; (18) Youravsky; (19) Troupp; (20) Haritonoff; (21) Kokicheff; (22) Leonid Sedneff.

Soon after we were transferred to Tobolsk horn Czarskoe-Selo two maids, Anna Utkina and Anna Pavlovna Romanova, joined us. The soldiers did not allow them to enter the house. They remained at Tobolsk and did not go to Yekaterinburg. I do not know where Hohriekoff came from. He was not educated and his capacities were not of a very high order. Previously he had been a stoker on a battleship, the *Alexander II*. He usually wore a black leather suit.

Neither do I know the origin of Rodionoff. He was about twenty-eight or thirty years of age, below medium height, not educated and produced an unpleasant impression. He seemed to be a cruel and cunning man. Baroness Buxhoevden assured us that she had seen him during her travels abroad. She met him on one occasion at a frontier station in the uniform of a Russian *gendarme*. I should say we still felt the *gendarme* in him, though he was not a good type of *gendarme* soldier, but that of a cruel man with the manners of a secret service agent

After his arrival Rodionoff searched Nagorny when the latter returned to the house from the train. He found a letter from Dr. Derevenko's son to the *czarevitch* and reported it to Hohriakoff, saying: "That is a nice sort of man; he said that he had nothing, and I found this letter." Then addressing me he added: "I am sure that during your time numbers of things were smuggled in." Hohriakoff was very pleased, saying: "I have been watching this rascal quite a time, he is a disgrace to us." That is what the sailor Hohriakoff was saying about the sailor, Nagorny. It could not be otherwise. One was "The beauty and the pride of the Russian Revolution."[1] The other was a man devoted to the imperial family, who loved the *czarevitch*, and who was loved by him, and for this reason he perished. Sedneff surely also perished for being "a disgrace,"' as he was also a sailor and also devoted to the imperial family.

After the departure of the imperial family I was cut off for a long time from all news and nobody could tell me anything about them. In June Omsk was taken from the Reds. The Omsk Bolsheviki escaped from Omsk on steamers and came to Tobolsk. Our Tobolsk Bolsheviki also ran away with them. Power in Tobolsk was taken into the hands of officers. Tumen continued to remain in the hands of the Bolsheviki. A fighting line separated us. Then I got news about Hohriakoff. He appeared to be in command of something on the river near Pokrovskoe (being a sailor, I suppose). They say that Matveieff was also in command. Tegleva told me afterwards that Hohriakoff was not permitted to go into the Ipatieff house, even though he was sure to be a *commissar* while there.

After Tumen was taken, most of the people who left Tobolsk with the imperial family returned, except the following: (1) Dolgoruky; (2) Tatischeff; (3) Derevenko; (4) Hendrikova; (5) Botkin; (6) Schneider; (7) Tegleva; (8) Ersberg; (9) Toutelberg; (10) Volk-off; (11) Nagorny; (12) Tchemodouroff; (13) Sedneff; (14) Troupp; (15) Haritonoff; (16) Leonid Sedneff; (17) Ivanoff.

They told us the following: During the journey of the imperial family they were treated in a disgraceful manner. While they were on a steamer Rodionoff forbade them to lock their cabin doors from the inside, but Nagorny and the *czarevitch* were locked in by him from the outside. Nagorny got very angry and quarrelled with Rodionoff, telling him that it was inhuman to a sick child. (Even here in Tobolsk Rodionoff displayed the same attitude, and would not allow the Grand Duchess Olga to lock the door of her bedroom or even to shut it.)

When the train arrived at Yekaterinburg the *czarevitch*, the Grand Duchesses Olga, Maria, Tatiana and Anastasia were transferred to the house. The emperor and empress were transferred also, with all the persons who accompanied them, except Dolgoruky, who was taken to prison. When the children came to Yekaterinburg the following per-

---

1. This is what Trotzky called the sailors of the Baltic Fleet after they had murdered their officers.—Translator's Note.

sons were immediately arrested: Tatischeff, Hendrikova, Schneider and Volkoff . Lately I heard from Gilliard that Sedneff and Nagorny were also removed from the house. Gilliard and Gibbes witnessed that. Derevenko remained in Yekaterinburg. Tegleva, Ersberg and Ivanoff stayed in Tumen; Toutelburg at Kamyshloff. The following persons remained in the Ipatieff house with the imperial family: Tchemodouroff, Sedneff (a boy), Troupp, Haritonoff, Demidova and Botkin.

Sometime after Yekaterinburg was taken Tchemodouroff came to Tobolsk. I saw him and talked with him. He came to Tobolsk absolutely destitute, a very aged man, suffering mentally and broken down. He died recently. His conversation was incoherent. He could only answer questions, but his answers were sometimes contradictory. I will tell you here the outstanding points of his conversation that I can recall: After the arrival at Ipatieff's house the emperor, empress and the Grand Duchess Maria were searched in a very rough manner. The emperor lost his temper and protested. He was rudely informed that he was merely a prisoner and that he therefore had no right to protest. Tchemodouroff noticed that Avdeieff was the senior.

The meals were very bad. The dinner was brought from a cheap lunch room, and they always brought it late, at three or four o'clock instead of one. They dined together with the servants. The pan was put on the table. There was a lack of spoons, knives and forks. The Red soldiers sometimes participated in the dinner. Sometimes a soldier came in and helped himself to the soup, saying: "Enough for you, I will take some myself." The grand duchesses slept on the floor as there were no beds for them. Roll calls were frequently made. When the grand duchesses went to the lavatory the Red soldiers followed them, saying it was on purpose to guard them. Even according to Tchemodouroff, who was not able to give the whole account, being so extremely depressed, it was clear that the august family was constantly subjected to intense moral tortures. Tchemodouroff did not believe that the family had been killed. He said that Botkin, Haritonoff, Demidova and Troupp were killed, but the family itself was taken away. He said that by killing the aforementioned people they simulated the murder of the family. He said that for the same reason the house was devastated, also some things were burned and others thrown into the waste basket. I remember he told me that somebody had found pieces of a holy image and an Order of St. Vladimir which was always worn by Botkin.

In a short time after this Volkoff came to Tobolsk. He said that

Hendrikova, Schneider and himself were taken from the railway car in Yekaterinburg and sent to prison. From there they were transferred to a prison in Perm. Afterwards they were taken out of the Perm prison, and led out to be shot, but he fled on the way and escaped. The others were executed.

In Tobolsk I heard for the first time about the murder of the imperial family. I saw it in the Omsk newspaper *Zaria*, or maybe in a Tobolsk newspaper *Narodnoe-Slovo*. The Bolshevik communication described the "execution" of the Emperor Nicholas "the sanguinary." In regard to the character and private life of the members of the imperial family, I state the following: The emperor was a very clever man, well informed, and very interesting to talk with; he had a remarkable memory. He was very fond of physical labour and could not keep well without it. He was very modest in his needs. Even in Czarskoe-Selo I saw him wearing old trousers and worn boots. He drank very little. During dinner he drank not more than one glass of port wine or Madeira. He liked the simple Russian dishes, *borsch, shchy* and *kasha*. I remember very well one day he came to the wine cellar and seeing some cognac, ordered Rojkoff to give it over to me and said: "You know, I don't drink it myself."

I never saw him drinking anything except port or Madeira. He was very religious. He hated, and could not stand Germans. The particular characteristics of his personality were kindness and a mild disposition. He was exceptionally kind. Of his own will as a man he would never cause any pain to anybody. This quality made a very strong impression upon other people. He was kind, modest, straight and frank. He behaved himself in a very modest and natural manner. In Tobolsk he played checkers with the soldiers. I am sure that many soldiers had very kindly feelings towards the imperial family. For example: when the soldiers (good regular soldiers) were leaving Tobolsk they went secretly to the emperor to wish him farewell and kissed him. The emperor's idea was that the Russian man was a mild, kind-hearted fellow; he did not understand many things, but it was easy to impress and influence him by kindness.

The *czar* himself was of this type. I often pitied him, for the soldiers frequently permitted themselves to act with rowdy manners, generally in the absence of the imperial family. They often made a number of dirty jokes in reference to the imperial family. Perhaps they were afraid to do it in their presence. And that was the reason why the august family did not realise the danger of their position.

The *czar* loved Russia and more than once I heard him express his fear of being taken abroad. He did not understand art, but liked nature and hunting extremely. It was painful for him to abstain from hunting for any length of time, and he disliked to have to spend his time indoors. A weak character was his fault and therefore he was influenced by his wife. I noticed that even in trifles, when he was consulted on some details, the usual answer was: "As my *wife* wishes. I will ask her."

The empress was very clever, extremely reserved and had a strong character, and her main feature was her love of power. Her looks were majestic. When you spoke to the emperor there were moments when you forgot you were speaking to the *czar*, but when you spoke to the empress the feeling that she belonged to a royal family did not leave you for a moment. Owing to her character she always took the leading part in all family affairs, and subdued the emperor to her opinion. Certainly she felt more keenly than he did their humiliating position. Everybody noticed how rapidly she was aging. She spoke and wrote Russian very correctly and loved Russia very much. She feared, as the emperor did, to be taken abroad. She had a talent for painting and embroidery. Not only was the German in her unnoticeable, but you might have thought that she was born in a country opposed to Germany. This was explained by her education.

After her mother's death, being still very young, she was educated in England by her grandmother, Queen Victoria. I never heard a single German word from her. She used to speak Russian, English and French. There was no doubt of her illness. Dr. Botkin explained to me the nature of it. Being the daughter of the Grand Duke of Hesse, it was something that she inherited from that family—weakness of the blood vessels. This malady produced paralysis following a bruise, from which the *czarevitch*, was suffering. The men got rid of this illness after arriving at maturity, when this trouble entirely disappeared. With women the illness only started after their climacteric and from this stage hysteria was progressive.

It was clear that the empress was suffering from hysteria. Botkin explained to me that this was the origin of her religious ecstasy. All her manual activities and all her thoughts were led by religious motives, and there was a touch of religion in her work. When she was making a present to anybody it always bore the inscription: "*God bless you and protect you*," or something similar to that. There is no doubt that she loved her husband, but she loved him not in the way a woman loves a man, but as the father of her children. She loved all her children, but her son she adored.

The Grand Duchess Olga was a nice looking young blonde, about twenty-three; her type was Russian. She was fond of reading, capable and mentally well developed; spoke English well and German badly. She had some talent for art, played the piano, sang, (she learned singing in Petrograd; her voice was *soprano*), and she painted well. She was very modest and did not care for luxury.

Her clothes were modest and she restrained her sisters from extravagance in dress. She gave altogether the impression of a good, generous-hearted Russian girl. It looked as if she had had some sorrows in her life and still carried traces of it. It seemed to me that she loved her father more than she loved her mother. She also loved her brother, and called him "The Little One" or "The Baby."

The Grand Duchess Tatiana was about twenty. She was quite different from her sisters. You recognised in her the same features that were in her mother—the same nature and the same character. You felt that she was the daughter of an emperor. She had no liking for art. Maybe it would have been better for her had she been a man. When the emperor and empress left Tobolsk nobody would ever have thought that the Grand Duchess Olga was the senior of the remaining members of the imperial family. If any questions arose it was always Tatiana who was appealed to. She was nearer to her mother than the other children; and it seemed that she loved her mother more than her father.

The Grand Duchess Maria was eighteen; she was tall, strong, and better looking than the other sisters. She painted well and was the most amiable. She always used to speak to the soldiers, questioned them, and knew very well the names of their wives, the number of their children, and the amount of land owned by the soldiers. All the intimate affairs in such cases were always known to her. Like the Grand Duchess Olga, she loved her father more than the rest. On account of her simplicity and affability she was given the pet name by the family of "Mashka." And by this term she was called by her brother and by her sisters.

The Grand Duchess Anastasia, I believe, was seventeen. She was overdeveloped for her age; she was stout and short, too stout for her height; her; characteristic feature was to see the weak points of other people and to make fun of them. She was a comedian by nature and always made everybody laugh. She preferred her father to her mother and loved Maria Nicholevna more than the other sisters.

All of them, including Tatiana, were nice, modest and innocent girls. There is no doubt they were cleaner in their thoughts than the majority of girls nowadays.

The *czarevitch* was the idol of the whole family. He was only a child and his characteristic features were not yet worked out. He was a very clever, capable and lively boy. He spoke Russian, French and English, and did not know a word of German.

In general, I could say about the whole imperial family that they all loved each other and were so satisfied with their family life that they did not need nor look for intercourse with other people. Never before in my life have I seen, and probably never again shall I see, such a good, friendly and agreeable family.

Now I can say that the time will come when the Russian people will realise what terrible tortures this very fine family was subjected to, especially when they consider how from the first days of the revolution the newspaper men insinuated a lot of scandalous stories about their intimate family life. Take, for instance, the story about Rasputin. I had many talks about it with Dr. Botkin. The empress was suffering from hysteria. This illness induced a religious ecstasy in her. Besides that, her only and beloved son was ill and there was no one who could help him. A mother's sorrow, on the basis of religious ecstasy, created Rasputin. Rasputin was a saint to her. Having a great influence over her husband, she converted him to her ideas in this matter. After I had lived with this family and been closely associated with them, I fully understood how unjust were the stories and the insults that were heaped upon them. They ought to have known that the Empress Alexandra, as a woman, had long ago ceased to exist. One can imagine how they all suffered in reading the Russian newspapers in Czarskoe-Selo.

They were even accused of treachery in favour of Germany. I explained to you before the feelings the emperor had towards the Germans. The empress also hated Wilhelm. She often said:

> I am always accused of liking and helping the Germans, but nobody knows how I hate Wilhelm for all the evil he has brought to my native country.

She had Germany and not Russia in mind when she said that. Tatischeff told me as an example of her broad vision that once when she was talking about the confusion in Russia, she prophesied that the same thing would happen in Germany. The grand duchesses had the same bitter feeling towards the Emperor Wilhelm. I remember that once the grand duchesses distributed amongst the servants the presents they received from Wilhelm during his visit on their yacht.

I cannot remember anything else. Well, yes, I remember the emperor used to keep a diary, though I could not say whether the empress kept one or not. All the grand duchesses used to keep diaries, but before their departure from Tobolsk, Maria and Anastasia destroyed theirs.

I read in a newspaper that while the emperor was in prison in Yekaterinburg somebody came to him and offered to save him, on certain conditions. After the emperor learned that the man was sent by the Emperor Wilhelm, he refused to parley with him. I cannot say from whence the Letts came who arrived at Tobolsk. But I draw your attention to the fact that the Lett detachment which took the children from Tobolsk, never returned. Hohriakoff also failed to return.

Miss Hitrovo visited Tobolsk. She was a young girl, and adored the Grand Duchess Olga. Her arrival created a whole story that was picked up and exaggerated by all the newspapers. She was searched but nothing was found.

My testimony has been read to me and it is written correctly

(Signed)   Eugene Stepanovitch Kobylinsky,
"   N. Sokoloff

4

EXAMINATION OF PHILIP PROSKOURIAKOFF

(The deposition of Philip Proskouriakoff possesses a certain amount of psychological interest as the testimony of a lad of seventeen who was suddenly confronted with death in one of its most violent and terrible forms. Proskouriakoff appears to have been a clever, restless youth with a distaste for settled employment, and who probably enlisted in the Workmen's Guards solely in the spirit of adventure.

His story of the murder of the imperial family is more horrible than the accounts given by the older men. Proskouriakoff's love of the morbid, and his slightly decadent mentality, is plainly shown in his account of the events of the night, when he was awakened from a drunken sleep and ordered to proceed to that sinister bullet-riddled room on the ground floor of Ipatieff's house. But his minute attention to many of the ghastly and often irrelevant details is valuable as documentary evidence, as it goes to prove most conclusively that these things actually happened and were retained as they happened in the mind of a person whose neurotic temperament enabled him to remember them accurately and vividly.—Original editor's note.)

From the first to the third day of April, 1919, the Investigating Magistrate for Cases of Special Importance of the Omsk Tribunal, N.

A. Sokoloff, in conformity with Paragraphs 403-409 of the Code of Criminal Procedure, conducted an investigation m the town of Yekaterinburg, in which the man named below, speaking as the accused, deposed: I am Philip Poliektoff Proskouriakoff. At the time that the crime was committed I was seventeen years old; I am a Russian peasant, belonging to the Orthodox Church, and single. For three years I went to the Sissert five-class school. My specialty is electrical fittings. In answer to your questions, I reply as follows:

For many years my father had been a foreman in the iron works, and resided all the time in the Sissert Iron Works. This was also my birthplace. I did not complete my studies in the Sissert school, and attended classes only during three years. It was very difficult for me to learn; at the same time my father got sick and took me away from school. At first he placed me in the blacksmith's shop of the factory, so that I might learn the trade. I was instructed by Vasily Afanasievitch Belonosoff. I left after I had worked for about a year in the shop: this work was too hard for me. My eldest brother found me a position in the Palais Royal Theatre where I began to study for a position of electrician. I stayed there for about a year, learned something about electricity and started in a business of my own—installing electric wires in town. Later I got a position in the central electric plant in Yekaterinburg. I worked there for about a month and, before Easter 1918, went home.

I remember quite well that on May 9th I met in the bazaar a friend of mine, Ivan Semenoff Talapoff . He told me that a certain *commissar*, Mrachkovsky, had started recruiting amongst our factory workmen for a special detachment that was intended to guard the *czar*. Personally, I did not see Mrachkovsky. I heard only that he was in command of some troops fighting against Dutoff—from whence he had come. I related to my father Talapoff's words. Both my father and my mother advised me not to enlist. My father's words were: "Philip, don't go, think it well over." I was anxious to see them so I ignored my father's advice and on the next day enlisted. The enlistment took place in the house of Vasily Erkoff, which is on the Tzerkovnaia Street, close to the soviet. The enlistment was conducted by one of our Sissert workmen, Paul Spiridonoff Medvedeff. Medvedeff told me that we should be paid four hundred *roubles* per month, that we should have to perform sentry duty, but that we should not be allowed to sleep while doing so! Such were the conditions explained to me, so I enlisted at once.

I heard at the time that thirty Sissert workmen altogether had enlisted. Later, some of them withdrew, but the number of those who did so was small and they were replaced by others, also workmen from our factory.

Eleven of these first thirty men, as I was told, belonged to the Bolshevik communist party.

In the second half of May we arrived altogether at Yekaterinburg. At first we were all quartered in the new "*Gostiny-Dvor*" (bazaar house), where the soldiers of the Red army also were located. We stayed there a few days without doing any work. At the end of May we were transferred to the Ipatieff house, where the *czar's* family lived. We were placed in the rooms of the lower floor.

Alexander Moshkin, a workman from the Zlokasoff's factory, was in charge of the house and our guard detachment was under his orders. Medvedeff was the senior in our party. He was our chief. Nobody had elected him, but he was in charge of the enlistment of our party from the beginning; he paid the wages and changed the sentries. Our salary was four hundred *roubles* per month; Medvedeff received six hundred. Avdeieff remained all the time in the house and occupied the *commandant's* room. Generally he arrived at nine o'clock a. m. and left at nine o'clock p. m. Moshkin stayed all the time in the *commandant's* room, where he lived. Medvedeff also always stayed with those two in the same room and spent the night there.

The sentry posts were as follows: (1) By the sentry-box near the gate. (2) By the sentry-box near the chapel. (3) Between two fences, by the window of the house. (4) In the front court, near the entrance to the house. (5) In the back court. (6) In the garden. (7) In the entrance room of the upper floor, by the commandant's room. (8) Near the lavatory, where the water closet and bath room were located. Besides that there were three sentry posts with machine guns: (9) Beside the window of the attic. (10) On the terrace that faced the garden. (11) In the middle room of the lower floor.

We were performing our duties for about a week when Avdeieff brought up about fifteen more men—all workmen of the Zlokasoff factory. I suppose he did it because he thought we were overworked, as we were obliged to be on duty four hours at a time; it was raining, and we were not accustomed to this sort of duty.

The Zlokasoff workmen lived with us in the upper floor. There were not any women in our detachment. We had our own male cooks, who prepared our food. At first Ivan Kategoff was the cook, later he was replaced by Andrew Starkoff.

At the end of time or maybe at the beginning of July Moshkin was arrested by Avdeieff, as he was suspected of stealing a small gold cross belonging to the *czar*. At the same time Avdeieff was also dismissed and replaced by Iourovsky. Nikoulin was appointed as his assistant.

Positively I do not know who Iourovsky and Nikoulin were. Both of them arrived at the house together. They always remained in the command-ant's room. Iourovsky arrived in the morning at eight or nine o'clock and left at five or six in the afternoon. Nikoulin practically lived in the *commandant's* room and spent the night there. Medvedeff also continued to spend the night in the same room. About a week after Iourovsky and Nikoulin assumed their duties all the Sissert and Zlokasoff workmen were transferred to Popoff's (or Oboukoff's) house, which was opposite the Ipatieff house. Instead of us the lower floor of the Ipatieff's house accommodated Letts, who were about ten in number.

Before the arrival of the Letts all the sentry duties were performed exclusively by the Sissert workmen. After their arrival all the posts on the upper floor, where the *czar's* family lived, were taken up by Letts. We, Russian workmen, were not allowed to go to the upper floor. Such were the orders of Iourovsky.

The machine gun teams, who performed no other duty than at the machine guns, were composed of our Sissert workmen.

At the time when Avdeieff was the chief all the other posts were occupied by the rest of the work-men. But after the arrival of Iourovsky and of the Letts, we workmen began to occupy only the posts outside of the house. All posts inside of the house were assigned to the Letts. Before the arrival of the Letts I, as well as other workmen, performed my sentry duties inside the house about six times, keeping guard by the *commandant's* room and the lavatory. I performed this duty in the morning, daytime, evening and night. During this time I saw all the imperial family: The emperor, the empress, *czarevitch*, as well as the daughters: Olga, Tatiana, Maria and Anastasia. I saw them very closely when they went for a walk or to the lavatory or passed from one room to another. They all used to walk in the garden, except the empress. I never saw her walking in the garden. The *czarevitch* I saw only once, as he was carried by the oldest daughter of the emperor—Olga. The *czarevitch* was ill all the time.

I can tell about the way they spent their time from the words of Medvedeff, who of course saw them more frequently than I did. They got up about eight or nine o'clock in the morning. They had family prayers. They all assembled in one room and sang prayers. They had dinner at three o'clock. They all dined together in one room; I mean to say that they dined with the servants that were with them. At nine o'clock in the evening they had supper and tea, after that they went to bed. According to the words of Medvedeff they occupied themselves in the following way: The emperor read, the empress also read, or sometimes embroidered or knitted something together with her daughters. The *czarevitch*, when he could, made little wire chains for his toy ship. They walked every day for about an hour or an hour and a half. They were not allowed to take any other physical exercise. I remember that Pashka Medvedeff once said that the Czar Nicholas Alexandrovitch once asked Iourovsky's permission to clean the garden. Iourovsky forbade it.

I heard their singing several times. They sang only sacred songs. On Sundays they had divine service, performed by a clergyman and a deacon, who I think were from the Verhne—Vosnesensky church.

At first the food was brought to them from a soviet dining-room; two women brought it; their cook heated it. Later, they were allowed to prepare their meals in the house.

Besides the imperial family on the upper floor of the house there lived with them the following persons, whom I have personally seen. There was a doctor, a stout man, with grey hair, aged about fifty-five. He wore spectacles, that had, as far as I remember, gold rims. There was a waiter, aged thirty-five, tall, slim, and dark. A cook stayed with them. He was aged forty, was short, thin, a little bald, he had black hair and small black moustache. There was also a maid with them, aged about forty, tall, thin, and dark; I did not see the colour of her hair, because she always tied a handkerchief on her head. There was also a boy with them. The boy was about fifteen, his hair was black and he wore it parted, his nose was long, his eyes black.

Two other men stayed with the imperial family. As Medvedeff explained to me, they also were servants. One of them was tall, thin, about thirty-five; his hair was light red, and cut short. He shaved his beard and trimmed his moustache; his nose was of medium size and straight; I don't remember his other distinguishing marks, but his skin was clear and looked as delicate as a woman's. The other was also tall, about thirty, his hair was black and parted. He was clean-shaven. The first man wore a black jacket, trousers and shoes. The second man wore a jacket, a stiff shirt, with a tie, trousers and shoes. I also saw the first man carry away a rubber pillow with the urine of the *czarevitch*.

These two men I saw only once, when I was on guard in the house during the first days. After that I did not see them. Medvedeff told me that both of them were taken to Number Two Prison, but what reason there was for imprisoning them I was not told and I was not interested either in knowing. On several occasions I have seen the Bolshevik Beloborodoff, who came to the house probably to inspect the life of the imperial family. Anyhow I was told by Medvedeff that such was the reason of his visits. Beloborodoff I recall very distinctly. He looked about twenty-five. He was of medium height, thin, his face was pale. Beloborodoff visited the house while Avdeieff was on duty there, as well as when Iourovsky was on duty.

Regarding the restrictions and treatment of the emperor and his family by the executives and the guards, as a matter of conscience I can say this: Avdeieff was a simple workman, very poorly developed, mentally. Sometimes he was intoxicated. But neither he nor the guards during his time offended or did any wrong to the imperial family. Iourovsky and Nikoulin behaved themselves differently. During their time the imperial family suffered more. They both used to drink in the *commandant's* room and while intoxicated they sang. Nikoulin played the piano (that was in the *commandant's* room) . Sometimes as Nikoulin was playing and Iourovsky's eyes were bleared with drink they both started yelling out songs, as: "Let us forget the old world; Let us shake its dust from our feet. We do not need a golden idol. We abhor the *czar's* palace." And so on. Or sometimes they sang: "You died as the victim of a struggle. . . ."

Moshkin also sometimes allowed himself to sing these songs but only in the absence of Avdeieff, who did not know anything about it; but the first two took things easy. In the time of Avdeieff women never entered the house, but Nikoulin had a mistress who came to see him and stayed with him after Iourovsky's departure. She was about twenty, was short, stout and blonde; her eyes were brown, her nose was small and straight. I do not know her name. I don't know either where she lived or from whence she came. Medvedeff told nothing about her. In the time of Iourovsky divine service was performed less often.

As a result the guards under the command of Iourovsky began to behave much worse. Fayka Safonoff began to behave indecently. There was only one lavatory for the imperial family. On the walls near this lavatory Fayka Safonoff began to write all sorts of bad words, that were very much out of place. He was seen writing those words on the wall near the lavatory by Alexeeff, who was on duty on the upper floor together with Fayka (Fayka occupied the post near the lavatory and Alexeeff near the *commandant's* room). After Alexeeff returned from duty he told us all about it. Once Fayka climbed up a fence which was quite close to the windows of the emperor's rooms and began to sing all sorts of vulgar songs.

Andrew Strekotin drew on the walls of the lower room numbers of indecent pictures. Belomoin participated in the drawing and he laughed and taught Strekotin how to draw better. I have personally seen Strekotin drawing those things.

Once I was walking near the house when I saw the youngest daughter of the emperor, Anastasia, look out the window. When the sentry on duty noticed it he fired his rifle at her. The bullet missed her and lodged above her in the woodwork of the window frame.

All of these unbecoming deeds were known to Iourovsky. Medvedeff reported to him about Podkorytoff but Iourovsky only answered: "They must not look out of the window."

As I said before, from the time that the Letts entered and joined the guards, they lived in the lower floor of the Ipatieff house, and we, work-men, were all transferred to the house opposite, belonging to Popoff (or Obouhoff). In this house we occupied all the rooms of the upper floor; the lower floor was taken up by tenants.

The Zlokasoff workmen were placed in the same rooms with us.

The last time I saw the imperial family, except the emperor, was a few days before they were murdered. On that day they all went for a walk in the garden—all of them walked— -except the empress. There were the emperor, his son, his daughters: Olga, Maria, Tatiana and Anastasia; there were also the doctor, the waiter, cook, maid, and the boy. I observed distinctly that the heir was dressed in a shirt and had a black leather belt, with a small metal buckle, around his waist. I saw that very distinctly because the Grand Duchess Olga carried him close past me. The heir was ill and the boy pushed his roller-chair. I could not tell you exactly the date when I saw them walking in the garden. But it was not long before their death.

The murder took place the night between Tuesday and Wednesday. I do not remember the date. I remember that we received our wages on Monday. So it must have been the 15th of the month of July, reckoning by the New Style. The day after we received the wages, at ten o'clock in the morning of July 16th, I was standing on duty by the sentry-box near to the Vosnesensky Prospect and Vosnesensky Lane. Egor Stoloff, with whom I lived in the same room, was at the same time on duty in the lower rooms of the house. After we finished our shift of duty, together with Stoloff we went to get some drinks in the house number eighty-five of the Vodotchnaia street.

We returned at dusk, as we had to resume our duties at five o'clock. Medvedeff noticed that we were drunk and put us under arrest in the bath-house, which was situated in the yard of Popoff's house. We fell asleep and slept till three a. m. At three o'clock in the night we were awakened by Medvedeff who said: "Get up and follow me." We asked him where and he answered: "They call you, so you must go." I am quite sure that it was three o'clock because Stoloff had a watch with him, and when I looked at this watch it was exactly three o'clock. We got up and followed Medvedeff. He brought us to the lower room of the Ipatieff house. All the workmen guards were there, except those on duty. There was a cloud of powder smoke in the room and it smelt of powder. In the rear room that had a barred window, which is situated close to the store-room, the walls and floor were pierced by bullets.

In one wall there were an especially large number of bullet holes, but there were also bullet marks in the others. There were no marks of bayonet strokes on the walls. In the places where the walls and floor showed bullet holes, there was blood around them; there were splashes and spots of blood on the wall and small pools on the floor. There were drops and spots of blood in other rooms that had to be passed on the way from the room that had the bullet marks, to the court yard. There were also traces of blood on the pavement of the courtyard on the way to the gate. It was obvious that quite recently before our arrival a large number of people had been shot in the room with the barred window. After I witnessed all that I began to question Medvedeff and Strekotin about what happened. They told me that just a few moments before, the whole imperial family and the people attached to them had been shot, except the boy.

Medvedeff ordered us to clean up the rooms. We began to wash the floor; several mops were brought in to remove the traces of the bloodstains. I cannot tell who brought them. Medvedeff ordered that some sawdust be brought. We washed the floor with cold water and sawdust, removing the bloodstains. The bloodstains on the wall we washed off with a wet rag. All the workmen participated in the cleaning except those that were on duty. A number of men did the cleaning in the room where the imperial family was killed. Amongst others I saw there Medvedeff and two Letts. I also helped to clean this room. In the same manner, using water, we washed the blood from the pavement of the courtyard. I did not find any bullets. If any bullets were found by other people or not I don't know.

When Stoloff and myself came down to the lower room we did not find anybody there except a few Letts. Medvedeff and our workmen were absent. Nikoulin at that time, as it was said by, Medvedeff, was in the upper room, the door of which leading to the lower rooms was locked from inside.

I saw no gold or any other valuable articles taken from the bodies of the murdered people in the lower rooms. I now remember that on Tuesday morning, when I was on sentry duty, I personally saw Iourovsky cane to the house at eight o'clock in the morning. Sometime after his arrival Beloborodoff entered the house. I left my post at ten o'clock in the morning; but Medvedeff told me that afterwards Iourovsky and Beloborodoff went for a ride in an automobile. At this time Nikoulin remained in the house. They returned before evening. During the evening Iourovsky told Medvedeff that in the night time the imperial family would be shot, and ordered him to notify the workmen and to take the revolvers from the sentries.

All this was not clear to me then. I cannot tell if it was true or not, as I did not think of questioning any of the workmen whether Medvedeff took their revolvers or not. Personally I don't understand why it was necessary; according to Medvedeff's words the imperial family were shot by the Letts and they all had Nagan revolvers. At this time I did not know that Iourovsky was a Jew. Being the instigator of the crime he may have selected the Letts to do the actual killing, having more confidence in them than in us Russians. Perhaps for the same reason he also wanted to disarm the Russian workmen that were on duty. Medvedeff faithfully performed Iourovsky's order, took the revolvers from the sentries, forwarded them to Iourovsky and at eleven o'clock in the evening notified the workmen that the imperial family were going to be shot. At twelve o'clock midnight Iourovsky awoke the imperial family, requesting all of them to dress and to go down to the lower room.

According to Medvedeff, Iourovsky explained to the imperial family that there would be danger during the night and that in case firing were to take place on the streets it would be dangerous to remain in the upper floors. So he insisted that everybody should come down. They complied with the demand and descended to the lower room, accompanied by Iourovsky, Nikoulin and Beloborodoff. There were the emperor, the empress, the heir, the four daughters, the doctor, the waiter, the maid, and the cook. The boy by order of Iourovsky about a day and a half before that, was transferred to the rooms where we were quartered, and I saw him there personally before the murder. All of them were brought into the room that bore the marks of bullets. They stood in two rows, Iourovsky started to read to them a paper. The emperor did not hear well, and asked: "What?" According to the words of Medvedeff, Iourovsky lifted his hand with the revolver and showing it to the emperor, answered: "This is what," and afterwards added: "Your race must cease to live."

I remember also that when telling about the paper which Iourovsky read to the emperor, Medvedeff called it a "protocol."

As soon as Iourovsky finished speaking he, Beloborodoff, Nikoulin, Medvedeff and all the Letts fired at the emperor and directly afterwards began to shoot at everybody else. They all fell dead on the floor. Medvedeff told me himself that he shot two or three times at the emperor and other persons whom they were executing.

After all of them were shot, Alexander Strekotin, as he told it to me himself, took all the precious things from the bodies; these were at once taken away from him by Iourovsky and carried upstairs. After that all the bodies were loaded on a motor truck and taken out somewhere. On this truck, along with the bodies of the killed, went Iourovsky, Beloborodoff and a number of Letts. No one from our workmen went with them.

After the cleaning of the rooms was over, together with Stoloff, we went to town, and sauntered about until evening. We did not meet any of our acquaintances and did not tell anybody about the murder. In the evening we came back to our quarters, had some food, and slept. At six o'clock in the morning on Thursday, July 18th, Medvedeff ordered me on duty on a post inside of the house by the *commandant's* room. Up to this time, after the arrival of the Letts, not a single workman ever was allowed to do sentry duty inside of the house while the imperial family was still alive. Now, after they were killed, we were again ordered on duty inside the house.

There was no sentry near the lavatory. Iourovsky, Nikoulin, Medvedeff and the Letts were already in the house when I took up my post. There was nobody from our or Zlokasoff's workmen. I remember very well that when I came to my post Iourovsky was already in the house. Probably he spent the night in the house. They were all ransacking the emperor's belongings; they were in a great hurry and were packing all the things that could be packed. I could not hear the conversation between Iourovsky, Nikoulin and Medvedeff. They were all calm but I had the impression that Iourovsky and Nikoulin were a little drunk.

During this day nothing was taken out—only packing was going on.

After I left my post I went to the guardroom, slept, ate, and went to see my brother Alexander who served in the militia. I did not tell anything about the murder to my brother. Until the evening I sauntered around the town and in the evening I returned to the guardroom. In the guardroom Medvedeff announced that we all had to leave Yekaterinburg.

On July 19th we were sent to the station Yekaterinburg First. Our party was assigned to guard the staff of the third Red army. The staff was in railway cars and we were posted by them. At this time I saw the emperor's belongings, loaded on trucks, being shipped to the station. There were the same things that had been previously packed in handbags and trunks. They were all brought to the station and loaded in a train of cars. The cars were big, of the American type.

I personally saw Iourovsky depart. As I remember, he left during the night of July 21st and .proceeded towards Perm. His family and Nikoulin accompanied him. I also personally saw all the Letts who lived in the Ipatieff house and killed the imperial family, departed with Iourovsky. We all left Yekaterinburg when the staff of the third army departed, at the time when the town was already being occupied by the Siberian forces. We went to Perm, but when the troops of General Pepelaieff were taking Perm the staff of the third army and all the workmen of our party left Perm and proceeded towards Viatka. I remained in Perm and after Perm was taken, returned to Yekaterinburg and stopped with my brother Alexander.

The secret service learned of my presence and I was ordered to come to the police station. An elderly official started to question me. I got very much afraid and began to lie to him, saying that I had never been amongst the guards of the imperial family. Afterwards, I confessed that I was amongst the guards, but I denied knowledge of anything. Now I have told you everything I know about this matter.

I fully realise how wrong I was not to follow the advice of my father and mother and to have enlisted in the guards. Now I realise what a wicked action it was to kill the imperial family and I understand that I was also wrong in washing out the bloodstains resulting from the crime. I am not a Bolshevik and I never was one. All that I did, I did because of my youth and stupidity. If at present I could help in any way to find and get hold of the people who committed the murder, I would spare no effort to do it.

All the workmen that performed duty had Nagan revolvers that were distributed by Medvedeff a few days before the murder. Iourovsky carried a Browning pistol; Medvedeff, a Nagan revolver.

I don't know what happened to the boy who was waiting on the imperial family and who was transferred to our quarters before the murder. He slept on my bed and I spoke to him. I don't know if he knew about the murder of the imperial family. He did not cry and we did not talk with him about the murder. He told me that the *commandant* intended to send him home and mentioned to me some district or other, but I have forgotten its name. At the same time he complained to me that Iourovsky took his clothes from him. I cannot name a single man among the Letts.

When I performed duty inside the house I never saw the empress enter the *commandant's* room. I do not think it ever happened, as Iourovsky treated them badly. The empress's rosary, which was found in the *commandant's* room, was probably forgotten there at the time of the packing after the murder.

Usually I saw the emperor wearing a grey or black jacket with a standing collar and brass buttons. He wore boots and grey hair was noticeable in his beard. When the grand duchesses walked in the garden they wore summer clothes, usually blouses and skirts of various colours.

I cannot explain anything more. My statement has been read to me and is written correctly.

Signed: Philip Proskouriakoff.
         "   N. Sokoloff.

Present at the examination:
Iordansky, Public Prosecutor.

5

EXAMINATION OF ANATOLIE IAKIMOFF

(*Anatolie Yakimoff whose deposition is now given, was a workman, who became one of the senior guards of the imperial family during their last days in Yekaterinburg. His statement bears the impress of truths and one gathers from it that he possessed some education and was more enlightened and tolerant in his views than were his fellows. Although Yakimoff never spoke to any of the members of the imperial family, we are able to see them vividly by his crude descriptions of their daily life. This workman-guard denies that he was present at the actual execution, but he insists that he and the others to whom it was related, were convinced that the czar and his family met their deaths in the manner described by Medvedeff.*

It is curious to notice the respect with which this peasant-workman always mentioned the imperial family, Avdeieff, so he say, referred to the imperial family as "They" and Yakimoff follows his example, but it is apparent that this implies no disrespect on his part,—Original editor's note.)

In 1919 from the 7th to the 11th of May, the Investigating Magistrate for Important Cases of the Omsk Tribunal sitting in the town of Yekaterinburg, examined, in accordance with Articles 403-409 of the Code of Criminal Procedure, Anatolie Alexandrovitch Iakimoff, peasant, thirty-one years old, belonging to the Orthodox Church, married. The accused deposed as follows:

I am a workman.

I specialised in work on milling machines; my father was also a workman. He was born in the Ugovsk factory of the Perm District. My mother's name was Maria Nicholaevna. I am the eldest son of the family.

When I was born my father worked at Motoviliha works. At eight I began my studies in a school that was attached to the ecclesiastical seminary. I went to school for three years. When my father died I was twelve. My mother sent me to the public school, but having passed the third grade, I left the school; we had no money to live on and at the same time I was not ambitious enough to study. I wanted to get some occupation and mother sent me to the Motoviliha works, where I was accepted as a bell boy in the drafting room. When I was sixteen I was transferred to the machine shop and began to learn to work on milling machines.

In 1906 I married the daughter of a workman of the Motoviliha factory. In 1916 I volunteered in the army and was recruited in the 494th Vereisky Regiment of the 124th Division. Our regiment fought on the Roumanian front. I participated in several battles but I was never wounded. In July, 1917, after the revolution, I was elected to the regiment's committee. You ask me the reason why I was chosen? I was chosen for the regiment's committee, as I understand, because I was better mentally developed than the rest of the soldiers. I never joined any of the political parties, but my sympathies were with the social democrats.

At the beginning of November, 1917, I got a position in Zloka-soff's factory in Yekaterinburg. The factory was still in the hands of its owners, the Zlokasoffs, but a committee of workmen existed and a *commissar* was commissioned to the factory also. The position of *commissar* was taken by Alexander Dmitrieff Avdeieff, a locksmith by trade. He was about thirty-four or thirty-five, was taller than the aver-age, thin, his face was thin and pale.

In December Avdeieff took to prison the owner of the factory, Nicholas Theodorovitch Zlokasoff. The owners were replaced by an "executive" soviet. This soviet began to rule the factory. The leading man of the factory was Avdeieff. The following workmen were the nearest to him: the brothers Ivan, Vasily and Vladimir Loginoff, Sergius Ivanoff Luhanoff and his son Valentine. The Loginoffs were from the Kishtym factory of the Yekaterinburg district. All those people were in extremely close relations with Avdeieff and occupied the privileged positions. They were either members of the factory's committee and executive soviet or had some other "easy" jobs, but did not work.

Alexander Michailoff Moshkin was also on good terms with Avdei-eff. As far as I remember, Moshkin was born in Semipalatinsk. He was twenty-seven or twenty-eight, short and husky. He was a locksmith. In April it became known in town that the *czar* had been brought to Yekaterinburg. This was explained by the workmen to be quite neces-sary, as somebody wanted to abduct the *czar* from Tobolsk and, there-fore, they had to transfer him to a reliable place such as Yekaterinburg. Such were the conversations amongst the workmen. In the first days of May, shortly after we heard of the arrival of the *czar*, we learned that our Avdeieff was appointed to take charge of the house occupied by the *czar*. At that time for some reason or other they used to call this house "The House of Special Purpose." It was said also that Avdeieff was appointed to be *commandant* of the house.

Shortly afterwards Avdeieff confirmed to us this news at a meet-ing, I cannot explain the reason for this appointment. Avdeieff was a true Bolshevik. He considered that the ideal life could only be realised under Bolshevism. On many occasions he openly said that the Bolshe-viki had destroyed the rich *bourgeoisie*, and had taken the power from Nicholas the "Sanguinary," etc. He always associated in town with the leaders of the local soviet. I believe that for this reason, being a violent Bolshevik, he was appointed by the local soviet to be commandant of the house of "Special Purpose." During the meeting which was as-sembled by him at that time he told us that together with Iakovleff he went to bring the *czar* from Tobolsk. Personally I do not know who Iakovleff was, but Avdeieff told us at the meeting that Iakovleff was a workman from the town of Zlatooust.

Avdeieff said very bad things about him; that Iakovleff wanted to take the *czar* out of Russia and, therefore, took him to Omsk But somehow the Yekaterinburg Bolsheviki learned about his intentions and also notified Omsk about them. Avdeieff raged when he spoke about the *czar*. He slandered him as much as he could, calling him: "The Blood Drinker." War was the main point of his denunciation; he said that the *czar* wanted this war and for three years spilled the blood of the "workmen" and that during this war a great number of workmen were shot for striking.

In general he said the things which were always said by Bolsheviki. It could be understood from his words that for his merits before the "Revolution," in other words, because he did not let Iakovleff take away the *czar*, he was appointed *commandant* of the house of "Special Purpose." It was seen that Avdeieff was very glad of his appointment. He was much pleased when he addressed us at the meeting and promised the workmen to show them the *czar*, saying: "I will take you all to the house and will show you the *czar*."

Judging by the words of Avdeieff, at the time when he was appointed commandant of the "House of Special Purpose," the guards of this house consisted of Magyars. Avdeieff spoke definitely about this and said he intended to relieve the Magyar guard by Russians. He spoke particularly about Magyar guards and not any others. Avdeieff kept his word to "show the *czar* to the workmen." Always workmen used to visit the house, but not all of them—only those that were chosen by Avdeieff. He used to choose only the workmen who were friendly with him, who did not perform guard duties at the house of "Special Purpose," but only "helped" Avdeieff, as his assistants.

They never came to the house all together, but only one or two at a time. They did not stay in the house for a long time, just a day or two. I think that their main ambition was money. For their being at the house brought them a special salary, amounting to four hundred *roubles* a month, excluding allowance for rations. Besides that they received salary in the factory, being members of the factory or business soviet. Altogether these workmen enjoyed their connection with Avdeieff and drew from it a lot of advantages.

On May 30th our factory committee received a letter from Oukraintzeff (the same Oukraintzeff who previously had been one of our workmen), the chief of the central staff of the Red army, wherein it was requested to detail ten men to perform guard duty in the "House of Special Purpose." Among the number I was selected.

When we arrived at the Ipatieff house the Magyar guard had already left. The guards that were there were workmen from the Sissert factory as well as workmen from various other works and factories: the Makaroff factory, Isset works and the mint. After our arrival the Sissert workmen remained in the house, but all the other workmen left. Together with the Sissert workmen we all took quarters in the lower room of Ipatieff's house. One could enter the upper floor from the lobby.

At the time of our arrival at Ipatieff's house there was no special chief amongst us Zlokasoff workmen or Sissert workmen. There were only seniors. During the first week I was the senior of the Zlokasoff workmen. The seniors of the Sissert workmen were Medvedeff and another man. It looked as if Medvedeff was altogether a leading man amongst the Sissert workmen, and I should say that it was he that gave them the orders; different questions were addressed to him; nevertheless he had no special power. Previous to this Nikiforoff occupied this position but soon he got ill and was relieved by Medvedeff. Such was the state of affairs only during the first days after our arrival at Ipatieff's house. About a week later this order was changed.

To begin with we were transferred to Popoff's house. Medvedeff became chief of all of us, in fact, of Zlokasoff's and Sissert's workmen. Three seniors were elected whose duties were shifting the guards. I was such a senior, as well as Benjamin Safonoff and Constantine Dobrynin. When shortly before the murder Safonoff became ill, he was relieved by Ivan Starkoff. In this manner, up till the time of the murder of the imperial family, the seniors were: Ivan Starkoff, Constantine Dobrynin, and myself.

The following were the duties of the seniors: We were eight hours on duty: from six a. m. till two p. m.; from two p. m. till ten p. m.; and from ten p. m. till six a. m. When on duty we shifted the guards and now and then inspected the sentries. Outside of that we were obliged to stay in the *commandant's* room and meet all the visitors to the house. Their arrival was announced to us by a bell rung by the sentry.

At the time of our arrival at Ipatieff's house there were altogether ten posts which were numbered as follows:

Post number one was situated in the first room of the upper floor adjoining the lobby.

Post number two was in the corridor that led to the bathroom and lavatory.

Post number three was situated in the court yard facing the street by the fence gate. The gate was always closed and had a little window to enable the sentry to see who came to the gate.

When we arrived at Ipatieff's house the house was already surrounded by two fences. The first fence was very close to the wall of the house. It began on the side of the Vosnesensky Lane, right from the wall of the house and separated the house from the Vosnesensky Lane, turning at an angle at the place where the lane crossed the Vosnesensky Prospect; after that it separated the house from the Vosnesensky Prospect and finished near the entrance leading to the upper part of the house. In this way the fence made a little courtyard in front of the house which could be entered only from the main entrance of the house which was facing the Vosnesensky Lane. In this court yard, just by the intersection of Vosnesensky Lane and Vosnesensky Prospect, stood an old sentry box.

The second fence also began near the Vosnesensky Lane. It started at the first fence and went further, also turning at an angle and separating the house from the Vosnesensky Prospect. It passed the gate, and finally ran into the wall of the house on the side that faced Vosnesensky Prospect. In this manner the second fence covered the main entrance of the upper floor of the house, as well as the gate and the wicket. This second fence had two gates—one facing the Vosnesensky Lane, the second right opposite them, in the opposite side of the fence, close to the gate of the house.

Both gates were shut from the inside of the fence.

There was only the gate which was near to the door of the house at the time we began to perform guard duty. At that time the gates that faced Vosnesensky Lane did not yet exist. They were built when we were there, as it was found that automobiles had much difficulty in leaving through the first entrance on account of a steep hill. That was the reason why the gates facing the Vosnesensky Lane were constructed. The motor cars entered through both gates, but they left only through the gate facing the Vosnesensky Lane.

The fence which was near the gate, and was built before our arrival, had a wicket with a little window.

On both angles of the exterior fence sentry boxes were constructed.

Post number four was situated outside of the outer fence by the wicket of the gates which were constructed at first

Post number five was situated by the sentry box, near to those gates, in a way that the sentry might observe the whole Vosnesensky Prospect.

Post number six was situated at the other sentry box, which was outside of the fence at the intersection of Vosnesensky Lane and Vosnesensky Prospect, just by the chapel.

Post number seven was situated by the old sentry box in the outer yard, between the walls of the house and the first fence.

Post number eight was in the garden. The sentry had to walk around the whole garden.

Post number nine was on the terrace, where a machine gun was mounted.

Post number ten was situated in a room of the lower floor.

At the time when we arrived at Ipatieff's house there were altogether ten posts.

We were transferred to Popoff's house at our own request. The Sissert workmen were especially insistent upon it. Their houses were far from town, so they were visited by their wives. At the same time, as strangers were not allowed at Ipatieff's house, the wives could not stop there. For this particular reason we were all transferred to Popoff's house.

Up to the second half of June we—Zlokasoff's and Sissert's workmen—performed guard duty on all the ten posts. From the second part of June a certain change took place. The reason was that a feeling of discontent towards Avdeieff grew very strong at that time amongst the Zlokasoff s workmen, so finally he was discharged from the position of *commissar* to the factory. He remained only *commandant* of Ipatieff's house. His group, consisting of the above-mentioned people, was also discharged from all the positions they occupied. After that Avdeieff took them all to Ipatieff's house. All the people mentioned by me came here: The three brothers Loginoff, Mishkevitch, Soloviev, Gonihkevitch, Koriakin, Krashensnnikoff, Sidoroff, Oukrainzeff, Komendantoff, Labousheff, Valentine Luhanoff and Skorohodoff. All of them, except Skorohodoff, who got sick and was removed to a hospital, took their places in the commandant's room and the lobby.

From their arrival at Ipatieff's house they began to perform duty on posts number rate and two. They all quartered in the commandant's room and the lobby and slept on the floor, for which purpose they took two or three mattresses from the storeroom.

In this way we performed duty until the first days of July, approximately until the third or fourth of July, when Avdeieff, Moshkin and the others were discharged.

This happened in the following way: Avdeieff was a drunkard. He liked drinking and did not miss an opportunity. He drank a sort of yeast paste which he obtained at the Zlokasoff's factory. He drank in Ipatieff's house. His followers drank also. When the latter moved to the Ipatieff's house they began stealing the emperor's belongings. Often they used to go to the storeroom and take out various things in sacks or bags. The bags they took away in a motor car or on horses. They took the things to their houses or flats. The fact of these thefts soon became the subject of gossip.

Our guards also began to speak about the stealing going on and especially Paul Medvedeff spoke about it. Thefts in the Zlokasoff's factory were also investigated and Avdeieff and Luhanoff were pointed to as the thieves. This was certainly right, as Avdeieff and his gang were suspected by the work-men at the time they were in the factory. Even at this time all of them stuck to easy jobs in the committee or business soviet. They got plenty of money and drank yeast. They continued this behaviour after they moved to the Ipatieff house: drank yeast and stole the *czar's* belongings.

About the third or the fourth of July, at the time I was on duty, Avdeieff went somewhere out of the house. I suppose he was called by telephone to the district soviet. Shortly after Moshkin also left. I know that he went to the district soviet whither he was called by telephone. Vasily Logoff remained in place of Avdeieff. Sometime after Avdeieff and Moshkin departed, Beloborodoff, Safaroff, Iourovsky, Nikoulin and two other men entered the house. Beloborodoff asked us who remained in the house instead of Avdeieff. Vasily Loginoff answered that he was staying instead of Avdeieff. At that Beloborodoff explained to us that Avdeieff was not a *commandant* any longer and that he and Mosh-kin were arrested.

The reason of the arrest was not explained by Beloborodoff. As far as I remember the same thing was told by Beloborodoff to Medvedeff, who at this time came from the Popoff house. Beloborodoff also explained to us that Iourovsky was the new *commandant* and Nikoulin his assistant. From this moment Iourovsky began to give orders in the house in the capacity of *commandant*. He immediately ordered Loginoff and others of Avdeieff's party—I can't remember which of them, at this moment, were in the house—to "get out."

I remember that all the people mentioned: Beloborodoff, Safaroff, Nikoulin, Iourovsky and the two men unknown to me, visited all the rooms of the house; they were in the rooms occupied by the *czar* and his family, but I did not accompany them to those rooms. They did not stay for a long time. I believe that Beloborodoff informed the family of the appointment of Iourovsky and Nikoulin. At that time Iourovsky questioned Medvedeff about the man who performed guard duty on posts numbers one and two. (Inside the house.) After he learned that those posts were kept by the "privileged" of Avdeieff's party, Iourovsky said: "For the present you will have to perform duty on those posts; later I will request men from the extraordinary committee for them."

In a few days the men from the extraordinary investigation committee arrived at the Ipatieff house. They were ten in number. Their baggage was brought on a horse. I could not identify the horse or tell the name of the coachman; but everybody at that time knew that the men came from the "*Tchresvytchayka*" (Institution of Secret Political Police) in the American hotel.

I cannot say why, but we used to call all those men Letts. But whether they were Letts none of us knew. It is quite possible that they were not Letts, but Magyars.

They took their quarters in the lower floor of the house, and had their meals in the *commandant's* room. They were in a privileged position in comparison with us. I think it would be right to say that we had three parties: the so-called Letts, the Zlokasoff and Sissert workmen. The Letts Iourovsky treated as equals. The Sissert workmen he treated a little better than us, and us worst of all. I account for the difference in his manner towards the Sissert workmen by the fact that he considered us as workmen from the Zlokasoff factory who had been discharged together with Avdeieff. Medvedeff also influenced his attitude. He ingratiated himself with Iourovsky and Nikoulin and made an effort to be very affable. That is why they had a better attitude towards the Sissert workmen.

At the beginning he increased the number of posts. He mounted another machine gun in the attic of the house and established a post in the rear yard. This post in the rear yard was number ten, the post by the machine gun, eleven, and the post in the attic twelve. Duties on posts numbers one, two and twelve, after the arrival of Iourovsky, were performed exclusively by Letts.

You ask me why I volunteered to guard the *czar?* I did not see at that time anything wrong in doing so. As I told you before, I read a little, different books. I read party pamphlets and had an idea about the views of the different parties. For example, I know the difference between the ideas of the social revolutionists and the Bolsheviki. The former believe that the peasants are a working-class and the latter consider them as *bourgeoisie* and believe that only workmen are real proletarians. My sympathies were with the Bolsheviki, but I did not believe that the Bolsheviki could build up by their methods of violence a "good" and "just" life. I still believe that a "good" and "just" life will exist only when there are not so many rich and so many poor people as there are at present; and this will only come when all the population are educated to the point where they understand that the life they arc leading at present is not the true one.

I believed the *czar* to be the first capitalist who would always play into the hands of capital and not into those of the workmen. For this reason I did not want a *czar* and thought that he ought to be kept under guard, or at least imprisoned, until the time when he could be judged by the nation and punished by it according to his crimes, after deciding: "Was he guilty before his people, or not?" I thought his imprisonment was necessary for the safety of the revolution, and if I had known before that he would be killed in the way he was, I never would have gone to guard him. I believed that he could be judged only by the whole of Russia, as he was the *czar* of the entire Russian nation. All that happened I consider a wicked deed, "unjust and cruel." The murder of the rest of his family I consider still worse. For what reason were his children murdered? I must also state that I joined the guards as I wanted to earn money. At that time I did not feel well and joined the guards because I thought it an easy job.

In this way we kept guard of the Czar Nicholas Alexandrovitch and his family. They all lived in Ipatieff's house—I mean to say the Czar Nicholas Alexandrovitch, his wife Alexandra Theodorovna, his son Alexis and his daughters, Olga, Tatiana, Maria and Anastasia.

Of the others who lived with them there were: Dr. Botkin, Demidova, "Freylina" we used to call her, Haritonoff, the cook, and Troupp, the waiter. The name of the waiter I remember very well because the list of all the people who lived in Ipatieff's house was hung up in the *commandant's* room.

Botkin was an aged man, stout, grey-haired and tall. He wore a blue suit: jacket, waistcoat and trousers, stiff shirt and tie; he always wore shoes.

Demidova was a tall and stout blonde; she was thirty to thirty-five, dressed herself very cleanly and nicely, not like a servant, wore a corset; and it was seen by her figure that she was very tight-laced.

The cook was about fifty. He was small, strong and had brown hair.

The waiter was about sixty; he was tall and thin.

There also lived with the imperial family a boy about fourteen, whose name I don't know. He was tall for his age, thin and his face was pale. He wore a dark grey jacket, with a high collar.

I cannot tell you anything as to how the imperial family lived and spent their time. I never entered the rooms where they lived, and I could not see anything from a distance, as the door from the lobby to their first room was always shut.

I don't know how the imperial family spent their time in the house. Dinner was brought for them by some women from the soviet dining-room that is located at the crossing of Vosnesensky and Glavny Prospects, in the place occupied now by the motion pictures and the Café Lorange. But later, during Avdeieff's time, permission was given to them to prepare their dinner in the house. For this purpose the provisions were brought to them from the district soviet by some special man. Nuns used to bring them from the monastery milk, eggs and bread. The only thing I personally observed in the life of the imperial family was their singing. I heard sometimes sacred songs which they sang. They sang the "*Herouvimskaya*" (cherubims) song. But they sang also a secular song. I could not get the words, but the tune was sad. This was the name of a song: "A Man Died in a Soldier's Hospital." I never heard men's voices singing—only women's.

The divine service was performed in the house, but during the whole time I was there divine service was performed only three times. Twice the clergyman Storogeff officiated at the service and once the clergyman Meledin. But there were services also before our arrival. I know this because I had to get a priest to officiate at the service. The first time I was sent to get a priest by Avdeieff he named the church from which the clergyman was to be asked. He did not give me the name of the priest. At the church I learned that it was Meledin who officiated. I wanted to get him but at this time he was busy. After that I called up Storogeff. I called him also later a second time.

When I was looking for a priest I used to address myself to the churchwarden who stood near the candle-box. I cannot tell who he was. But once he asked me if he couldn't officiate instead of a deacon, saying: "I would like so much to see the *czar*." In the time of Avdeieff, when I was in the house, two services were held. While Iourovsky was there, only one. Personally I was never present at divine service. We were not allowed in the room. Avdeieff and Iourovsky were present at the service. From the distance I heard men's and women's voices during the service; probably they sung themselves. I saw all the members of the imperial family, as well as all the people who lived with them.

I saw them in the house when they passed to the toilet room, or went for a walk in the garden, as well as during the walk itself. They passed near the *commandant's* room and close to post number one as they went to the toilet room. They could also go to the toilet room through the kitchen. I don't know the reason, but they never did it. If the heir was not with them, they used to go for their walk by the staircase that led down from the toilet room, through the lobby that led into the yard and from the yard to the garden. Sometimes when the heir went with them to walk they all went through the main entrance of the house to the street, then through the gate (and not the wicket) to the yard, and then to the garden. He was probably ill and he was carried out to his roller chair, which was brought up to the main entrance. The *czar* used to carry him personally. I never saw him carried by anyone else.

Personally I could not observe the attitude of other people towards the emperor and his family, though I watched Avdeieff, who had to deal with them. Avdeieff was a rough and uncouth man and a drunkard; his soul was not kind. If on any occasion during the absence of Avdeieff any member of the imperial family asked Moshkin for a favour, he always used to answer that they would have to wait the return of Avdeieff. When Avdeieff returned and their plea was made to him, Avdeieff's answer was: "Let them go to hell." Sometimes returning from the imperial family's room, Avdeieff used to say that they asked him for something or another and he refused. Apparently the process of refusal gave him much pleasure. He spoke about it, looking very happy. For example, I remember that he was asked once for permission to open the windows—telling us about it, he said that he forbade it.

I cannot say how he addressed the *czar*, but in the *commandant's* room he referred to the imperial family as: "They"; the *czar* he used to call "*Nikolashka*." I have told you already that as soon as he got into the house he began to bring in his favourite workmen, who moved into the house altogether, after being discharged from the committee and soviet. All those people had a merry time with Avdeieff in the Ipatieff house. They drank and stole the emperor's belongings. Once Avdeieff got so tight that he fell in one of the lower rooms of the house. At the same time Beloborodoff arrived and called for him. Someone of Avdeieff's favourites lied to Beloborodoff that Avdeieff had gone out of the house. It appeared that he fell drunk in the lower floor directly after he had visited the imperial family, whom he went to see in that state.

The drunkards made a great noise in the *commandant's* room; they shouted, slept one on the other as they toppled over and were very dirty in their habits. The songs they chose for their singing, of course, could not have been agreeable to the *czar*. They all sang: "You fell as a victim in the struggle," "Let us forget the old world," "Get cheerfully in step, comrades." Oukrainzeff could play the piano which was in the *commandant's* room and accompany the singers. Knowing Avdeieff was a Bolshevik and also a harsh man, who was always drunk, I believe that he treated the imperial family badly. He could not treat then well, as it was against his nature and behaviour. After I watched him in the *commandant's* room I believed the way he treated the imperial family was insulting. I also remember that Avdeieff spoke with his friends about Rasputin. He spoke about the same things which other people discussed and which were written a number of times in the newspapers.

Not a single time did I speak with the *czar* or anyone of his family. I met them only occasionally, and we never spoke. Only once I saw and heard the *czar* speaking to Moshkin. They were walking in the garden. The *czar* walked in the garden. Moshkin sat in the garden on a bench. The *czar* approached him and said something about the weather.

Though I did not speak when I met them I still got an impression, that entered my soul, of all of them. The *czar* was not young anymore; he had grey hair in his beard. I have seen him wearing a *"gimnasterka"* (soldier's shirt), an officer's belt, with a buckle, around his waist. The buckle was yellow and the belt was yellow, not of a light yellow colour, but of a dark one. The colour of the *gimnasterka* was khaki. His trousers were the same colour and he had old worn-out boots. His eyes were kind and he had altogether a kind expression. I got the impression he was a kind, modest, frank and talkative person. Sometimes I felt that he would speak to me right away. He looked as if he would like to talk with any one of us.

The *czaritza* was not a bit like him. Her look was severe. She had the appearance and manners of a haughty and grave woman. Sometimes we used to speak about them amongst ourselves, and we all thought that Nicholas Alexandrovitch was a modest man, but that she was different and looked exactly like a *czaritza*. She seemed older than he was. There was grey hair on her temples and her face was not the face of a young woman. He looked younger when they were together. I cannot describe the way she used to dress.

Tatiana looked like the *czaritza*. She had the same serious and haughty look as her mother. The other daughters: Olga, Maria and Anastasia, had no haughtiness about them. One had the impression that they were modest and kind. I also cannot describe the way they dressed, as I did not notice it.

The *czarevitch* was sick all the time. I can tell you nothing about him. The *czar* used to carry him up to his roller chair, and there he lay covered with a blanket. I cannot describe his clothes either.

I thought a great deal about the *czar* after I stayed a certain time amongst the guards. After I personally saw than several times I began to feel entirely different towards them: I began to pity them. I pitied them as human beings. I tell you the entire truth. You may believe me or not. I had the idea in my head to let them escape, or to do something to allow them to escape. I did not tell anybody about this, but I had an idea to tell it to Dr. Derevenko, who visited them at that time, but I was doubtful of him. I cannot tell you why I was doubtful. I just thought: "I don't know what type of man he is."

When he left them his face did not express anything, and he never spoke a single word about them, so I got doubtful. I am relating to you the exact truth. I had in my head the thoughts I am expressing now. Previously, when I first entered into the guards, I did not see them and did not know them. I was also a little guilty before them. When Avdeieff and the "*Tovaristchy*" (comrades) used to sing the revolutionary songs, I also used to join a little in the chorus, but after I learned how the matter stood, I stopped it and all of us, or if not all then a great number, condemned Avdeieff for his behaviour.

In the time of Iourovsky we were not allowed into the house. I never used to stay longer than necessary in the *commandant's* room, as I did during the days of Avdeieff. Whenever a bell rang (an electric bell was connected with the *commandant's* room and Popoff's house), one used to come to the *commandant's* room, get an order and immediately retire. We seniors did not have to go to the *commandant's* room to answer the bell ring. It was always Medvedeff who went and we were asked for through him. Iourovsky was always with Nikoulin; Medvedeff also made his best efforts to be in their company. The Letts from the Tchresvytchayka were also near to them. That is why I cannot describe to you how Iourovsky felt about the *czar*. Avdeieff was nearer to us, as he was the same sort we were—a workman, and he lived with us. Iourovsky behaved himself like a chief and did not let us in the house.

I can only say that immediately after he got in command of the house he mounted a machine gun in the attic and established a new post in the rear yard. He stopped all drunkenness and I never saw him drunk or intoxicated. Nikoulin was visited by a girl whose name was "Seveleva" but she was never let into the *commandant's* room. But on one occasion Iourovsky either changed or forbade altogether the donation of the nuns to the imperial family; he did something that made the position of the imperial family worse, but what he changed or forbade, I do not remember. Something that I could not understand happened also in regard to the priest. As I remember, in the time of Iourovsky there was only one divine service. I was called by Iourovsky, who ordered me to get "any" priest.

At first he asked me who were the priests that officiated. I named Father Meledin and Father Storogeff. After that he ordered me to get one of them. As Father Meledin happened to be the nearest, I called him up the same day, on Saturday evening. In the evening I told Iourovsky that I called up Meledin. Next day, in the morning, Iourovsky called me up and again asked me the name of the priest I had told to come. I answered that I called up Father Meledin. Hearing that, Iourovsky asked me: "Is that the one who lives on the Vodotchnaya in the place where Dr. Tchernavin lives?" I answered that it was the same one, after which Iourovsky sent me to inform Meledin that he should not come. "Go and tell Meledin that there won't be any service, service is postponed. If he should ask you who postponed the service, you will say that they did it and not myself. Instead of Meledin, fetch Storogeff." Well, I went to Meledin and told him there would be no service. He asked me why? I answered in the way I was ordered by Iourovsky: that "they" postponed it. Directly after I went to Storogeff and asked him to come.

What the reason was for all that, and why Iourovsky preferred Storogeff to Meledin, I don't know. Towards me also he acted very arbitrarily, neglecting the desires of the men. On July 12th the men elected me instead of Medvedeff to be chief. On Sunday, July 14th, I returned after my leave later than it was allowed, so Iourovsky dismissed me and appointed Medvedeff instead to be chief. So it continued till the end.

The last time I saw the *czar* and his daughters was on July 16th. They were walking in the garden about four o'clock. I don't remember whether I saw the heir. The *czaritza*, I did not see, as she did not walk at that time.

On Monday, July 15th, the boy who lived with the imperial family and used to push the roller chair, appeared in our quarters at Popoff's house. I specially noticed this fact. Probably the other guards also noticed it. But nobody knew why the boy was transferred to our house. There is no doubt that it was done on Iourovsky's orders. On July 16th I was on duty. My hours at that time were from two p. m. up till ten p. m. At ten o'clock I placed the sentries on all the eight posts (duties on posts numbers one, two, eleven and twelve were not performed by us). The sentries that I placed at ten p. m. had to be relieved at two a. m. by the new senior, Constantine Dobrynin, to whom I shifted my duties.

After I was relieved I went to our quarters. I remember that I had tea and afterwards, at about eleven o'clock, went to bed. Klescheeff, Romanoff and Osokin were in the same room with me. About four a. m., when it began to be daylight, I was wakened by Klescheeff's voice. Romanoff and all the other men, including Osokin, who slept in the same room with me, were also awakened. Klescheeff was saying in a nervous voice: "Get up fellows, I will tell you the news; get out into the other room." We got up and followed him to the next room where there were more men, and when we all got assembled, Klescheeff announced: "Today the *czar* was shot." We all started to ask how it happened and he and Deriabin told us the following mutually completing each other's narrative.

At two a. m. a notice was given to them by Medvedeff and Dobrynin whilst they were standing on their posts, that they would have to perform their duty longer than two o'clock a. m., as during the night the *czar* was going to be shot. After receiving the notice Klescheeff and Deriabin approached the windows: Klescheeff, to the window of the lobby of the lower floor which was opposite to the door that led to the room where the murder took place; and Deriabin to the window of the room that faced the Vosnesensky Lane. Shortly afterwards, they say it was a little past midnight by the Old Time, or a little past two by the New Time (instituted by the Bolsheviki, who changed the time two hours ahead), some persons entered the lower room and proceeded to the room where the murder took place. The procession was seen very well by Klescheeff. Iourovsky and Nikoulin went ahead and were followed by the emperor, empress and the daughters—Olga, Tatiana, Maria and Anastasia, as well as by Botkin, Demidova, Troupp and Haritonoff, the cook.

The heir was carried in the arms of the emperor. Behind them went Medvedeff and the Letts, the ten men that lived in the lower room and were requested by Iourovsky from the *"Tchresvytchayka."* Two of the number carried rifles. When the imperial family were in the room, they placed themselves as follows: In the middle of the room stood the *czar*, the heir was seated on a chair to the right of the *czar*, to the right of the heir stood Dr. Botkin; behind them against the wall stood the empress with her daughters; at one side of the empress stood the cook and the waiter; on the other Demidova.

Besides them, the following people were in the room: Iourovsky, Nikoulin, and the Letts. Behind the Letts stood Medvedeff.

Deriabin couldn't tell the words with which Iourovsky addressed the family, he didn't hear them, but Klescheeff positively affirms that he heard Iourovsky's words and that Iourovsky said to the *czar*: "Nicholas Alexandrovitch, your relatives are trying to save you, therefore we are compelled to shoot you." The same minute several shots were heard. All the revolvers were fired.

A woman's scream and loud cries of several women's voices were heard after the first shots. They executed the victims one after the other. The emperor fell first, after him fell the heir. Demidova was tossing herself about, but was dispatched by bayonets. After they all fell they were examined and some of them who gave signs of life were again shot and pierced by bayonets. Of the members of the imperial family they mentioned Anastasia as being pierced by bayonets. After that they again started to examine the dead: unbuttoned their clothes, looking for jewellery. All the things found on the dead persons, Iourovsky took himself and carried upstairs. Somebody brought from the upper rooms a few bedsheets and the dead were wrapped in those and carried out into the yard through the same rooms through which they had passed to their execution.

From the yard they were carried to a motor truck which was standing behind the gate of the house. All of them were transported on a truck; some cloth was taken from the store room and spread on the truck; the bodies were put cm the cloth and covered with the same cloth. Sergius Luhanoff was the driver. The truck with the bodies was taken out by Luhanoff through the gates that opened on the Vosnesensky Lane. Iourovsky and about three Letts went out with the bodies. After the bodies were taken out of the house two Letts began to mop up the blood and wash it with water and sawdust The narratives of Klescheeff and Deriabin about the murder sounded so much like truth and they both were so excited by everything they had seen, that nobody had even a shadow of a doubt that they were speaking the truth.

Deriabin felt especially upset about it; he swore and called them murderers, butchers, and spoke about them with profound disgust. On one of the following days, either Medvedeff or somebody who heard him, told me that Luhanoff took the bodies to the Verkh-Issetsk Works. The truck went through a wooded country. The ground began to get soft and swampy. The car was proceeding with difficulty, as its wheels sank into the mud. With many difficulties the automobile arrived at its destination, where a hole was already dug. All the bodies were laid in the hole and covered.

All that I am telling is the exact truth. Neither myself nor any other of our Zlokasoff workmen knew anything in the evening about the intended murder. After that evening Medvedeff did not come to our quarters and did not explain anything to us. I admit that some of the Sissert workmen may have known about it through Medvedeff, but the Sissert workmen were holding themselves aloof from us, and we from them. Among the Sissert workmen there was a greater number of Bolsheviki than among us.

Regarding the weapons, I can say the following: Iourovsky had two revolvers; one of them was a big Mauser and the other a Nagan. Besides that I have seen a big revolver in the *commandant's* room and it is possible that it was a Colt. All the Letts had revolvers and judging by the holsters they had Nagans. Besides that a few more revolvers were brought from some place at the time Iourovsky was *commandant*.

The description of the murder of the *czar* and his family impressed me very much. I was sitting trembling. I did not go to bed, and at eight o'clock in the morning I went to see my sister, Kapitolina, with whom I was on very good terms. So I went to her to share my feelings with her. I was deeply pained in my soul. I found my sister alone; her husband was working in the *commissariat* of justice. When my sister saw my distressed expression she asked me: "What is the matter?"

I answered her: "The *czar* is shot." My sister asked me: "Is it possible that you were there?" I told her the same thing I am telling you, but not in such detail. I told her the imperial family were shot by decision and order of the "district soviet of workmen deputies." I have the same opinion at present; it could not be possible that Iourovsky did it on his own decision. As at that time all the power was in the hands of the district soviet, I believe that the murder was done by the order of the soviet.

Previously among the Red Guards there was the following conversation: "What will happen if the Czechs enter the town? What will they do with the imperial family?" Some suggested that they would execute the family.

I remember that Deriabin said that Demidova had about thirty bayonet wounds. I told that to my sister.

At about ten o'clock in the morning I returned from my sister's to the Popoff house. I do not remember what I did until two p. m., when my duty commenced. I placed the guards on all the posts and entered the *commandant's* room. There I met Nikoulin, two Letts and Medvedeff. They were not gay, any of them; they looked preoccupied and depressed. None of them was speaking. A large number of precious things were placed on the table. They were pins, stones, earrings, beads and all sorts of jewels. A part of them lay in boxes, which were all open. The door from the lobby leading to the rooms where the imperial family used to live was closed as before, but there was nobody in the rooms; not a single. sound was heard. Before, when the imperial family used to live there, sounds of life were always heard in those rooms. There was not any life there at present.

Only their little dog was standing near the door in the lobby, waiting to be let into those rooms. I remember very well that I thought at the time: "You are waiting in vain." Before the murder there was a bed and a couch in the *commandant's* room. On this day at two o'clock of July 17th, when I came to the *commandant's* room, I noticed there two more beds, on one of which a Lett was lying. Later Medvedeff told us that the Letts did not want to live any longer in the room where the murder took place (they had lived before in this room). Obviously this was the reason why the two beds were transferred to the *commandant's* room.

From two o'clock p. m. up till ten o'clock p. m. on July 17th I performed duty. On this day I did not see Iourovsky in the house.

The same day Medvedeff told us that all of us guards would be sent to the front. So, on July 18th, I went in the morning to the Zlokasoff factory for the purpose of drawing the money that was due me. At two o'clock of the same day I again went on duty. On this day the *czar's* belongings were being taken from the Ipatieff house and loaded on an automobile. Beloborodoff was sitting in the automobile. A number of things were also taken away on carriages.

On July 18th I saw Iourovsky in the house about six o'clock in the evening; he was constantly coming and going. At about eight o'clock in the evening he called up Medvedeff and gave him the money for our wages. On July 18th all the things had been taken out of the house.

On July 20th, during the night, together with the other guards, I was sent to the station Yekaterinburg First. A part of the guard remained in the Ipatieff house.

At the end of July we arrived at Perm and about a week after our arrival we were joined by the remainder of the guards from the Ipatieff house. All were assigned to the command of the *commissar* of supplies of the third army, by the name of Gorbounoff, and taken on a steamer to Levshino. Klesscheeff alone did not go with them to Levshino as he had to stay in Perm owing to illness from venereal disease.

For about a month I was guarding the steamer and railroad cars of the *commissar* Gorbounoff. On November 1st, of my own will, I went to Motoviliha and remained there. After the place came under the rule of the supreme ruler I was mobilised, participated in battles with the Reds and finally was arrested.

I remember another fact in the life of the emperor. On one occasion I entered the *commandant's* room and met there Nikoulin and Kabanoff. I heard Nikoulin asking Kabanoff what he spoke about with the *czar* during the time of his walk. Kabanoff replied that the emperor asked him if he had not been previously in a certain *cuirassier* regiment. Kabanoff answered that he had been and added also that once, during the time he was in the regiment, the regiment was reviewed by the *czar*. We were all surprised at the *czar's* memory.

I cannot say what became of the boy who stayed with the imperial family. On one of the days immediately following the murder I saw the boy from a distance; he was sitting in the room where the Sissert workmen were dining and was weeping bitterly so that his sobs were heard by me. I did not go towards him, nor did I ask him any questions. I was told that the boy learned about the murder of the imperial family and began to cry.

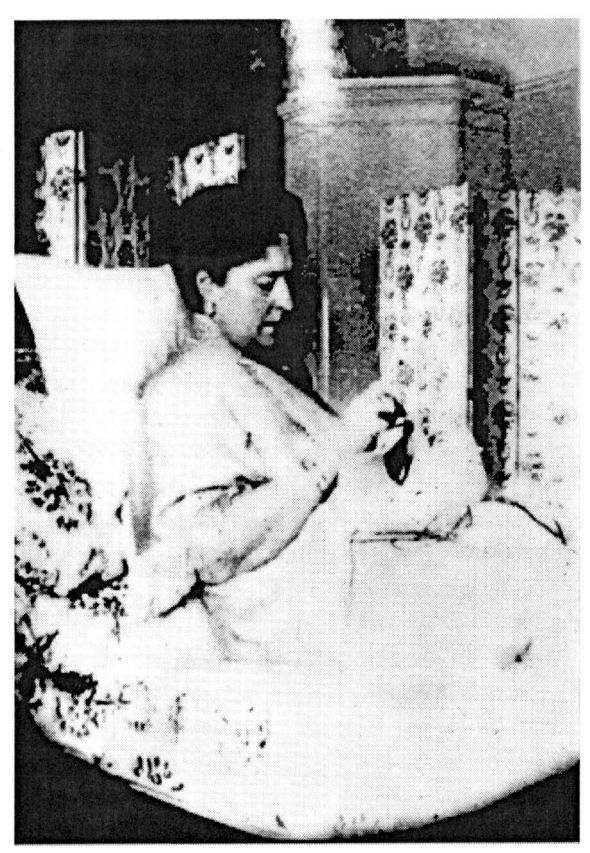

EMPRESS ALEXANDRA FEODOROVA IN TOBOLSK

X

THE IPATIEV HOUSE IN EKATERINBURG
(GENERAL VIEW)

(X) The Basement room in which the
murders took place.

YANKEL YUROVSKY,
THE MURDERER

He shot the Tsar and the Tsarevich
with his own hand.

THE IPATIEV HOUSE: SHOWING THE STOCKADE AROUND THE HOUSE

The above photograph was taken in May, 1918, directly after the arrival of Nicholas, Alexandra and Maria. Their jailers had had time to put up only the inner fence. The outer stockade, erected later, inclosed the gateway and approaches to the house. Machine-guns were mounted at different points within the inclosure and in the garret. Note the shrine on the left.

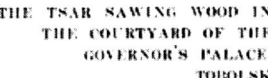

THE TSAR SAWING WOOD IN THE COURTYARD OF THE GOVERNOR'S PALACE, TOBOLSK

It is winter. He wears the papaha (military fur hat) and felt boots.

BEDROOM OF THE EMPEROR AND EMPRESS IN THE IPATIEV HOUSE

On July the 17th, after I became calmer, I went to Medvedeff's room. In this room I met another man who had previously obtained the supplies for the imperial family and the guardsmen. I began to question Medvedeff about the murder. Medvedeff told me that shortly after twelve in the night, Iourovsky woke up the imperial family and said to the *czar*: "An attack is being prepared on the house, I must transfer you all to the lower room." They all came down. In reply to my question who did the shooting, Medvedeff answered that it was the Letts. When I asked where the bodies were taken, he told me that the bodies were taken by Iourovsky and the Letts on an automobile to the Verkh-Issetsk Works and there in a wooded place by the swamp all the bodies were put in one hole that was previously prepared and covered with earth. I remember he said that the automobile sank and only with great difficulty arrived at the grave.

I know that; Avdeieff, before being appointed *commandant* of the Ipatieff house, went to Tobolsk to get the *czar* and his family. He was accompanied by Hohriakoff, who was afterwards killed at the front and buried with great ceremony in Perm by the Bolsheviki.

I also remember that when I went to Yekaterinburg I heard in the car two workmen saying that the *czar* had left Yekaterinburg. All of us who were of the guards began to tell them that the *czar* had been shot.

I can't explain anything else. My testimony has been read to me, and is correct.

| (Signed) | Anatolie Alexandrovitch Lakimoff. |
| " | N. Sokoloff. |

6
EXAMINATION OF PAVEL MEDVEDEFF

(The deposition of Pavel Medvedeff, the former workman at the Sissert Factory, reveals a more hardened character than that of Yakimoff. He regards events in the cold light of reason, and offers no comment either of pity or of dislike. As he informed the member of the District Courts the fate of the czar and his family did not "interest" him. But it is worthy of notice that this unemotional workman insists that he took no part whatever in the actual murder, which implies that the tragedy was repugnant even to a man of his type.

His account also bears the imprint of truth. It is evident from it that Medvedeff possessed no imagination, and he describes the bloodstained room, and the bleeding corpses exactly as everyday occurrences. There is no attempt to impress his interrogator. His standpoint is: "I saw these things, this is how they happened. I have nothing more to say."

His account of the disposal of the corpses differs from that of Yakimoff. It agrees, however, that the route taken by the motor lorry was in the direction of the Verkh-Issetsk Works.—Original editor's note.)

On February 21, 1919, in the town of Yekaterinburg, a member of Yekaterinburg district court, J. Sergeeff, examined the person named below as one of the accused, in accordance with Article No. 403–409 of the Code of Criminal Procedure. The accused deposed as follows:

I am Pavel Spiridonovitch Medvedeff, thirty-one years of age, and belong to the Orthodox Church; able to read and write; born a peasant of the Sissert factory of the Yekaterinburg district. I have a house belonging to me at the factory.

In September, 1914, I was mobilised and assigned to the Opolchenskaia Drujina (33rd territorial battalion), located in the town of Verhotourie. I stayed with the battalion for two months. I was then discharged and exempted from military service, on account, I believe, of being employed as a munition worker.

After the February revolution, in April, 1917, I joined the Bolshevik party, as the majority of the workmen in our factory did. During three months I paid to the party treasury one *per cent* of my wages. Then I ceased to pay because I was not willing to participate in the activities of the party.

After the October revolution, in January, 1918, I was enlisted in the Red army and in February they sent me to the front to fight against Dutoff. Commissar Sergius Mrachkovsky was in command of my detachment. We were fighting in the vicinity of Troizk, but our fighting was not a success, as we did more wandering on the *steepes* than actual fighting. In April I came home on leave and spent three weeks there. In the second half of May the abovementioned Commissar Mrachkovsky came to our factory and began to recruit workmen for a special detachment which was assigned to guard the house where the former emperor, Nicholas II, and his family lived. The conditions appeared attractive to me and I enlisted. Altogether thirty workmen were enlisted.

On May 19, 1918, the detachment recruited by Commissar Mrachkovsky came to Yekaterinburg and was quartered in the Novy Gostiny Dvor (new market house), where we lived till May 24th. According to the order of the Ural district soviet, we elected from amongst our number two seniors. Alexis Nikiforoff and I were elected.

121

On May 24th our detachment was transferred to new quarters, to the lower floor of the Ipatieff house. The same day the former emperor with his family arrived. They were placed in the upper floor of this same house. The whole upper floor of the house was at their disposal, except one room (to the left from the entrance), which was occupied by the *commandant* of the house and his assistant. Alexander Avdeieff, workman of the Zlokasoff factory, was the *commandant*. Moshkin (I don't remember his Christian name) was his assistant. Two other men were also quartered in the *commandant's* room. I do not know their names, but I know they were Zlokasoff workmen.

As soon as our party arrived at the Ipatieff house the *commandant* ordered me, as I was senior, to receive the prisoners. Together with Avdeieff and Moshkin I entered the corner room (the *czar's* bedroom). The following persons were there: The emperor, his wife, son, four daughters. Dr. Botkin, the cook, the waiter and a boy. (I do not know their names.) After having counted the party and finding that they were twelve in number, we left, without having spoken to them. In the room adjoining the *czar's* bedroom were placed the *czar's* four daughters. At first there were no beds for them. After two or three days the beds were put in. The *commandant* was in charge of the internal life in the house; the guards performed only sentry duty. At first the guards were on duty in three turns, but later in four.

We stayed in Ipatieff's house two or three weeks, after which we were transferred to Popoff's house, which was exactly opposite Ipatieff's house. In a few days after this the guard was augmented by fourteen more workmen from the Zlokasoff factory, which is situated in Yekaterinburg. These Zlokasoff workmen also elected their senior, by the name of Iakimoff. There were altogether eleven sentry posts; two were inside the house; two by the machine guns; and four outside the house. Every day the *czar's* family used to walk in the garden. The heir was sick all the time and the emperor carried him to his wheelchair. At the beginning, dinner for the family was brought from the Soviet's dining-room; but afterwards they were allowed to prepare their own dinner in the kitchen of the upper floor.

The seniors' (guard captains') duties were to take charge of the food and supplies of the guardsmen, to change the sentries, and supervise them. When on duty the senior had to stay in the *commandant's* room. At first the seniors took turns every twelve hours in performing their duties. Then the third senior was elected, Constantine Dobrynin, and after this we did duty in eight-hour shifts. At the end of June or at the beginning of July (I don't remember exactly), the *commandant*, Avdeieff, and his assistant, Moshkin were removed (it seems that they were suspected of stealing the *czar's* belongings). A new *commandant* was assigned; his name was Iourovsky. The new *commandant's* assistant arrived with him. His name I do not remember. In the evening of July 16th the time of my duty had just begun, when between seven and eight p. m. the *commandant*, Iourovsky, ordered me to take all the Nagan revolvers from the guardsmen and to bring them up to him. I took twelve revolvers from the sentries as well as from some other guardsmen and brought them to the *commandant's* office.

Iourovsky announced to me: "We will have to shoot them all tonight; notify the guardsmen not to be alarmed if they should hear the shots." I understood that Iourovsky had in mind to shoot the whole of the *czar's* family as well as the doctor and servants who lived with them, but I did not ask him where or by whom the decision was made. I must tell you that the boy who assisted the cook, in accordance with Iourovsky's order, was transferred in the morning to the guardsmen's rooms in the Popoff house. The lower floor of Ipatieff's house was occupied by the Letts from the Letts commune who took up their quarters there after Iourovsky was made *commandant*. They were ten in number.

At about ten o'clock in the evening, in accordance with Iourovsky's order, I informed the guardsmen not to be alarmed if they should hear firing. About midnight Iourovsky woke up the *czar's* family. I do not know if he told them the reason they were wakened and where they were to be taken, or not, I positively affirm that it was Iourovsky who entered the rooms where the *czar's* family was. Iourovsky had not ordered me or Dobrynin to waken the family. In about an hour the whole of the family, the doctor, maid and two waiters got up, washed and dressed themselves. Just before Iourovsky went to wake the family up, two members of the extraordinary commission arrived at Ipatieff's house.

Shortly after one o'clock in the night the *czar*, *czaritza*, their four daughters, the maid, the doctor, the cook and the waiter left their rooms. The *czar* carried the heir in his arms. The emperor and heir were dressed in "*gimnasterkas*" (soldiers' shirts) and wore caps. The empress and the daughters were dressed, but their heads were uncovered. The emperor with the heir proceeded first. The empress, her daughters and the others followed him. Iourovsky, his assistant, and the two above-mentioned members of the extraordinary commission were accompanying them. I was also present.

During my presence nobody of the *czar's* family asked anybody any questions. They did not either weep or cry. Having descended the stairs to the first floor, we went out into the court, and from there by the second door (counting from the gate) we entered the lower floor of the house. When the corner room, adjoining the storeroom with a sealed door, was entered, Iourovsky ordered chairs to be brought. His assistant brought three chairs. One chair was given to the emperor, one to the empress, and the third to the heir. The empress sat by the wall with the window, near the back pillar of the arch. Behind her stood three of her daughters (I knew their faces very well, because I saw them every day when they were walking, but I didn't know them by name).

The heir and the emperor sat side by side, almost in the middle of the room. Dr. Botkin stood behind the heir. The maid, a very tall woman, stood by the left post of the door leading to the storeroom; by her side stood one of the *czar's* daughters (the fourth). Two servants stood at the left from the entrance of the room, against the wall separating the storeroom. The maid had a pillow. The *czar's* daughters also brought small pillows with them. One pillow was put on the empress's chair; another on the heir's chair. It looked as if all of them guessed their fate, but not a single sound was uttered. At the same time eleven men entered the room: Iourovsky, his assistant, two members of the extraordinary commission, and seven Letts. Iourovsky ordered me to leave, saying: "Go to the street, see if there is anybody there and if the shots can be heard."

I went out to the court which was enclosed by a fence, and before I could get out to the street I heard the firing. Immediately I returned to the house (only two or three minutes having elapsed), and on entering the room where the execution took place, I saw all the members of the *czar's* family lying on the floor, having many wounds in their bodies. The blood was running in streams, the doctor, the maid and the waiters were also shot. When I entered the heir was still alive and moaned. Iourovsky went up and fired two or three more times at him. The heir grew still.

The aspect of the murder and the smell and sight of the blood made me sick. Before the assassination Iourovsky distributed the revolvers; he gave me one also, but, as I said before, I did not take part in the murder. After the assassination Iourovsky said to me that I was to bring some guardsmen to wash up the blood in the room. On the way to Popoff's house I met two seniors, Ivan Starkoff and Constantine Dobrynin. They were running in the direction of Ipatieff's house. Dobrynin asked me: "Has Nicholas II been shot?" I answered that Nicholas II and the whole of his family had been shot. I brought twelve or fifteen guardsmen with me. These men carried the bodies to the motor truck that stood near the entrance of the house. The bodies were carried on stretchers that were made from bed sheets and shafts of sledges taken from the court. When loaded on trucks they were wrapped in soldiers' clothing. The driver was Luhanoff, a Zlokasoff workman. The members of the extraordinary commission sat on the truck and the truck went away. I do not know in what direction the truck went, neither do I know where the bodies were taken.

The blood in the room was washed out and everything was put in order. At three o'clock in the morning everything was in order. Then Iourovsky went to his room and I went to the guardroom.

I woke up after eight o'clock and went to the *commandant's* room. I met there the president of the district soviet, Beloborodoff and Commissar Goloschekin and Ivan Starkoff; the last-named was on duty (he had been selected to be senior two or three weeks before). All the rooms in the house were in disorder. Things were scattered. Suitcases and trunks were opened. Piles of gold and silver things were laid on the tables of the *commandant's* room. Objects of jewellery which were taken from the members of the *czar's* family just before the murder, were also there; as well as things that were on them after their death, such as bracelets, earrings and watches. The precious objects were put into trunks that were brought from the coach house. The assistant *commandant* was present. In one of the rooms I found under the Holy Bible six ten-*rouble* bank notes and appropriated them. I took also several silver rings and a few other trifles.

On the morning of the 18th my wife arrived and I went with her to the Sissert factory. I was instructed to distribute wages to the guardsmen's families. On July 21st I returned to Yekaterinburg. All the *czar's* belongings were already taken from the house and the guards relieved. On July 21st I left Yekaterinburg together with the *commissar*, Mrachkovsky. In Perm the Commissar Goloschekin assigned me to the party that was in charge of preparations for the destruction of the stone bridge, in case of the appearance of the White troops. I had not time enough to blow up the bridge, according to the instructions received by me, and furthermore I did not wish to do it either, as I was to surrender myself voluntarily. I received the order to blow up the bridge when it was under the fire of the Siberian troops and I surrendered voluntarily.

Answering the question as to where the bodies of the killed were taken, I can say only the following: On the way from Yekaterinburg railway station to the Alapaievsk I met Peter Ermakoff and asked him where the bodies had been carried. Ermakoff explained to me that the bodies were thrown down the shaft of a mine near the Verkh-Issetsk works and after that the shaft was destroyed by bombs or explosives in order to fill it up. I do not know and never heard anything concerning the wood piles that were burned near the shaft. I do not know anything more as to where the bodies are. It did not interest me on whom depended the fate of the *czar's* family and who had the right to dispose of them. I executed only the order of those in whose service I was. The above is all that I can tell in reference to the accusation that is made against me. I cannot say any more. My testimony has been read to me and it is taken correctly.

(Signed)   Medvedeff.

Member of the Yekaterinburg District Courts

J. Sergeeff.

Resolution:

On February 22, 1919, in the town of Yekaterinburg, a member of the District Tribunal, Sergeeff, having questioned the peasant, Pavel Medvedeff, prosecuted as an accomplice in the assassination of the former emperor and the members of his family, and considering what measures must be taken to prevent his escape from further inquiry has found:

(1) That Medvedeff is indicted for a crime that may be punished by a very serious penalty;

(2) that before having been arrested, he was hiding himself in the Red army; and, previous to that, he escaped from Yekaterinburg just before the said town was taken by government troops.

On account of the foregoing, it was resolved to put Pavel Medvedeff, thirty-one years old, under arrest in the Yekaterinburg prison.

(Signed)

Member of the Yekaterinburg District Courts

J. Sergeeff.

RECEIPT OF BELOBORODOFF FOR THE ARRESTED
RUSSIAN IMPERIAL FAMILY

The workmen's and Peasants' Government
of the
Russian Federative Republic of Soviets
Ural District Soviet
of the
Workmen's, Peasants' and Soldiers' Deputies

Presidio

Yekaterinburg, April 30, 1918.

On the 30th of April, 1918, I, the undersigned. Chairman of the Ural District Soviet of Workmen's, Peasants' and Soldiers' Deputies, Alexander Georgievitch Beloborodoff, received from the *commissar* of the All Russian Central Executive Committee, Vasily Vaselievitch Iakovleff, the following persons transferred from the town of Tobolsk: (1) The former *czar*, Nicholas Alexandrovitch Romanoff; (2) former *czaritza*, Alexandra Theodorovna Romanova; (3) former grand duchess, Maria Nicholaevna Romanova—all of them to be kept under guard in the town of Yekaterinburg.

(Signed)   A. Beloborodoff,
Member of District Executive Committee,
D. Didkovsky.

CHAPTER 1

Prologue

The true story of the martyrdom of Nicholas II., ex-*Tsar* of Russia, and of his wife and family is told below.

It is based upon evidence obtained by a properly constituted legal investigation. The signed depositions of eye-witnesses are in the writer's possession, but he does not disclose their identity because many of the deponents are still in the power of the Soviets. The day will come when the guilty will be called to account, but a long time may elapse before the day of retribution dawns. The writer has sought to present the opening for the prosecution, fully confident that the eventual hearing of the evidence before a Court of law will substantiate his statement and impose a verdict of "Guilty."

At Ekaterinburg, on the night of July 16, 1918, the Imperial family and their faithful attendants—eleven persons in all—were led into a small room in the house where they had been imprisoned and shot to death with revolvers. There had been no trial of any kind. Before their death, the captives were subjected to ill-treatment, amounting to horrible torture, mental if not physical. After death, the bodies were taken to the woods and completely destroyed. These acts had been premeditated and the murders elaborately prepared.

The actual arrangements for the crime began some weeks before the advent of anti-Bolshevist forces. Neither fear of rescue by the Whites nor plots to release the captives—the existence of which is doubtful—can be reasonably alleged in explanation of the slaughter.

The official statement issued by the Moscow Government on July 20— four days afterwards—spoke of the shooting of Nicholas as an act of necessity, but categorically affirmed that the ex-empress and the children had been conveyed out of the city. These deliberately concocted reports of the safe removal of the family were intended. to circumvent any investigation—and did so at first.

It is established beyond doubt that the ex-*tsar* fell a victim to his loyalty. He had refused offers from the enemies of Russia's Allies, proposing that he should endorse the Treaty of Brest-Litovsk.[1]

Attempts to inveigle him into an unholy alliance undoubtedly preceded the murder. All the Romanovs who died violent deaths were, like the *Tsar*, inconvenient to German as well as to internationalist plans. So many tales have been circulated regarding the fate of the Romanovs, in most cases without the slightest approach to the truth, that I consider myself bound to relate the circumstances which have (1) placed in my possession the complete history and documents of the case; and (2) imposed upon me a moral obligation to publish them to the world.

In March, 1919, returning from Omsk for a short visit to Vladivostok, I met General Diterichs, an old acquaintance, of the Russian Western Armies. After the Revolution he had piloted the Czechs to Siberia and then taken charge of the Uralian front. By one of the fateful blunders that have marred intervention in behalf of Russia he had been superseded by inferior leaders, and was devoting his energies to the investigation of the *Tsarskoe delo* (*Tsar* case). Knowing Diterichs, I felt sure that, sooner or later, he would again become commander-in-chief of the armies, then fighting the Reds with British and Allied assistance. Personal regard and journalistic considerations equally prompted me to follow his fortunes, good or bad. I have not had cause to regret my decision.

General Diterichs was found to be indispensable and recalled to his command, when it was too late. From the first he had seen only too clearly the rocks ahead and warned everybody concerned, and he knew that the fate of Kolchak's attempt to restore Russia was sealed. Yet he accepted the leadership. With equal perspicacity he had also long ago realised the enormous importance of the *Tsar* case. Thanks to his efforts much was accomplished before the Reds, having recaptured the Urals, could obliterate all traces of the crimes committed there. He continued to follow the case even after his appointment as commander-in-chief and after the *débâcle*.

1. Cf. Ludendorff's *War Memories*, Vol. II. "We could have deposed the Soviet Government, which was thoroughly hostile to us, and given help to other authorities in Russia which were not working against us, but indeed anxious to cooperate with us. This would have been a success of great importance to the general conduct of the war. If some other government were established in Russia, it would almost certainly have been possible to come to some compromise with it over the Peace of Brest."

On my arrival at Ekaterinburg a month later, I met the investigating magistrate who had been specially appointed by the Supreme Ruler (Kolchak) to conduct the inquiry into the *Tsar* case—Nicholas Alexeievich Sokolov. He had left his home and family in Penza to avoid service under the Reds, and had managed, after innumerable hardships and hair-breadth escapes, to cross, disguised as a peasant, into Siberia. He walked the last twenty-five miles foodless, his feet one mass of sores and blisters. An ardent sportsman, he had lost an eye through the carelessness of a comrade. He had made a name for himself in the investigation of famous criminal cases. He was relentless, tireless, full of resource in the pursuit alike of murderers and beasts of prey. The *Tsar* case called for the exercise of all the skill that the most genial and courageous of magistrates could display. Sokolov never faltered. It is thanks to him that an overwhelming mass of evidence has been built up into a structure that cannot be overthrown—that still continues to grow.

At all the centres of interest for the investigation—Ekaterinburg, Perm, Omsk, in field or forest, amid the disused iron mines which hid so many a gruesome record of Bolshevist "justice"—I was for many months in constant touch with the course of the inquiry, and personally took part in the search for the remains of the victims. Besides Sokolov and Diterichs only two persons signed the more important *process-verbaux*—I was one of the two.

When the fall of Omsk appeared to be imminent, N. A. Sokolov departed eastward, taking with him all the documents, material clues, etc., which by right could be in no other hands save his. I followed later with General Diterichs, after he had resigned his command, in despair over Kolchak's suicidal decision to defer the evacuation of the city—a decision that entailed the loss of countless lives and the death of the Supreme Ruler. We found Sokolov at Chita, persecuted by the myrmidons of the redoubtable Ataman because they personally desired that the Romanovs should be alive for certain obscure purposes of their own, and therefore wished to get rid of Sokolov for proving the contrary. After many vicissitudes and adventures he reached Harbin, whither I had also made my way, and was joined by General Diterichs.

The ultimate fate of the *dossier* there had to be decided. On all sides were hostile or doubtful organizations. To leave the originals behind and take away only duplicates was, to say the least, risky. Sokolov's life being in danger, he hid the *dossier* in my car, which had the protection of the British flag. General Lokhvitsky rendered invaluable assistance in bringing about a decision. I must express my feelings of gratitude and personal regard for this very gallant soldier and gentleman, who here in the midst of a veritable bedlam preserved his unruffled courtesy and calm just as he had done in the turmoil of battle in France and of disaster in Siberia.

With the knowledge and approval of the three distinguished men above-mentioned—representing the Russia that was and that we all hope will be again—I took charge of the *dossier*, it being understood that, given certain contingencies, I should be free at my own discretion to make it public in whole or in part. The contingencies have arisen, and I am free. But that is not all. I consider the circumstances of today render it an imperative duty to let the Allies and the Russians know the truth. Too many hostile interests are served by deliberately concocted lies and legends regarding the fate of the Romanovs. It is time to let the light of day into this tragic and gruesome history.

When I first came into personal touch with the *Tsar* case many points were still obscure. I refer to the actual circumstances of the murder itself, not to extraneous aspects—political and international—that were only vaguely hinted at, and that have since attained extraordinary proportions. The confusion then existing was due to two causes: first, to the inexperience of the officials who took charge of the investigation; secondly, to the activity of Bolshevist agents who remained in the city or were concealed among the ranks of the White Administration.

The official version of the events of July 16th-17th, given out by the Reds before they fled from Ekaterinburg, was that Nicholas Romanov had been executed "after trial," but that the family had been removed "north." This legend became engrafted upon the minds of a great many people and still continues to exercise its luring appeal. Every sympathiser with the Soviets considered himself or herself bound to foster this version, since no Russian, however hostile to the ex-sovereigns, could find the slightest excuse or pretext for "executing" a whole family of five children who had never taken, or been able to take, the slightest part in politics. The Russians who still belonged to the German "orientation" were also—curiously enough—disposed to credit any tale of a miraculous escape. They seemed to think that a restoration of the monarchy—which formed the basis of their political creed—would be furthered by the "miracle" theory. Some of them had more practical aims, as will be shown later on.

N. A. Sokolov was not deceived for an instant. If, supposing, the family had been removed, their death was, to him, none the less a moral certainty. He had precise information that every other member of the Romanov kin had been murdered, although they were just as unconcerned in politics as the boy Alexis and his sisters. But the evidence of eyewitnesses, coupled with and corroborated by countless material proofs, could leave no doubt as to the fact of a wholesale murder at Ekaterinburg. All the efforts of the organisers and the supineness of the earlier investigators could not completely tangle the threads. But it became a harder task to assemble the evidence that would secure a conviction in a court of law.

I visited the house where the victims had lived. It belonged to a certain Ipatiev, a merchant who held the rank of captain in the Engineers. By one of the ironies of Fate he bore the name of the monastery whence the first Romanov sallied to assume the Crown of All the Russias. The Ipatiev of Ekaterinburg was, however, of Jewish origin.

The engineer department of the Siberian Army was installed in the upper story. Directly after the occupation of the city by the Czechs General Gaida had forcibly taken possession of the premises, despite the vehement protest of the judicial authorities, alarmed by the risk of losing possible clues. The rooms underwent extensive alterations. This was, of course, a flagrant violation of the most elementary principles of criminal investigation.

The lower floor was tenanted by Ipatiev himself, on the understanding that no strangers should be admitted. The small basement room—the scene of the murders—was sealed up. I saw it a few days later. Sokolov took me over the premises, explaining step by step the enactment of the tragedy. We stood in the little room, noted the trace of the bullets, the direction of the bayonet thrusts, and the splashes of blood on the walls. The room had been a shambles, and all the washing and scouring that, according to the evidence, had followed the murders could not remove tell-tale signs. We knew from the depositions of witnesses and the mute, gruesome language of the death-chamber where each of the victims sat or stood when the assassins fired their revolvers. The bullet-holes in the walls and in the floor had been carefully cut out; human blood had been found in the wood and on the bullets.

Obscene drawings and inscriptions covered the upper walls. Obviously they were the work of uncultured peasants. Their character showed only too clearly how deeply the conscience of the people had been revolted by the Razputin scandal. There were other inscriptions—in Hebrew, in German, in Magyar. Regarding them I was to learn much at a later date.

Soon afterwards I was in the woods, ten miles north of the city, where the peasants had found jewellery and other relics of the murdered family. I saw the tracks, still clear, of heavy lorries crashing through the trees to a group of disused iron-ore shafts. All went in one direction, ceasing near a pit round which a vast collection of clues had been discovered; precious stones, pearls, beautiful settings of gold and platinum, some hacked, broken, bearing traces of fire; metal buckles, hooks, buttons, corset-frames, pieces of charred leather and cloth, a human finger intact, a set of false teeth. The character, condition, and numbers of these various articles were in themselves sufficient to indicate the sex and ages of the victims and the manner in which their bodies had been disposed of.

First on the scene had been the peasants. For three days and nights they were cut off from the city by a cordon of Red Guards placed around the wood. Knowing that the Whites were at hand, they thought the Reds were burying arms. Vague rumours had reached them of the death of Nicholas II. As soon as the cordon had been removed they rushed to the spot. Woodcraft and native astuteness quickly opened their eyes. "It is the *Tsar* that they have been burning here," they declared. On this very spot, a year later, I found topaz beads, such as the young princesses wore, and other gems, by scratching the surface of the hardened clay surrounding the iron pit.

Led off on a false scent, the earlier investigator had neglected the unerring sagacity of the peasants and had even failed to make an immediate examination of the wood and pits—perhaps afraid to leave the city, because Red bands were reported to be in the neighbourhood. He was following the red-herring trailed by Soviet agents, that, to wit, the family had escaped or been removed. These agents did not know the truth themselves. They merely related what they had been instructed to say. The local Soviet had not known the facts. There had been no trial. The murders had been the work of a separate organization which directed everything from a distance. Misled by the versions thus spread, the investigator had lost himself in the maze of conflicting rumour in Ekaterinburg.

When Sokolov took over the case—in the early months of 1919—it was almost at a standstill because of the initial mistakes and incapacity of the investigator. Yet evidence had come from another quarter that should have compelled him to take the right course. From one of the Imperial servants who had escaped from a Red shooting squad it became known that several grand dukes and the Grand Duchess Elizabeth had been murdered immediately after the Ekaterinburg shooting, and that some of the bodies had been found in disused iron pits. In no case had there been any semblance of a trial. It was evident the wholesale extermination of the Romanovs had been pursued, and that all theories of the miraculous survival of the children should be abandoned.

CHAPTER 2

The Stage and the Actors

Some idea of the crime of Ekaterinburg is now in the reader's possession; but, in dealing with the evidence in all its aspects, it is necessary to give an account of conditions that prevailed in the country then, and of the chief actors in the drama. The murder of the *Tsar* and his family, even after his abdication, may not be regarded as a simple act of vengeance or casual precaution.

In 1917, the Germans had sent Lenin with a horde of Jewish revolutionaries to take possession of Russia. A Red Government, composed of persons selected in Berlin, was now in power; but they were vassals. Count Mirbach, representing the suzerain State, figured in Moscow as the virtual ruler, before whom the apostles of Karl Marx bowed the knee. At the period under review, the Reds had displayed no overt disposition to throw off the German yoke. They conformed with all the humiliating clauses of the Treaty of Brest-Litovsk, dutifully sending the tribute gold to Berlin which had been demanded as "war indemnity," plundering the national Exchequer and resources by order of their German masters. Apparently everything was going well with the German plan of "peaceful" conquest, whatever secret hopes the Red leaders may have nurtured. Instead of a redoubtable foe, Russia was now a willing handmaid.

Ludendorff has related frankly, disingenuously, how simple and wonderful had been this operation.[1] Not only was Russia out of the

---

1. Ludendorff. *War Memories*, Vol. II:—"From October, 191 7, onwards, Bolshevism in Russia obtained an even firmer hold. "I could not doubt that the disintegration of the Russian Army and nation involved an extraordinary risk for Germany and Austria-Hungary. All the greater was my anxiety when I thought of the weakness of our Government and theirs."By sending Lenin to Russia our Government had, moreover, assumed a great responsibility. From a military, (continued next page),

war; the foodstuffs obtained from the Ukraine had literally saved Germany and her allies. Hetman Skoropadsky already ruled the Ukraine for Germany. Krasnov, at the head of the Cossacks, and Alexeiev with the gallant Volunteer army remained neutral. Ludendorff hoped to lure them into his net—a radiant combination that assured dominion over Russia and her vast resources. He explains why it was not realised. The German Government was to blame, it appears. There was a divergence of views between Berlin and G.H.Q.

The latter considered that the Reds had "done their work;" so the Reds "must go," and Krasnov and Alexeiev be diverted at once from their sympathies with the *entente* in order to preclude any possibility of a revival of the Eastern front. For this purpose it was necessary to order the German divisions in the South of Russia to march on Moscow. Ludendorff felt quite sure that even Alexeiev would not be able to resist the temptation to join hands with the enemies of Sovietdom. But the obstinate, slow-witted bureaucrats in Berlin could not adapt themselves to these lightning changes. Ludendorff stormed at them: Were they blind not to see that the Reds were hoodwinking them? Did they want proofs? Were the Czech prisoners of war not proceeding eastward with the avowed object of reinforcing the French Army?

This concrete accusation could not be denied. Lenin's organization had promised Professor Masaryk to permit the Czecho-Slovaks to leave the country by way of Siberia provided they went peacefully. It was an easy riddance of possible enemies. The Czechs were proceeding quietly to Vladivostok, carefully abstaining from violence even when sorely tried by the impudence of local Soviets, giving up

point of view his journey was justified, for Russia had to be laid low. But our government should have seen to it that we also were not involved in her fall."
"In Russia events had developed along lines of their own, illustrative of the lying propensities of the Soviet Government. With the consent of the government the Entente had formed Czecho-Slovak units out of Austro-Hungarian prisoners. These were intended to be used against us, and were therefore to be conveyed to France by the Siberian railway. All this was sanctioned by a government with whom we were at peace, and we actually took it lying down! At the beginning of June I wrote to the Imperial Chancellor specially on the subject, and pointed out the dangers which threatened us from the Soviet Government."
"I had got into touch with him (General Krasnov) in order to prevent his joining the Entente. The situation was complicated by the fact that I could not put difficulties in the way of the home government's, pro-Bolshevik policy, of which, of course, I was informed, and Krasnov regarded the Soviet Government, and not the Entente, as his enemy."

their arms to bribe the Reds.

Mirbach received instructions to call his Red henchmen to account; at the same time messages were conveyed from the two *kaisers* to their warriors imprisoned in Siberia, enjoining upon them the duty of organising resistance to the "invaders." How the German and Magyar officers enrolled Russian convicts and flung themselves athwart the Czech retreat with the energetic concurrence of the Soviets is a matter of history. But the connection between this circumstance and all that preceded and followed is less known. Ludendorff feared above all the re-establishment of the Eastern front, yet it was Ludendorff and his government that brought about the very consequences that they least wanted.

Had the Czechs been allowed to depart it is certain that there would have been no military help from the Entente side, and the chances of seducing the Russian anti-Bolshevist leaders might not have been still-born. As it was, the whole edifice of guile, duplicity, and deceit, raised with such labour and cost, fell to the ground. The murder of Mirbach sounded the call of its collapse.

But at the time when the fate of the *tsar* and his family hung in the balance, Germany was absolute mistress of the situation, and, had there been unity of method as well as of purpose between the German High Command and Berlin, the fate of Russia and, perhaps, of the war would have been changed. Berlin wanted to continue to rule Russia through the Soviets under Mirbach; Ludendorff aimed at the overthrow of the Soviets in order to enlist the support of the Cossacks and Volunteers. As might be expected, the conflict between them resulted in a fatal compromise—an attempt to run with the White hare and hunt with the Red hounds.

Ludendorff's plan was to substitute a more agreeable form of government in the place of the Soviets and to modify suitably the Treaty of Brest-Litovsk. Here we have the key to the removal of Nicholas II. from Tobolsk. But all that subsequently happened was conditional upon another set of forces. Sovietdom asserted itself. The working and organization of the Soviets fitted in admirably with German requirements, and incidentally subserved the plans of the murderers. New names, devised to appeal to the fancy of the mob, concealed familiar institutions. There were three principal bodies—*Sovnarkon*, *Tsik*, and *Chrezvychaika*, these names being abbreviations of *Soviet narodnykh kommisorrov* (Council of People's Commissaries), *Tsentralny ispolnitelny komitet* (Central Executive Committee), and *Chrezvychainaia komisia dlia borby z kontr-revoliutsiei* (Extraordinary Commission for Combating Counter-revolution).

Under the old regime the *Duma*, the Council of Ministers, and the Okhrana had occupied the same relative positions. Instead of the former ranks and dignities there were *komisary*, all supposed to be elected, but in reality appointed by an inner and occult body. *Sovdeps* (Councils of Deputies) and *Komitety bednoty* (Poor Commissions) took over the functions of the old *zemstvos* and municipalities, grouped into regional communes, just as it had been proposed to group the *zemstvos* according to separate *oblasti* (regions). Sovietdom (in Russian *Sovdepia*) had invented no new forms. It is still in the grip of the Red Okhrana.

As there was no apparent authority, the local bodies often acted independently; indeed, Lenin encouraged this tendency. *Vlast na mestakh* (*every place its own master*) was his motto. Lenin did not rule; the Soviet system was governed by other people, the fellow-passengers who came with him under German auspices. Though he delivered impassioned harangues before the Sovnarkom and received deputations from minor Soviets, the real power was elsewhere—in the Tsik and Chrezvychaika; and, just as it had been in the Old Russia, the last word was always with the Police-*Okhrana* organisation.

Mirbach received his daily report from the Chrezvychaika. He was murdered by two men who said they came from that office. Lenin had as little to do with his death as he had with the murders, a week later, of the ex-*Tsar* and his family. The Red Okhrana and the inner circle of the Tsik were the veritable authors of the crime of Ekaterinburg, and probably of Mirbach's assassination.

Nonentities, figureheads of the Sovnarkom, do not interest us. We are concerned with great, if maleficent, personages in the Red world. Most of them are still unknown outside the ranks of the professional revolutionaries. A goodly proportion of the hundred Jews who came out of Germany with Lenin, and the hundreds who came from Chicago, deserve to be included in this gallery, for they undoubtedly held Russia under their sway. To enumerate and describe them would require a small volume. I need sketch only those who act prominently in the drama of Ekaterinburg. The most important were:—Sverdlov, Safarov, Voikov, and Goloshchekin, and the murderer-in-chief Yurovsky.

The names of Safarov and Voikov figure in the list of Lenin's fellow-passengers. Both are very powerful Bolshevists, holding high places in the executive and police branches. Sverdlov is—I use the present tense because all these persons continue to wield their influence to the present day—the uncrowned *tsar* of the Soviets. His authority is really much higher than that of Lenin or even Trotsky. He dominates the Tsik, and his creatures rule the Chrezvychaika. Sverdlov's name appears in the Bolshevist Government as approved by Germany. The direct connection between Sverdlov and the murders of Ekaterinburg is established beyond doubt.

Goloshchekin was the representative of the above-named conclave in the regional soviet of the Urals and kept that rather recalcitrant body under secret subjection to his chiefs. The Uralian Reds were particularly self-willed and jealous of Moscow because the population consisted almost entirely of miners and metal-workers—a very advanced and independent class, having little in common with the peasant-farmer, for whom they professed contempt. Goloshchekin did whatever Sverdlov wished. A stratagem had given him absolute power. The president of the regional soviet was a Russian named Beloborodov.

He was arrested by the *chrezvychaika* and imprisoned on a charge of appropriating 30,000 *roubles*. The punishment would be death. Together with Safarov and Voikov, Goloshchekin arranged to release him. Beloborodov resumed the presidency of the regional soviet as if nothing had happened. Dishonesty was so rampant among the *komisars* that the transition surprised no one. But after that, Beloborodov gave up all attempts to resist Moscow—if he had ever done so. He was henceforth a mere man of straw, kept in his place to deceive the obstreperous Uralian miners, who did not wish to be ruled from Moscow, much less by Jews.

The closest personal bonds had existed for many years between Goloshchekin and Sverdlov. They had been together in prison and exile. Goloshchekin ranked as an internationalist of the most pronounced type. He had been selected for the rulership of the Urals with an eye to other than political activities. He was bloodthirsty in an abnormal degree, even for a Red chieftain. People who knew him at Ekaterinburg describe Goloshchekin as a homicidal sadist. He never attended executions, but insisted upon hearing a detailed account of them. He huddled in bed shivering and quaking till the executioner came with his report, and would listen to his description of tortures with a frenzy of joy, begging for further details, gloating over the expressions, gestures and death-throes of the victims as they passed before his diseased vision.

Yurovsky had a humbler task; he was not one of the mighty ones of the Soviet. When the German plan to restore Nicholas as a vassal sovereign had failed, and the Jewish conclave in Moscow was free to carry out its vengeful purpose, Yurovsky was installed as chief gaoler and tormentor of the doomed family. The Russian *commandant* and guards were dismissed, ostensibly because they were pilfering. Magyarised-German soldiers under a Jewish commandant took their places and were able to rob wholesale the unfortunates whom they were supposed to protect.

The origins of Yurovsky have been fully investigated. His parents and relatives—all poor Jews—remained in Siberia after the murderer and his chiefs and accomplices had fled from Ekaterinburg. He had been a watchmaker at Tomsk, scarcely able to make ends meet. Naturally ambitious, he despised the people around him. He was waiting for an opportunity. It came suddenly and mysteriously. Yurovsky disappeared. This was before the war. He is next heard of in Ekaterinburg as a photographic dealer. It leaked out that he had been to Berlin and become possessed of some capital. When war came, he evaded service in the trenches by qualifying as a Red-Cross assistant (*feldsher*) and remained in Ekaterinburg. When the Bolshevists seized the government, Yurovsky became one of the local agents of the new power.

At a time when he was seeking any and every means of advancement, Yurovsky had been baptised into the Lutheran church. He used to attend prayers in Ipatiev's house. He even chatted pleasantly with the sick boy Alexis, whom, a few days later, he shot with his own hand.

CHAPTER 3

No Escape: Alexandra Misjudged

Apart from the bald assertions of parties interested in spreading false reports, there is no evidence of any attempt on the part of the Romanovs to escape from any of their prisons. All the compromising "documents" produced by Soviet apologists on this subject are transparent fabrications. Loyal Russians wished to save the *tsar* from the Soviets, knowing full well the danger of treachery that he incurred, and there were several organisations, working independently, but none ever begin putting a plan into execution.

During the captivity at Tobolsk some money reached the prison-house secretly. It helped the prisoners to eke out the starvation allowance ordained by the Soviets. Attempts to render further aid were frustrated by a German-Bolshevist agent stationed at Tiumen. This person, a Russian officer who had married a daughter of Razputin, ingratiated himself with doubtful travellers for Tobolsk and betrayed them to the Soviet. The Germans had thus taken elaborate precautions not to allow the ex-*tsar* to slip out unawares. Perhaps they thought that the Allies of Russia might try to rescue him! At Ekaterinburg nothing could be done. The Reds claim to have intercepted some letters between the captives and conspirators.

But it may be pointed out that not a single person was arrested there for conspiracy to help the exiles. Remembering the lavish repressions ever applied by the occult powers of the Chrezvychaika, it will be conceded that they would have missed no opportunity to exert them in such a cause. The British Consul (Mr. Preston), remaining gallantly at his post throughout the Red terror, and rendering incalculable service to the victims of Bolshevist oppression, was unable to do anything to alleviate the sufferings and torture of the Romanovs. Yet, strange to relate, a monarchist organisation had its agents in the city.

It even succeeded in conveying some food and comforts through the nuns of the local monastery. Beyond that, it was unable to go. There is no evidence to show that at any time during the captivity was any active attempt made to rescue the Romanovs. This applies equally to the ex-sovereigns and to their kinsmen.

At Tobolsk, Ekaterinburg, Perm, and Alapaievsk the pretext for wholesale murder was always the same; an alleged attempt to escape or rescue. And from the testimony of persons who were in daily intercourse with the imprisoned family, it is clear that, had any serious efforts to procure their escape been made, they would have met with no encouragement. Nicholas II. repeatedly said that he would not leave Russia; Alexandra hated above everything the idea of going to Germany. At that time Russia offered no sure place of refuge.

The Razputin propaganda had poisoned the minds of the people, but not all the people. In the villages, among the old folk, feelings of loyalty still held sway, ready at the first signal to assert themselves openly. The volumes of evidence in my possession prove this statement. Many of the witnesses were peasants who, consciously, willingly risked their lives in order that the truth about the fate of the *tsar* should be established. Who knows how many of these simple souls have been martyred for their boldness?

Among the obscenities that disfigured the walls of the Ipatiev house, one inscription struck an opposite note. In uncouth peasant writing and spelling the author—evidently one of the guards—asked how long were the people going to put up with the *komisars*, and urged the *Tsar* to come forward and drive away the horde of usurpers that were ruining the country!

I cannot help thinking that the Razputin legend did not suffice to kill the people's faith in the *tsar*. It certainly discredited Alexandra, and he shared her disgrace; but that was not enough to account for the virulence of popular clamour against Nicholas II. His fate would not have been so much a matter of indifference to the multitude had the vile story of Razputin not been preceded by blunders that deeply incensed the popular conscience. I recall the dreadful murder of women and children before the Winter Palace on Bloody Sunday. That crime was prepared by the Okhrana and attributed to the *tsar*. It seems to me that had it not been for that hideous slaughter of innocents no one would have ever dared to raise a hand against the *tsar* and his children. I wish to be quite fair to the Russians, without in any way extenuating the heinousness of the crime of Ekaterinburg.

The ex-empress was the object of special hatred. She completely dominated her spouse in the imagination of the people, and occupies a place apart in the evidence. Many new facts have been brought to light substantially modifying the current estimate of her life and character. Several trunks full of papers and effects belonging to his victims were taken by Yurovsky to Moscow after the murder. Sverdlov then announced that all would be published, so that the people should see what manner of persons had ruled them. That promise has not been kept, and for a good reason: the diaries and correspondence of Nicholas and Alexandra contained no hint of treachery. They proved two things—unbounded loyalty to Russia and to the Allies; and, alas! complete subserviency of Nicholas to his wife. But neither of these matters interested the Soviet leaders, and most of these priceless documents have been suppressed in Moscow. Many others were overlooked or forgotten in Ekaterinburg, and figure in the *dossier* of the *Tsar* case. Among them is a collection of Alexandra's letters to her maid-of-honour.

There are also the depositions of servitors and members of the household. Analysing this mass of first-hand evidence, one obtains a true picture of Alexandra, Proud, domineering, self-restrained, gifted, mystical she had been from youth. Her troubles, mental and physical, had distorted these characteristics. Nicholas fell in love with her when she was fifteen, and waited patiently for her eight years. Even as a girl she dominated him. After their marriage there was never any doubt who was master. Her dominion was not even challenged. Nicholas never acted without his wife's approval, except when he was separated from her—for instance, when he signed the writ of abdication. These were not the best qualifications for *tsardom* at a time of transition. Alexandra could not attain popularity, nor would she admit the necessity of it for herself or the *tsar*. Indeed, as the years passed she became less and less responsive to the demands and requirements of public opinion, which cannot be defied with impunity even by an autocrat.

Many Russians attributed these failings to the Hesse disease (*bolezn Gessenskikh*), the hereditary taint that had carried off many of Alexandra's relations.[1] The fact that her only son suffered from and might at any moment die of it only made her own trouble worse. The disease is dangerous to boys and adult women; girls do not feel its effects till they

---

1. Haemophilia, the disease from which the *Tsarevich* suffered, is as a general rule transmitted through the females to the males. The females do not suffer from it themselves.

are grown up, whereas boys become immune after reaching manhood. In the case of women it is apt to prey on the mind, aggravating and intensifying any morbid predisposition. Hysteria in its worst forms is an almost invariable accompaniment. She also suffered intensely from heart trouble. Her life must have been one long agony

Alexandra was not normal. Her belief in Razputin indicated as much. The evidence of Dr. Botkin is explicit. People who suffer from hysteria in an acute congenital form repel and estrange all persons that do not blindly accept their domination. Razputin had to be treated as a saint because Alexandra imagined him to be one. The Court of Russia became peopled with time-servers and nonentities.

I shall deal with Razputin presently. The new materials in my possession show that he was simply a peasant afflicted with a pathological condition. The legend that has grown up regarding his occult powers can be traced not to Razputin, but to his "friends." He was a mere tool. Alexandra wanted him—to cure her son; others used him for personal or political intrigues because Alexandra, the veritable Autocrat of All the Russias, had need of him. In the tragedy of the Romanovs every thread leads us to this Woman of Destiny.

The very exhaustive records of their life before and after the Revolution give a true presentment of the family, such as no individual could furnish even if he or she had been in the closest intimacy with Nicholas or Alexandra. One is struck by the almost superhuman secretiveness of the ex-sovereigns. They did not trust anyone completely. Most of the persons who were supposed to be particularly attached to them knew little or nothing of their inner life and thoughts. This explains, perhaps, why so few decided to follow them into exile. Only between themselves does there appear to have been no reserve.

Alexandra's personality is reflected in her family—Nicholas, like herself, an embodiment of all the domestic virtues, religious to the verge of mysticism, expert in dissimulation, never showing anger, perhaps never really feeling angry, incapable of a decision—so utterly had he surrendered himself to his wife; the daughters relegated to the background entirely unprepared to take their proper place in the world; Alexis monopolizing all the care and attention of his mother; the children ashamed of her belief in Razputin, yet not daring openly to resent it.

Among the court favourites, male or female, nobody exercised any real influence except in so far as it suited the empress. Only one person appears to have been admitted for any length of time to the

Imperial confidence. That person was Anna Vyrubova. Regarding her Razputin used to speak in the crudest terms to the companions of his tavern-revels, who, of course, repeated his drunken boasts. That was the origin of her infamous notoriety. She herself could not have devised a surer way of retaining Alexandra's favour. The detractors of Vyrubova had also dared to retail the foulest stories about Alexandra, alleging the same source. Alexandra rightly considered herself a victim of slander, and naturally included Anna under the same designation.

The fact is, Anna Vyrubova was Razputin's accomplice—nothing more. She kept him in touch with everything, especially with the boy's health. It was at her house that Razputin saw the emperor and empress when it became too scandalous for him to appear daily in the palace—after the dismissal of governesses who had raised an outcry against Razputin's familiarities with their charges.

Another person deserves mention. It is not positively shown how far his influence was felt, but certainly he played an important part in the Romanov tragedy. He was in many ways a mystery man—a doctor of Thibetan medicine, by birth a Buriat, named Badmaiev. Besides dispensing nostrums that cured all ills—often bringing relief where modern science had failed—he dabbled in politics, and who knows what dark forces were served by him? Razputin was one of his best clients. According to Razputin one could immediately regain all the vigour of youth by swallowing a powder composed of Thibetan herbs; another kind of powder made one quite indifferent to worry. Badmaiev reserved these specifics for people whom he could trust. The first-named kind was for Razputin, but who was the recipient of the "dope" that "made you forget"—who if not the hapless Nicholas? And once it is admissible that the peasant had taken to drugs for unmentionable purposes, one may seriously entertain other accusations against him and his accomplices.

According to indications contained in the evidence, Anna Vyrubova arranged the "miracles" of healing that Razputin performed on the sick boy. It was not difficult. The malady always followed the same course. A slight bruise set up internal haemorrhage. The patient suffered terrible pain while the blood flowed, clotted, and finally began to be reabsorbed. Anna knew from experience how to read the symptoms. Razputin would come to pray when the crisis was over, so that it should seem as if his intercession had brought relief. Things happened in this way on several known occasions. Razputin did not wish to lose the empress's favour. He and Vyrubova took their precautions.

And Badmaiev's powders may here also have been used with benefit to all concerned. Alexandra's eyes were never opened to the fact that Razputin's prayers did not affect the disease.

It will be argued by those who knew Vyrubova that she was too garrulous to keep a secret, too child-like to conceive or carry out any intrigue, and still less any act affecting the empress in whose hands she was as wax. To have lived for twenty years in the confidence of such a woman as the empress presumes the possession of no ordinary faculties, whether of extreme innocence combined with serpent wisdom or of profound guile hidden under an appearance of candour. Vyrubova's apologists would have us believe that she was nothing better than an idiot. The skill with which she crept into the good graces of the Imperial family, ably seconding all the moves of the practised courtier Taneiev, her father, shows the absurdity of such a theory and sufficiently denotes her real disposition.

Woman-like, the empress regarded all things from a personal standpoint. Her malady only served to intensify her likes and dislikes. One of her particular aversions was Wilhelm of Prussia, first, because the Hohenzollerns had been exalted at the expense of her own house; secondly, because Wilhelm had not counted with her. Germany, ruled by Wilhelm, was ever the foe of Russia ruled by Alexandra. She could not admit the possibility of a compromise or truce with Wilhelm's Germany, any more than she would permit the *tsar* to summon a ministry composed of Razputin's detractors and enemies. A complete and ludicrous misapprehension prevailed in Russia and among the Allied peoples about the alleged pro-German tendencies of the ex-empress. She hated Germany with a bitterness and a fervour equalled only by her contempt and loathing for the Russians—always excepting the peasants, whom she "imagined" to be endowed with all the virtues and qualities that Razputin was supposed to possess.

Wilhelm was described by her as "that low comedian" and "man of falsehood," who had "stooped to associate himself with Bolshevists." With fierce and joyful anticipation, she foresaw his punishment: "The day will come when they will destroy him!" She did not live to see her vision fulfilled.

Such was the so-called pro-German empress. It is easy to recall the outcry that was raised in *entente* countries in the spring of 1917 when it became known that the Romanovs would be permitted to come to England. "How can we tolerate this friend of Germany in our midst?" The public had been so deeply affected by the Razputin propaganda, that they would not hear of Alexandra coming to this country. And as the family could not be disunited, they had all to remain in Russia. The ex-*tsar's* servants had even prepared his English uniforms. Sorrowfully, without understanding the reasons, they obeyed the order to pack them away. Thus, after depriving them of the throne, Razputin's foul influence took from the Romanovs their hope of an asylum and left them to suffer a shameful death.

CHAPTER 4

Razputin the Peasant

The walls of Ipatiev's house epitomised the Revolution. One name and one effigy predominated: the name of Grishka, the silhouette of Razputin, loathsomely caricatured. One met, here and there, allusions to the "*tsar*-bloodsucker" and other catchphrases of the Revolution, but one felt that they were perfunctory. The one and only unpardonable crime in the eyes of the Red guards had been the preference shown by the empress for a peasant—a common man like one of themselves. What a commentary on the blindness of the unfortunate Alexandra!

Political propaganda had represented Razputin as a monster of iniquity and occult powers, whereby he held the empress under his thraldom. The *dossier* kills this legend—it is nothing more.

Gregory Razputin was forty-five at the time of his death (1916). Till the age of thirty-four he had lived as an ordinary peasant in his native village of Pokrovskoe, between Tobolsk and Tiumen. He had a wife and three children, a comfortable home, and enough land to feed himself and family. Grishka—to use the familiar diminutive of his Christian name, as is customary in the villages—was a fair type of the Siberian peasant-farmer. They are endowed with an abundance of mother-wit, wield the vernacular with consummate skill, and are fine, upstanding fellows, able to do a day's work or celebrate a festival equally well. Such was Gregory Razputin. Nothing indicated a future for him different from the rest. He might be expected to plough, drink vodka, beat his wife, trick his neighbours, and pray before the Holy Ikons in the usual sequence till one day the Voice or the Reaper gathered him in.

One day he heard the Voice. It happened to peasants now and then in youth, sometimes in the prime of life, and often in their old age.

After that they left their mundane affairs, and prepared themselves for Eternity. Grishka had been "called" when he was fourteen, and in an ecstasy had tried to mutilate himself. But he had fallen from grace. Now twenty years later, the call came again. Grishka was "converted" by Dmitri Pecherkin, a *strannik* (wanderer), who had deserted his home in the same province of Tobolsk to pray at the Holy Places. In 1905 Razputin turned over his farm to his wife, son, and daughters, and joined Dmitri in his wanderings. Together they visited Mount Athos, Jerusalem, Kiev, Moscow, and Petrograd.

I have a copy of his work, *My Thoughts and Reflections* (published in Petrograd, 1915), describing his pilgrimages. It is an assortment of stereotyped phrases, texts from Scripture, homely proverbs—just the conversation of an ordinary *strannik*. One is struck with wonderment that the "author" of such utter commonplace should have influenced the destinies of a vast empire, or could for one moment impose upon the cultured intellect of an empress.

I believe that Razputin was quite sincere in following Pecherkin, and that during his earlier days in the capital he was still an earnest *devotee*. Bishop Feofan met him in Petrograd and was impressed by his sincerity. But even at this time (about 1907) he was already inclining once more towards wordly things. Pecherkin tried in vain to persuade him to take the vows and join him in a monastery. Razputin had a fancy for the drawing-rooms of the great city, where he was petted and paraded by hostesses in search of a sensation. And thus it came to pass that, with the help of Feofan and the Grand Duchesses Militza and Anastasia (the Montenegrin princesses who had already introduced various "saints" to the mystically disposed sovereigns), Razputin came to the court.

The diaries and depositions of his daughter Matrena form part of the *dossier*. Amidst a mass of verbiage one is able to discover here and there precise landmarks of the Razputin history. One sees the "saint" gradually drawn into the multiple cog-wheels of court intrigue; bound firmly to the family chariot, as his daughters are put to fashionable schools; having to make money for the girls; obliged to remain a peasant in garb and language to please his protectress. But a peasant who is divorced from his normal occupation and has disobeyed the Voice takes to drink. There is no alternative.

The unhealthy life of the city set its mark on him. "Fish-soup, bread and *kvass* with onions, were his daily fare, but he drank red wine and Madeira . . . always jolly in his cups, singing and dancing as the villagers do;" "whenever we remonstrated with him, he would say that he could never drink enough to drown the sorrow that was to come." That is the description given by his daughter of Razputin "at home" in Petrograd. But these mild debauches were constantly supplemented by swinish orgies outside. Many a peasant, placed in the same position, would have acted in the same way.

Razputin was just an ordinary peasant, except for a certain pathological propensity, traceable to his attempted self-mutilation. He was rustic even in the measure of his "perquisites." In his native Pokrovskoe it was not considered dishonourable to cheat one's neighbour, but always in a small way, of course. So here, this man, who could have amassed a colossal fortune, contented himself with dabbling in small "affairs" that brought in a few hundred *roubles*. His whole estate at the time of his death did not much exceed £10,000. Matrena declares most positively that he never possessed or attempted to display at home any occult gift of mesmerism, healing, or clairvoyancy.

This drunken immoral peasant nevertheless played a political *rôle*. He gave advice to the *Tsar* on all sorts of important matters. He even had the audacity to stamp his foot at Nicholas for not heeding it. We know that at least on one occasion he directly influenced the *tsar* to take a fatal decision. For the Imperial fete day, December 6/19, 1916, all political Russia, nobles, burgesses, and peasants, expected the *tsar* to go to the *duma* and announce the formation of a ministry enjoying public confidence. Alexandra was, of course, violently opposed to any concession, but she feared the influence of the army on Nicholas, and Razputin was produced for the occasion. He succeeded in dissuading the hapless Monarch, to his undoing and to the ruin of the army and of Russia.

I do not propose to rehearse the well-known stories about Razputin's influence on the dismissal or appointment of ministers or prelates. Those stories are true only in so far as they represent Grishka acting as the instrument of another person's will, in most cases Alexandra's. He was too ignorant, too petty, to understand political questions. For instance, he was always urging the emperor to come into direct contact with the people. "Get rid of the ministers. They lie to you. Address yourself direct to the people. You will then know the truth and everything will right itself."

Nicholas became rather tired of this parrot-like repetition. He had heard it all so often from his wife. One day he told Razputin:—"It sounds very nice, but how is it to be done? You know quite well that if I took your advice I should very soon lose my life."

"No, never," was the reply. "You will be killed by an intellectual, not by a peasant"—not a convincing or cheerful response.

On one point Razputin took what seemed to be a line of his own: he was against the war with Germany. "She is too strong. We must be friends," he declaimed. This view did not reflect the mind of the empress. Who had instilled it into him? It is not difficult to guess. His daughter and her husband are known to have been acquainted with one of the secret agents of Germany. Besides, there were also Badmaiev and a number of other doubtful personages around him. When war broke out Razputin was lying wounded at Pokrovskoe. The *Tsar* telegraphed to him about the war. Grishka fell into such rage that his abound reopened.

He served the German interest in a more subtle and redoubtable manner. His very existence was bringing about the collapse of Russia by destroying the faith of the people in the *tsar*. All the foremost supporters and friends of the "saint" were of the German orientation. That was not a coincidence. Everyone who even tolerated Razputin was helping the enemy.

It being pretty well established that Razputin was the direct cause—in the empress's hands—of the Revolution and the downfall of Russia, I would ask what the Ludendorffs and their Russian dupes have to say in justification of the argument that it was the *entente* that brought about the Revolution, Razputin's relationship to the defeatists was so clear to everybody in Russia that people—Russians as well as Allies—fell naturally into the mistake of supposing that the empress must be pro-German, since she supported Razputin. Who magnified Razputin before the war? The *Cologne Gazette*. Who was his archapologist? The pro-German Witte. The Germans had almost as much to do with the Razputin scandal as they had to do with Lenin and the exploits of his hundred Jews.[1]

The murder of Razputin evoked the greatest outburst of popular rejoicing that any act had ever produced. "*Ubili!*" (they have killed) was the universal greeting. People did not stop to ask who had been killed. They knew. The whole nation had desired his death, and one

1. Ludendorff. *War Memories*, Vol. II. "... The *Tsar* was overthrown by the Revolution, which was favoured by the *entente*. The *entente's* reasons for backing the Revolution are not clear. At all events, it is certain that the *entente* expected the Revolution to bring them some advantage in the war. They wished at least to save anything that could be saved and, consequently, did not hesitate to act. The *Tsar*, who had begun the war in order to please the *entente*, had to be removed."

wonders that he so long survived. But his murder was, none the less, a mistake, since he was merely an ignorant tool, and the circumstances of his end—the lawless joy that it evoked—only helped the revolutionaries. Thenceforth, the empress's name was in the gutter, and there was only one hope of salvation for the *tsar*—to dissociate himself from his wife. To do that—to put her away into a monastery as Tsar Peter Alexeievich would have done—was quite beyond the capacity of a gentle soul like Nicholas Alexandrovich. . . .

It had been suggested before the Revolution that she should go alone to England "on a visit." This argued complete ignorance of the inner life of the sovereigns. The Razputin scandal had arisen because Alexandra morbidly imagined that the destinies of Russia depended upon their joint faith and prayers—hers and the "saint's." Also she was convinced that without her constant presence and support Nicholas would be lost. Sooner would she have died than go away, particularly after the death of her "saint."

There had been plots to kill Alexandra and even the *Tsar*. It is curious, indeed, that her life should have been spared. One must bear in mind the probability of German "protection." It is evident that Alexandra's death would have put an end to the Razputin scandal and therefore been unprofitable for Germany. As for Nicholas, the people were on his side to the last—till the Revolution extinguished in men's minds the last vestige of all that was seemly.

The manner of Razputin's murder is known to all. The man who killed him is no more. His diary has been published. It gives almost a complete account of the murder. One feature has escaped attention, and I mention it because it gives point to the true version of Razputin's character as related above. The accomplices had prepared a most elaborate scheme for killing him, yet in the end it was Purishkevitch with a vulgar revolver that effected the deed. Poisoned tarts, "doctored" wine, and even a revolver shot had been in vain. The conspirators had innocently administered an antidote with the poison; the shooter's hand had trembled so that he had failed to hit Razputin standing a few paces away. But why all this rigmarole? The fact is the conspirators were affected by the Razputin propaganda; they also believed that the man was more than mortal. Purishkevitch thought that the devil was in him till the third bullet brought him down. That was an epoch-making shot.

Razputin was fond of identifying his own well-being with that of Russia. In this, as in other things, he merely copied the empress.

When Khionia Guseva, incited by the monk Iliodor, who had fallen out with Grishka, stuck a knife into the "saint," he announced that "much blood would flow" and that there would be "woe unutterable if and when he died." But he was ever prophesying all sorts of things, good and bad, like the proverbial tipster. It suited the interested or superstitious to proclaim him infallible. Anyhow, it did not require much acumen to read the signs of coming disaster in Russia. Grishka was no fool, and he must have had a shrewd idea what his own friends and supporters were doing. But charlatanism "paid," and he had a family to support and lots of "friends" coming for assistance, all of which flattered Grishka's cheap little soul and kept him on his daily round of prayer and debauch.

Razputin the monster is a fiction, bred in the busy brains of politicians and elaborated by the teeming imagination of sensational novelists. Razputin the saint is an imaginary product of a woman's diseased mind. Even the stories of the sanctifying baths and other *khlyst* (flagellant) doctrines, supposed to have been applied by a demoniacal Grishka, turn out to be imaginary. It is not unusual for the peasants in certain parts of Russia to take the steam bath in common. No strangers are admitted, and there is nothing unseemly in the practice. It was quite appropriate for a native of Tobolsk. In this and in his gross familiarities with the other sex Grishka was merely Razputin the peasant, a village satyr.

CHAPTER 5

Captives in a Palace

Before the Revolution, propagandists of all descriptions aimed their poisoned shafts at the empress. Her fatal belief in Razputin rendered her an easy prey. The revolutionary section watched over Grishka, just as their German accomplices "protected" Alexandra. Nicholas was left alone, comparatively speaking. After the Revolution all the energies of the dark forces involved were concentrated upon him. It was not enough that he had voluntarily abdicated; he had to be shorn of all prestige, so that the inveterate devotion and loyalty of the people, which had formed the very foundation of Russia's existence, should be swept away forever. "The *tsar* was a traitor; he and his wife had been in secret communication with the Germans." In city, village, and camp this poisonous rumour spread.

Blindly, the Provisional Government did nothing to stop it. The order of the day to the armies, in which Nicholas, bidding goodbye to his soldiers, proclaimed his unshaken loyalty to the sacred cause of Russia, and besought them never to lay down their arms to Germany, was suppressed by telegram from the War Office in Petrograd. (See note following). Evil deeds come back to roost whence they have issued. The people who besmirched the *tsar* to please the revolutionaries were themselves punished. One does not undermine the faith of a whole nation without destroying all authority.

Note. Here is the text of the suppressed document:

My dearly loved troops, I address you for the last time. After my abdication, for me and for my son, from the Russian throne, the power is transferred to the Provisional Government which rose on the initiation of the *duma*. God help them to lead Russia on the way of glory and prosperity. God help you also, valiant troops, to hold our native land firmly against the evil enemy. During two and a half years you endured, daily, the hardships of active service. Much blood has been shed, many efforts have been made, and the hour is already near when Russia, bound to her valiant Allies, by one general impulse to victory, will break the last efforts of the adversary.

This unprecedented war must be brought to a full victory. He who thinks now of peace, who wishes it—that man is a betrayer of his Fatherland, a traitor. I know that every honest soldier thinks thus. Then fulfil your duty, defend our native land valiantly, submit yourselves to the Provisional Government, obey your commanders, remember that every weakening of discipline in the service is only an advantage to the enemy.

I firmly believe that the infinite love of our great native land has not died out of your hearts. May God bless you and Saint George the great Vanquisher and Martyr guide you.

Nicholas.

(The order was counter-signed by General Alexeiev, Chief of Staff.)

When the empress and her sick children were proclaimed prisoners of state, and a few days later Nicholas arrived under custody at Tsarskoe, this foul charge of treachery hung over them, poisoning their lives by the mental and even physical torture that ensued. It was because of this abominable lie that the ex-sovereigns were first treated like common malefactors, kept in separate rooms, and forbidden to see or communicate with each other; and the soldiers and officers of the guard considered themselves justified in persecuting and insulting them, and even their followers deserted them.

After the overhauling of all their private papers by a special court of inquiry instituted by order of the revolutionary chieftain, Kirbiss-Kerensky, even he had to amend his demeanour. "*Tsar chisf* (the *tsar* is clean), he declared. The Russian phrase means more than "innocent;" it is really "beyond reproach." But the Jewish Press and the Soviet did not recant their foul slanders. No justice could be shown to the man whom they hated. Captivity lost some of its worst forms after the innocence of the ex-*tsar* had been established. But Tsarskoe Selo was only a prelude to worse martyrdom.

I do not wish to go over the details of the first captivity, a good deal being already known about the five months at Tsarskoe-Selo. Only the more important episodes are given here, based upon the depositions of members of the Imperial household. But before relating these sad memories, I would take the reader a little farther back, and touch upon fateful incidents that have not yet been recorded in their proper bearing.

I have referred to the estrangement of nearly everyone of the ex-empress's friends as a consequence of her malady. This exodus of intimates included kinsfolk as well as humbler people. Even the Montenegrin Princesses Anastasia and Militza[1] were no exceptions to the rule. Coldness between the wives in this case was bound sooner or later to affect the husbands. Alexandra resented the popularity of the Grand Duke Nicholas as a personal affront. In the end she succeeded in persuading her husband to dismiss him and to assume the chief command. But she punished herself. The *tsar* at the *Stavka* (G.H.Q.) began to do things without her knowledge and consent. He actually listened to dreadful stories about the "saint," dismissed Stuermer, and might go further. Razputin's death helped the empress to reassert her usual influence.

Then, once more, the *Tsar* went off to Mogilev, and anxiety crept again into the mind of Alexandra. The illness of the children—they all contracted measles in a very bad form—caused her worry of another sort. For a time the autocrat was forgotten in the mother; and so, when the rumbling of the Revolution was already loud, she did not discern it. Protopopov, the friend of the departed "'saint," was assuring her that nothing serious had occurred. When the children were out of danger, she had leisure to take stock of affairs. Realizing that Protopopov was not to be trusted, she sent for the Grand Duke Paul. Rumours about the *tsar* tormented her. He was going to abdicate. The idea of such a surrender made her frantic. Paul could not help. She tried to get into communication with her husband by aeroplane. A trusty flying officer was summoned, but even this venture failed.

Remaining outwardly calm, she showed the measure of her anxiety by abandoning the reserve that she had always displayed. Thus she herself came out to the guards battalions and units that had been concentrated around the palace, and actually made a speech to them.

On the morning of the 21st of March, General Kornilov came to

---

1. They are the wives of the Grand Dukes Nicholas and his brother Peter and sisters of the Queen of Italy. At one time they were very friendly with the empress and through them Razputin came to the notice of the court Afterwards they became enemies of Razputin.

DINING ROOM IN THE IPATIEV HOUSE
This photograph was taken before the arrival of the
Imperial family

THE GRAND DUCHESSES' ROOM IN THE IPATIEV HOUSE

THE COMMANDANT'S ROOM IN THE IPATIEV HOUSE

THE HALL AND DRAWING ROOM IN THE IPATIEV HOUSE
This photograph was taken before the arrival of the
Imperial family

inform Alexandra "that upon him had fallen the painful duty of announcing the ordinance of the Council of Ministers that from that hour Her Majesty must consider herself to be under arrest." This announcement was made to the empress in the children's play-room in the presence of Colonel Kobylinsky, the new commandant of the Palace. Then General Kornilov asked to speak to the empress alone. He assured her that there was no danger, and then gave instructions for the treatment of the prisoners, based upon kindness and courtesy.

The meeting between husband and wife was a very affecting one. Nicholas came straight to the nursery. They embraced each other tenderly, "forgetting the world and its troubles in the joy of reunion with their children." Prison rules, rigorously applied, thenceforth prevented any communication with the outside, and for a time even between the prisoners.

Kerensky set about trying to discover some evidence of collusion with the enemy. Alexandra was isolated. A creature of Kerensky's, named Korovichenko, came to search the Imperial papers. The *tsar* politely offered to help him, but met with a rude rebuff, after which he left Korovichenko alone. Having satisfied himself that no such evidence existed Kerensky somewhat altered his demeanour. At his first meeting with the ex-*tsar*, he had adopted a tone of haughty familiarity. Later, he became polite, even respectful, addressing him as "your Majesty," instead of plain "Nicholas Alexandrovich."

Although the soldiers guarding the palace were not supposed to enter its precincts, the prisoners did not enjoy immunity from their prying gaze and offensive curiosity. They broke into the palace and pilfered, ransacking trunks. On one occasion they rushed into the sitting-room where the family had assembled. One of the girls sat between the light and the window, doing some sewing. Her movements silhouetted outside had been suspected to be signals.

An officer accompanying the Minister of War (Guchkov) on one of his visits loudly accused the occupants of the palace of being "sold to the enemy" (*Vy vsie prodazhnyie*) , The fact that he was intoxicated did not lighten the insult. It showed what unworthy suspicions animated people in the ministries. The ignorant soldiers who imbibed their daily dose of revolutionary lore from the Soviets were not better or worse than their chiefs. By dogging the ex-*tsars* footsteps when he went out for exercise, by shooting the boy's pet goats, and taking away his toy rifle, and by other acts of the same kind the soldiers were merely copying their officers. These demonstratively donned red badges and ignored the *tsar's* salute.

Senseless clamour had led to daily espionage of the family. Officers of the guard went into the dining-room at lunch time to see if the prisoners were all in the palace. The *tsar* always greeted them. On one occasion an officer declined the extended hand. Nicholas, deeply hurt, asked him: "Why?" The man, putting his hand behind his back, declaimed: "I am of the people. When the people stretched their hands out to you, you did not meet them!"

★★★★★★

At the end of July the captives heard that they would shortly go away. It was impossible to leave them there any longer. The Soviets of Petrograd and Kronstadt had tried to obtain possession of them by force and by stealth. Once an individual attired in uniform, styling himself Colonel Maslovsky, had made his appearance, and, producing a paper signed Chkeidze, demanded, in the name of the Soviet of Petrograd, the transfer of the prisoners to the fortress of SS. Peter and Paul, threatening to call in the troops if his demands were not immediately complied with. It was with the greatest difficulty that Colonel Kobylinsky averted the danger.

The provisional government could not afford to let the Soviets obtain the custody of such valuable hostages. It had to remove them to a place of safety—above all to a place where the Soviets could not easily reach them. Perhaps this explains the selection of such a remote place as Tobolsk. It was chosen by Kerensky without the knowledge of the captives. They thought, till the train was conveying them eastward, that they were bound for the south. The ex-*Tsar* did not like his destination. He suspected a trap, though what should have made him suspicious is not known.

Permission had been given to the banished sovereigns to choose the persons who were to accompany them into exile. Nicholas selected his *aide-de-camp* Naryshkin, but as this favourite hesitated, he at once crossed out his name and proposed Ilya Leonidovich Tatishchev, who, with Prince Vasily Alexandrovich Dolgoruky remained with him to the end, paying for their loyalty and devotion with their lives. In a separate chapter I shall describe the heroism, sufferings, and end of those who were faithful unto death—of the two whom I have just named, of Dr. Botkin and of young Countess Anastasia Vasilievna Hendrykova, angel of purity and grace, whose mere presence at the Court of Alexandra should have kept away all things evil, and of devoted Mlle. Schneider, and of the humbler servitors. The ex-empress

161

was not permitted, for some unexplained reason, to take her favourite maid.

The evil genius of the household, Anna Vyrubova, had been locked up in the fortress. She and Voeikov, the ex-palace *commandant*, had been subjected to the most searching interrogation by the members of the "Extraordinary Commission of Inquiry regarding the Dark Forces." Such was the high-sounding title invented by Kerensky to mobilise all methods of bringing home to the *Tsar* the abominable charges invented against him. Nothing could be proved, because there was nothing to prove. But Kerensky had his spies all the time at the palace and sent one to Tobolsk.

Young Alexis celebrated his thirteenth birthday on the eve of departure. The family attended a special service and afterwards offered up the customary prayers for a safe journey. They were going into the unknown. Here in their own familiar surroundings life had not been so terrible towards the end of their captivity. What had the future in store? The war was still in progress. They could not leave the country. Perhaps when peace came, some quiet refuge would open its gates, and they could live happily together. The girls and the boy were delighted like all young things over the prospect of a journey. Alexis and his sisters had quite recovered from their illness.

At midnight of the 13th August Kerensky came to the palace, assembled the soldiers who had been selected to escort the family, and made them a speech. "You have guarded the *tsar's* family here," he said, "you also will have to guard them in the new place where they are going by order of the Council of Ministers. Remember, one does not hit a man who is down. Bear yourselves like men, not like cads."

He then entered the palace. The ex-*tsar's* only brother, the Grand Duke Michael, had been permitted to come to say goodbye. Kerensky gave him ten minutes with Nicholas, remaining in the room with them. The brothers were never to meet again. Michael did not see any other member of the family.

Learning that the *tsar's* family was to be removed from Tsarskoe-Selo the men employed at the railway station refused to let out the engine. All night the exiles waited for the train. It came at six o'clock in the morning.

CHAPTER 6

Exile in Siberia

The period between autumn, 1917, and the following spring furnishes much material for this tragic history. It was during their exile in Siberia that the fate of the Romanovs was decided—not in the Urals. It was at Tobolsk, in the close intimacy that misfortune naturally brings, that the true character of each captive, high and low, asserted itself. Thus, invaluable *data* has been obtained for the historian.

At first the captives enjoyed the respite of remoteness from the storm centre of Petrograd. But many circumstances gradually impaired this advantage. They began to suffer privations even before the Reds captured the government. The remittances promised by Kerensky did not arrive. After the Bolshevist usurpation, the captives were allowed starvation rations, and had to eke out their livelihood by needlework, drawings, etc. Then the boy fell ill with one of his periodical attacks, aggravated by the exhausting effects of the Siberian winter and inadequate diet.

At Tobolsk Alexandra showed herself to be strong, brave, gentle. Adversity seemed to bring out all that was best in her nature. Yet here the family physician, who had followed them into exile and afterwards shared their fate in Ekaterinburg, became entirely convinced that she was not quite normal. It required only a chance remark on political topics to provoke a hysterical outburst. As usual, she could see nothing bad in the peasants, even when the peasant soldiers of the guard were constantly behaving "like cads"—despite Kerensky's exhortations.

Nicholas sawed wood and gave lessons to the children. Indeed, with the help of Mr. Sidney Gibbes and M. Gilliard and other teachers, they were making up for time lost in their education.

With so many and such powerful influences interested in their existence, it was only to be expected that efforts would be made to enter into communication with the exiled monarchs. Each of the parties then fighting for power in Russia had its spies and emissaries in Tobolsk. It is certain that the Germans were represented in many ways. It is equally certain that the *entente* had nobody. The talk of a rescue by some bold Englishman ascending the Ob and Irtysh from the Arctic Ocean and wafting away the prisoners is not only unfounded, it is the merest moonshine. Winter in Siberia lasts seven months, during which time there is no means of reaching the northern shores except on sleighs. Any attempt to enter or leave the country would have been easily discovered and notified by telegraph, which was wholly in the hands of the Soviets.

One comfort was not denied to the captives—they sent and received letters, in some cases without censorship. They were also able to get newspapers and other literature. Thus they were in touch with the happenings of the outer world. These did not bring them much consolation, it must be admitted. Nicholas never recovered from the blow of learning in this manner of the Treaty of Brest-Litovsk. Up to that time he had, in spite of everything, kept alive some hope for the future of his country. Thenceforth he was a man without hope, and all that happened afterwards left him indifferent. If he could have died without causing pain to his wife and children, he would have died gladly, unable to live down the stain of dishonour.

The exiles suffered unconsciously from the senseless if not traitorous behaviour of a man in whom they naturally trusted—the local priest, Father Vasiliev. Base cupidity may have been his only motive, but it is certain that he caused incalculable harm and must be held accountable for the tales of alleged plots to escape from Tobolsk. The Reds used him as their tool. Perhaps he was not altogether blind. There were other "friends" who proverbially, proved to be worse than enemies. On the other hand, many instances of disinterested loyalty and devotion consoled the captives in their afflictions.

From Tsarskoe to Tobolsk, the journey under normal conditions required not more than a week. The Imperial exiles reached their destination on August 19th, within six days of departure. They travelled in comfort in sleeping cars with a whole retinue of servants. The list of the passengers as officially approved numbers forty-five all told. Two trains conveyed them and their effects. Stoppages were not made at the large stations because local workmen and Soviets were disposed to interfere. They had done so at Zvanka, the first important station on the Vologda-Viatka route, by which the party travelled. The deputy

Vershinin, who had brought the *tsar* a prisoner from Moghilev, acted again in the capacity of representative of the Provisional Government during this journey. He had the greatest difficulty in overcoming the resistance at Zvanka. The workers did not wish to allow the trains to pass.

At Tiumen two steamers awaited the party for the river trip to Tobolsk. They passed by the village of Pokrovskoe. Alexandra called the children to look at the birth-place of the "saint" on the banks of the stream in which he had fished. She was fond of comparing him to the fishermen of Galilee, humble men like him. The children dutifully complied and joined their mother in prayer—not because they liked or regretted Grishka, but out of love and obedience to their mother. To her diseased imagination this coincidence between the scene of their exile and the home of Razputin had a mystical meaning.

The voyage had been as pleasant as it could possibly be. The tedium of the long days of travel had been relieved by frequent stoppages amidst forest or field. All who wished could alight and walk, while the train followed slowly. Such comforts are possible only in Russia. Descending the tributaries of the mighty Irtysh, the exiles had a wonderful picture of the Siberian autumn, with its splendour of colouring and teeming bird life. At Tobolsk they had to remain a whole week in the steamers, because the houses intended for them were not ready. They were, of course, under constant guard, but allowed to take exercise ashore. .

On August 26th they moved into their new prison. Alexandra was suffering more than usual from heart trouble. She drove in a comfortable carriage. The *tsar* and the family and household walked. With the exception of a few servants, all found accommodation in two houses: one a warm, roomy stone building, formerly the residence of the governor; the other adjoining it and known as the Kornilov house. The ex-sovereigns and their children took up their quarters in the upper storey of the governor's house. Here were the *tsar's* study and the bedchambers of the imperial couple, of Alexis and of the grand duchesses. Here also was the drawing-room. Downstairs were the schoolroom, servants' rooms, and the quarters of the *commandant* and officers on guard duty. The suite and other servants lived in the Kornilov house. Later, the soldiers expelled many of these occupants without reason, and, as some of them had to be accommodated in the governor's house, there was no small discomfort from overcrowding.

Both houses faced the main street, which had been renamed Ulitza

Svobody (Liberty-street). People passing by could see into the lower rooms. It became a custom to bow to any member of the family who happened to be visible, and some of the citizens would demonstratively make the sign of the cross. Behind the governor's house was an immense enclosure, surrounded by a high wooden fence. Here the family took their exercise; here the *tsar* chopped and sawed wood, and with his own unaided efforts built a sort of wooden terrace, where the captives loved to sit whenever the weather permitted.

Early rising was the rule. All except the empress were ready for breakfast by 8:30. Alexandra's health was so bad that she seldom left her room before lunch-time. Breakfast, as usual among Russians, was a slight meal of tea and bread. The *Tsar* had it in his study with his eldest daughter Olga, who of all the children most resembled him in character. The other children and members of the household assembled in the dining-room, situated on the ground floor of the governor's house. The empress had coffee in bed.

Till eleven o'clock Nicholas read or wrote his diary, while the children had lessons. From eleven till noon father and children were in the courtyard. He worked with axe or saw and the young folks played games. At twelve o'clock all went to the school-room and had sandwiches, after which the *tsar* left his children to continue their lessons. The family and household met at one o'clock at lunch—a simple meal—after which they were in the open air, weather permitting, till four p. m. The empress seldom left the house. Olga and Tatiana, the two elder grand duchesses, helped their father in his manual work. Alexis generally had a short sleep after lunch, and then followed the others into the courtyard with his tutors.

Five o'clock tea was served in the *tsar's* study. Then followed an interval for reading or games, then two hours for preparation of lessons. Dinner at eight consisted of soup, fish, meat, sweet-dish, and coffee. It was prepared by the Imperial cook, Haritonov, and during the earlier period differed little from the customary repast of old times. Everybody met in the drawing-room after dinner. There were reading and conversation. Court etiquette being forgotten. Alexis retired to rest early. At eleven o'clock tea was served, and soon afterwards all lights were out.

Despite her poor health, Alexandra was seldom idle. In the morning she gave lessons to the children and did needlework. When she remained alone in the house she would play the piano. Often, when the heart trouble was severe, she had dinner also in her room, and then

Alexis kept her company.

The company at table included besides the family only the persons already mentioned as forming the household—namely, Countess Hendrykova, Mlle. Schneider, Prince Dolgoruky, General Tatishchev, Mr. Gibbes, M. Gilliard, and Dr. Botkin. On Sundays came Dr. Derevenko and his son Kolia.

The *tsar* gave lessons to Alexis in history, a favourite subject, in which Nicholas was extremely well versed. Alexandra instructed all the children in religion, and taught her favourite daughter Anastasia German—a language that none of the children understood. Anastasia was ambitious to know everything. She studied history with the help of Countess Hendrykova. Another teacher, Mme. Bittner, came afterwards to help in the schoo-room. To relieve the monotony of their lives, the children were encouraged to take up private theatricals. Several plays, English and French, were produced with great success.

To the empress's intense joy, they were permitted to attend church. Her greatest sorrow at Tsarskoe had been the interdict on church-going, the nearest place of worship being outside the precincts of the palace and therefore inaccessible to the prisoners. Here at last they could go to church, after a lapse of more than four months. But the sacred edifice was closed to other worshippers when the exiles attended it.

Unhappily, this source of spiritual comfort was not unalloyed with temporal drawbacks. Father Vasiliev, the incumbent, did a very rash thing one day. Without consulting anybody, he suddenly intoned the prayers for the sovereigns, as if they were still on the throne. The exiles were powerless to interfere. Of course, the incident came to the knowledge of the whole garrison immediately afterwards, and led to the sort of reprisals that one might have expected: church-going was stopped for ever, and, what was worse, the soldiers insisted upon having a representative inside the house at all religious services, to see that the above named practice was not repeated. Thus all the efforts of Colonel Kobylinsky, the good-hearted commandant, to keep the soldiers out of the house were defeated.

Within a month of their arrival in Tobolsk the exiles were placed under the observation of special emissaries of the Provisional Government: the Komisar Pankratov and his assistant, Nikolsky. The former enjoyed high confidence and renown in revolutionary circles, having spent fifteen years in the Fortress of Schlusselburg and twenty-seven years in exile in Siberia. A typical theorist, dangerous in his teachings, he was personally the best-hearted of men. He adored children, and was the playmate of the young Romanovs, whom he literally enthralled with stories of his prison years. His particular favourite was Maria. Nikolsky, on the other hand, was uncouth, uncultured, brutal, and stupid, and took an apparent delight in bullying the young folks, especially Alexis. With permission from the government, some medicinal wine had been sent to Tobolsk from Tsarskoe. Nikolsky took the bottles and smashed them.

As a matter of fact, the delightful but not very far-sighted Pankratov caused much more harm than the bestial Nikolsky. True to his revolutionary principles, he immediately proceeded to indoctrinate the soldiers. Perhaps he feared the personal influence and charm of the ex-*Tsar*. Pankratov talked with them by the hour on the wonders of the Socialist-Revolutionary programme, and, as so often happened in Russia, the ignorant listeners became not Socialist-Revolutionaries but Bolshevists. Anyhow, they very soon lost all respect for authority in the persons of their *commandant* and officers, and began to ill-treat the prisoners. They sank so low that even the young grand duchesses suffered insult. Lewd drawings and inscriptions disfigured the posts of the swing that was their only outdoor pastime. Later, these hooligans broke up the ice-hill that the girls and their father had put up in the yard.

The day came when they included the ex-*Tsar* in their deviltries. Nicholas wore the simplest garb—a soldier's khaki shirt and overcoat, retaining only his colonel's shoulder-straps and his Cross of St. George. Suddenly the soldiers decided that he must take off his badges of rank. In vain Kobylinsky remonstrated with them. They threatened violence if their "orders" were not carried out at once. It hurt the ex-*Tsar* to the quick to cut off his shoulder-straps. Thenceforth the cross alone remained to symbolise his fidelity to Russia and her allies. He kept it ever on his breast to his dying day.

Some of the old soldiers remained immune from Pankratov's influence, and when the time came for them to be relieved, they visited the ex-*Tsar* by stealth to bid goodbye. These were affecting scenes. The men fell on their knees and prayed, and then embraced the captive and blessed him. Of course, Nicholas related all this to Alexandra, whereby her invincible belief in the peasants gathered new strength.

On several occasions violent disputes arose between Alexandra and one of the ladies, because the latter spoke of the horrible behaviour of the soldiers.

Alexandra lost all control over herself, and cried: "They are all good! They are all good! They are led astray by Jews.....The people will come to their senses, and there will be order.... The soldiers are all right. I wish the officers were more energetic."

In November, while Kerensky was still at the head of the government, no money had as yet been received, in spite of all his promises. The funds of the household had run out, and Dolgoruky and Tatishchev, having expended their own substance, had to borrow from charitable souls in the town, giving their note of hand in return. Two months later, word came from the Soviet Government that it had no money to spend on the prisoners. They would be allowed to occupy their houses free of charge, would receive soldiers' rations, and have to work if they wanted anything more. Sorrowfully, they faced the situation. One-third of the servants were at once released, each receiving a certain sum out of the scanty remnants. Nicholas and Alexandra never knew how their faithful followers had to pinch and contrive in order to keep the household from starvation.

Alexis astonished the household by his precocious understanding. "I begin to know the truth here. At Tsarskoe everybody told lies," he remarked one day. "If I become *tsar*, no one will dare to tell me lies. I shall make order in the land." He combined his mother's will with his father's charm. Those who came to know the boy at Tobolsk are confident that he would have justified his words.

To a visitor at his bedside when he was ill, he spoke his thoughts about Razputin. The "saint's" portrait had been placed by Alexandra near her sick son's pillow. The visitor accidentally upset it. "Do not pick it up!" cried Alexis. "The floor is the place for it."

★★★★★★

Towards the end of their exile, some, if not all, of the captives realised the desperate nature of their position, and had scant hope of surviving Bolshevist rule for any length of time. Pathetic evidences of their attitude were found among the papers that remained at Tobolsk and came into the hands of the investigating magistrate. Among them are two prayers written in verse—apparently composed by Countess Hendrykova and transcribed by the Grand Duchess Olga. Here is an approximate rendering of some of the verses:—

Grant us Thy patience, Lord,
In these our woeful days.
The mob's wrath to endure.

The torturers' ire;
Thine unction to forgive
Our neighbours' persecution.
And mild, like Thee, to bear
A blood-stained Cross.
And when the mob prevails.
And foes come to despoil us,
To suffer humbly shame,
O Saviour aid us!
And when the hour comes,
To pass the last dread gate,
Breathe strength in us to pray,
"Father forgive them!"

CHAPTER 7

The Last Prison

The intimate connection between Berlin and Moscow yielded many living examples among the visitors to Tobolsk. Many, if not all, of the spies, emissaries, and other agents appearing there had been at one time or another in the German capital. Yakovlev, the special commissary sent to remove the prisoners from Tobolsk, was no exception to the rule.

His appearance was preceded by certain events which must be related here. The soldiers forming the guard at Tobolsk grew tired of Pankratov and his everlasting speeches. By the end of the first week in February (1918) they had decided to get rid of him and of Nikolsky. On the 9th they turned them out of the Kornilov house and drove them out of the town. They then telegraphed to Moscow, reporting what they had done, and asked that a proper *commissary*—not an appointee of Kerensky—should be sent. But Moscow remained obstinately silent. The time for action had not yet arrived. Meanwhile, the Soviet at Omsk, representing Western Siberia, sent a representative to Tobolsk. He arrived on March 24th. This man was a certain Dutzmann, a Jew. He did not interfere with the prison *régime*; indeed, he never came near the governor's house.

At the end of March, Alexis had a severe attack of his illness—the worst ever known. Both legs were paralysed. The pain was excruciating and unremitting. Day and night he cried aloud in his agony, and the aged and infirm mother had to sit by and comfort him. After a whole month of suffering the patient began to improve and the pains grew less, but he was still a cripple and could not be moved without serious danger. At this juncture appeared the Soviet emissary, Yakovlev. Neither the soldiers nor the captives were surprised. Only a few days later they understood what an important part he had come to play in their lives.

Yakovlev reached Tobolsk with an escort of 150 horsemen late in the evening of April 22nd and unobtrusively took up his residence in the Kornilov house. Colonel Kobylinsky saw him next morning. Yakovlev handed him an order from the *Tsik*, signed by Sverdlov, intimating that the bearer was entrusted with a mission of the highest importance and that he must be implicitly obeyed, but no hint was given as to the nature of the mission. Yakovlev then had the men of 'the guard mustered and showed them a similar document, by which they were informed that any disobedience to him would be punished with death. To sugar the pill, Yakovlev told them that he had brought them a lot of money, the Soviet having decided to pay at the rate of three *roubles* a day instead of fifty *kopecks*, the rate fixed by the Kerensky Government.

Altogether, Yakovlev showed himself to be an expert in the art of handling peasant soldiers, but he had to overcome opposition of a more subtle kind from a Jew named Zaslavsky, who had insinuated himself among the guards as the representative of the Uralian Soviet. This man had previously caused no end of trouble by "discovering" "plots," and had almost persuaded the soldiers on one occasion to insist that the Imperial captives should be transferred to the town lockup. In fact, here once more it was only the coolness of the resourceful Kobylinsky that had saved the situation.

But this noxious individual did not have things all his own way. The Omsk Soviet also had its representative among the guard—a Russian named Degtiarev. Now the two Soviets—that of Omsk and the one at Ekaterinburg—being constantly at odds, their emissaries were naturally jealous of each other. Thus it was enough for Zaslavsky to take one view in order that Degtiarev should take the opposite one. Zaslavsky had for some reason immediately stirred up opposition to Yakovlev and tried to persuade the soldiers that he was a spy come to deliver the prisoners. With Zaslavsky was an Ekaterinburg workman named Avdeiev, who figured prominently in subsequent events.

It is noteworthy that Yakovlev came to Tobolsk by way of Ufa—a roundabout journey from Moscow—apparently in order to avoid Ekaterinburg. Yakovlev had friends in Ufa. It is probable that he had met Avdeiev there. He appears to have imagined that Avdeiev might help him to prevent or allay suspicion in Ekaterinburg. In this he was mistaken.

At a meeting of the soldiers on the 24th, Degtiarev, backed by Yakovlev, attacked Zaslavsky with such vim that the men threw him out, and he made haste to escape to Ekaterinburg to relate a purely imaginary story of Yakovlev's designs to release the Romanovs. But there is evidence to show that he first communicated by wire with Sverdlov. Zaslavsky's poisonous character may have been the only prompting necessary, but it is not impossible that he may have been "inspired" from Moscow to play a part in the intricate conspiracy that was to exterminate the Romanovs. Certainly Yakovlev underrated his capacity for mischief, as will appear later. Sverdlov tried to make the world believe that Nicholas II. was to be brought to Moscow for trial. But this may have been only an afterthought. In any case, it was easy to have him intercepted by playing upon local ignorance and suspicion through Zaslavsky.

Meanwhile, during these two days (the 23rd and 24th), Yakovlev had been repeatedly inside the governor's house, and on each occasion had gone to the boy's room, appearing suddenly, looking fixedly at the patient, and then going away. Nobody noticed his strange behaviour at the time. They remembered it afterwards. No one knew as yet what he had come for. On the night of the 24th Yakovlev went to the telegraph office, taking with him an expert operator who had come with him from Moscow, and had a long conversation over the wire with Sverdlov, the substance of which—as transpired later—dealt with the boy's sickness and the impossibility of moving him. Sverdlov gave him "new instructions" to the effect that he was to bring Nicholas and that since the boy could not come he would have to be left behind for the present.

From the telegraph office, Yakovlev went straight to Colonel Kobylinsky and, for the first time, disclosed the object of his mission. "But what about Alexis?" remonstrated the commandant. "That is the trouble," was the reply. "I have satisfied myself that he is really too ill to travel, so my orders now are to take the ex-*tsar* alone and leave the family here for the present. I propose to start tomorrow. Arrange for me to see him at once." It should be explained that as the roads would, in a few days, become impassable, and the river-ice break up any moment, owing to the advance of spring, it was necessary to leave Tobolsk at once or wait several weeks till the rivers were clear of ice. Hence Yakovlev's haste. But as he was apparently well acquainted with the character of the empress, he insisted that Nicholas should receive him alone.

The ex-*tsar* appointed two o'clock on the following day for the interview. Alexandra became furious on learning that she was not to be present. When Yakovlev entered the drawing-room, she met him with flaming eyes and asked him how he dared to separate husband and wife. Yakovlev, with a shrug of the shoulders, addressed himself to Nicholas:

"The Moscow Central Executive Committee have sent me as Commissary Extraordinary with power to remove the whole family, but as Alexis Nikolaievich is ill I have received orders to leave with you alone."

The *tsar* replied: "I shall go nowhere."

Yakovlev remonstrated: "You must not say that. I have to carry out orders. If you refuse to go, I must either use force or send in my resignation, and then someone else will come who will be less humane. Have no anxiety; I answer for your life with my head. If you do not wish to go alone take anybody you like. Be ready to leave tomorrow at four." Yakovlev thereupon left without addressing the empress.

Kobylinsky remained in compliance with a request from the ex-*Tsar*. Alexandra and Tatishchev and Dolgoruky stood by.

"Where do they want to take me?" asked Nicholas.

"To Moscow," was the reply. "Yakovlev let it slip out when I inquired how long he would be away before returning to fetch the family."

The ex-*tsar* nodded, as if the news confirmed his own knowledge. Turning to his followers he declared: "You see they want me to sign the Treaty of Brest-Litovsk. But I would rather cut off my hand than do so."

Alexandra, much agitated, interposed: "I am also going. Without me they will persuade him into doing something, as they did once before. . . ." And she fired a volley of abuse at Rodzianko for his part in the abdication. But in the stress of the moment she had forgotten her sick boy. The hours that followed will ever be recalled by all who survive as the most painful of their memories. This distracted mother, too feeble to stand for more than five minutes, paced her room like a caged tigress. She summoned her favourite daughter Tatiana and burst into a storm of weeping. For the first time her attendants saw her lose all self-control. In broken sentences she disburdened herself of her sorrow, revealing in her distress the innermost thoughts of her mind:

"The Germans know that their treaty is valueless without the *tsar's* signature. . . . They want to separate him from his family in order to frighten him into some disgraceful act. . . . He will be afraid to refuse on our account. . . . It will be a repetition of Pskov. . . ."

She wrestled with herself, praying that she might not have to choose between her husband and her son, hoping that the river might suddenly open and prevent any travelling. At last she came to a decision, and, jumping up, cried: "It is enough, I go with the emperor." Nicholas entered the room. She greeted him with the words: "I shall not let you go alone."

"As you will," was his reply.

Volkov, the empress's confidential manservant, deposes that he saw her in the Tsarevich's room, and as she was going out inquired what was the matter. Alexandra replied: "*Gosudar* (the *tsar*) is to be taken away to Moscow. They want him to conclude peace. But I am going with him. I shall never permit such a thing. What would our Allies say?"

Madame Bittner spoke to the *tsar* at this same juncture. She suggested that "they," meaning the Germans, would take him "out of the country."

He replied: "God grant that it be not so. Only not abroad!" This witness deposes that the whole family dreaded the idea of being sent abroad, *i.e.*, to Germany.

In this connection I recall a remarkable passage in one of the depositions. Some member of the household at Tobolsk was reading out of a newspaper the statement that the Brest-Litovsk treaty contained a clause assuring the safety of the Imperial family. The empress broke in with an angry exclamation in French: "I had rather die in Russia than be saved by the Germans." (*Je préfère mourir en Russie que d'être sauvée par les allemands.*)

It was then settled that the party with the *tsar* should include: Alexandra, the Grand Duchess Maria, Prince Dolgoruky, Dr. Botkin, and the servants Chemodurov, Demidova, and Ivan Sednev. On receiving the list, Yakovlev said: "It is all the same to me." The soldiers were again assembled on the evening of the 25th to be informed of the Tsar's removal. To forestall any objections, a number of them were selected to accompany the party.

★★★★★★

The vehicles that were to convey the travellers to Tiumen, where they would find a train, did not differ from the ordinary Siberian *tarantass*—a large basket swung upon long flexible poles uniting two springless axles, the baskets being filled with straw. Into these vehicles the travellers tumbled and disposed themselves as best they could. Alexandra had a *troika*, the others a pair of horses. She beckoned to the *tsar* to mount with her, but Yakovlev sent Maria to join her mother, and shared his *tarantass* with Nicholas.

The roads were terrible. No traveller who has not experienced springtime travel in Russia can have any idea of them. At some places the party had to alight and walk through deep slush. The empress was better off than the others as she had a stronger team. Yakovlev was hurrying as fast as horseflesh could go. Relays waited at stated intervals. The travellers passed from one *tarantass* into another. It was better to lose no time as every day the roads became worse, but there was another reason; Yakovlev was evidently afraid of being stopped by the local Soviets and wished to rush past before they had had time to oppose him.

Throughout the trip he conversed with the ex-*tsar* on politics, endeavouring to talk him over to a certain point of view—but the *tsar* would not give way. This much the coachman who drove them could swear to, although he could not catch all the details of the conversation. He noticed that Nicholas did not "scold the Bolsheviks," but somebody else.

They reached Tiumen on the 28th at 9 p.m. A special train was in waiting. They started westward, but had not travelled far when at a wayside station Yakovlev heard that Ekaterinburg would intercept him. What he feared had happened. The only hope lay in circumventing Ekaterinburg. For this purpose it was necessary to return, go east as far as Omsk-Kulomzino, and thence switch on to the Cheliabinsk-Ufa railway. But he was too late. The soviet at Ekaterinburg had wired to Omsk that the ex-*tsar* was escaping eastward, and a cordon of Red guards stopped the train at Kulomzino. Yakovlev detached the engine and went across the Irtysh to Omsk, and there, with the help of his private telegraphist, spoke with Moscow. He was ordered by Sverdlov to proceed *via* Ekaterinburg. As might be expected, they were met by a strong force of fanaticised Red guards at the station at Ekaterinburg (April 30th). Yakovlev's authority was flouted and the escort and guards that were with him imprisoned till he had departed empty-handed on his way to Moscow. The unfortunate Romanovs thus came into the hands that were to massacre them and take their belongings.

Yakovlev had no hand in this foul conspiracy. He had been quite sincere and consistent in his efforts to bring the whole family safely to Moscow. There is no indication whatever, in all he said, that the object of this removal was to bring the Tsar to trial. On the contrary, the conversations with the *tsar*, continued in the railway carriage, where, again, he was separated from Alexandra, gave additional colour to the version already given by Nicholas himself—that it was intended to restore the monarchy under certain conditions.[1] Speaking of Yakovlev, the ex-*tsar* afterwards said: "Not a bad sort—evidently sincere." Alexandra did not cease to bewail her misfortunes, weeping over her son and her husband.

On reaching Moscow, Yakovlev must have had some doubts about the sincerity of the *Tsik*. Anyhow, he resigned his *commissaryship* and eventually joined the White forces, and then mysteriously disappeared. An interview with him, published in a Red organ at the time of his journey in charge of the Imperial captives, contains some very instructive features. It passes over in silence the attempt to evade Ekaterinburg and falsifies the dates of arrival and departure at Tiumen so that the glaring discrepancy between this and the arrival at Ekaterinburg (two days instead of half a day) should not be noticed; ignores, in fact, all the local soviet intrigues and protests, quite needlessly, that he did not mention politics in his conversation with Nicholas. Vasily Vasilievich Yakovlev had been a naval officer and was therefore of Russian noble blood. He had committed some political offence, had spent many years abroad—in Berlin. Who were his real chiefs? It is not difficult to guess.

Two other *commissaries* went to Tobolsk to remove the remainder of the family—Tatiana had been left in charge of the invalid and household. Olga, the eldest daughter, did not enjoy her mother's confidence in the same degree. She took far more interest in literature than in the practical affairs of life, and would hide herself in a corner with a book or tell stories to the soldiers, utterly forgetting domestic trifles. Anastasia, still a child, and rather backward, could be left in Tatiana's care.

---

1. It must be borne in mind that the virtual ruler in Moscow was Count Mirbach (see chapter 2), the Bolshevist leaders being appointees and vassals of Germany, though, perhaps even then, secretly conspiring against their masters. Further, it is known that many influential Russians were intriguing with Mirbach (May, 1 9 1 8) to restore the Monarchy. This movement collapsed because the two "orientations"— German and *Entente*—could not agree. The "Germans" wanted Alexis; the "*Ententes*" favoured Michael.

"We could have deposed the Soviet Government, which was thoroughly hostile to us, and given help to other authorities in Russia, which were not working against us, but indeed anxious to cooperate with us. This would have been a success of great importance to the general conduct of the war. If some other government were established in Russia, it would almost certainly have been possible to come to some compromise with it over the Peace of Brest"

Maria went with the Imperial couple because she was too grown-up to remain under her sister's care. She was a very attractive girl, and it used to be rather a joke among the grand duchesses to twit her on her "conquests" among the *komisars*.

The two successors of Yakovlev were:—A sailor named Hohriakov and a certain Rodionov. The latter was afterwards identified as a former *gendarme* officer. He used to inspect the passports at the German frontier, and served sometime in the Russian Embassy at Berlin as a spy on Russian revolutionaries. When taxed with it, he admitted the impeachment. The sailor, a typical good-natured peasant, soon made friends with all the children. Rodionov, on the contrary, went out of his way to torment and ill-treat them. He forbade the grand duchesses to lock their doors at night, informing them with a leer that he had a perfect right to come into their rooms whenever he liked. With every appearance of enjoyment, he announced that in Ekaterinburg they would have to observe stricter rules, which he himself had devised. Hohriakov was nominally senior to Rodionov, but the latter did what he pleased.

Here must be recorded a circumstance which was destined to play an important part in the detection of the murders of Ekaterinburg. Before separating, it had been understood between mother and daughters that they would take measures for safeguarding the jewels that had been brought with them from Tsarskoe, worth not less than a million gold *roubles* (£100,000). A letter from the maid Demidova from Ekaterinburg gave the necessary indications. The grand duchesses were "to dispose of the medicines as had been agreed." This meant that the jewels had to be secreted in the clothing in such a way as to escape search (Nicholas, Alexandra, and Maria had been "searched" very thoroughly and brutally). For some days the grand duchesses and their trusty servants worked at the task, sewing up the valuables in their bodices, in their hats, and even inside their buttons. The empress had few if any valuables with her—possibly because there had been no time to secrete them—but thanks to the precautions now taken, the grand duchesses managed to smuggle all that was of greatest value into their last prison-house. Womanlike, they clung to these relics of former happiness, and perhaps deep down in their hearts slumbered some hope that the gems might help them to escape.

Leaving Tobolsk by steamer on May 20th the family and household reached Ekaterinburg on the 22nd without incident.

In handing over his prisoners to the Ekaterinburg Soviet, Yakovlev

**THE IPATIEV HOUSE: THE ROOM IN THE BASEMENT
WHERE THE IMPERIAL FAMILY WAS MURDERED**

A vaulted semi-basement, 18 by 16 feet. Photographed from the spot where the so-called "Lett" soldiers stood while firing their revolvers. The Tsar and his son sat in the center of the room and behind them was the Empress, also seated. The other victims stood at the further wall.

YANKEL (JACOB) SVERDLOV, THE RED TSAR

He organised the murder of the Romanov family, and was despised and later killed by Russian workmen. He was President of the "Tsik", i.e., Prime Minister and Ruler of the Red Inquisition. He posed for his portrait with his portfolio at the entrance of his palatial offices in the Hotel Metropole in Moscow, located on the square which is named after him. He is dressed in a short shirt and shabby overcoat with only a cap of expensive fur to befit the high office of the wearer.

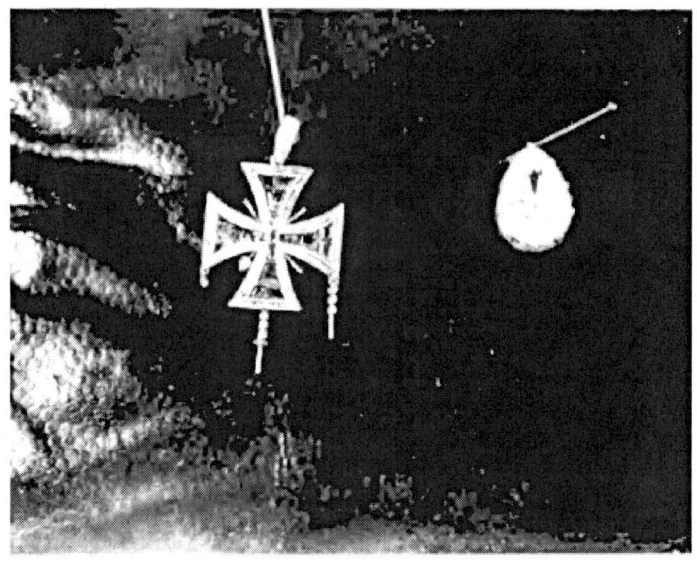

RELICS FOUND NEAR THE PYRES
A pectoral cross, set with emeralds, belonging to the Empress, and the Empress's
great diamond pendant.

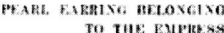

PEARL EARRING BELONGING
TO THE EMPRESS

IKONS (HOLY IMAGES), BELONGING TO THE EMPRESS AND HER DAUGHTERS

THE ENTRANCE TO THE SHAFT NEAR EKATERINBURG

obtained the following written acknowledgment:—

Russian Federal Soviet Republic. Uralian Regional Council of Deputies. Receipt. 30th April, 1918. I, the President of the Regional Uralian Council of Deputies, Beloborodov, have taken over from the member of the All-Russian Tsik comrade Yakovlev the interned: former Tsar Nicholas Romanov, the former Tsaritsa Alexandra Feodorovna, the former Grand Duchess Maria Nikolaevna, and the persons accompanying them. All these persons are under arrest and under guard. The President of the Uralian Regional Sovdep. (Signed) Beloborodov.

CHAPTER 8

Planning the Crime

Nothing had been done at Ekaterinburg to prepare for the arrival of such prisoners as the ex-*tsar* and his family till April 27th (*i.e.*, two days after the spy Zaslavsky had denounced Yakovlev). The arrangements then taken consisted in requisitioning Ipatiev's house and putting a rough hoarding around it. Zaslavsky reached Ekaterinburg in company with a Russian workman named Alexander Avdeiev, who had been with him at Tobolsk and become imbued with the Jew's tale of Yakovlev's alleged treachery. In return for his support and blind subserviency, this man received the post of commandant of the new imperial prison and promises of further promotion.

Isai Goloshchekin, the intimate friend of Yankel Sverdlov, took charge of the prisoners on their arrival. Isai played the part of a Bolshevist Poohba, being a *komisar* many times over, but above all he loomed largely in the local *chrezvychaika*. He supervised the removal of the prisoners from their railway carriage, completely ignoring Avdeiev, and took them away in his motorcar. On reaching the Ipatiev house, Goloshchekin told the imperial trio to descend, then pointing to the door, said:—"Citizen Romanov, you may enter." In the same manner he let the ex-empress and Maria pass the threshold.

Prince Dolgoruky, who was of the party, did not meet with Goloshchekin's approval. "You go to another prison," said he, and straightway Dolgoruky was removed, never to be seen again.

When, three weeks later, the other children and remainder of the household arrived, the same procedure was adopted. Once more Avdeiev was ignored, the person in charge being Rodionov. His brutalities at Tobolsk had earned him distinction. Here he excelled himself. It was raining heavily and the platforms were slimy with mud. He would not permit anyone to help the grand duchesses to carry their own luggage. Nagorny, one of the imperial servants, was knocked over for daring to extend a hand to Anastasia, dragging a heavy bag.

Nobody had permission to share the new prison with the Romanovs except the physically weak or mentally undeveloped. The only exception was Dr. Botkin. Those who did not enter the house went to other prisons, the two foreigners excepted. Their fate is described elsewhere.

The family, once more reunited, had need of all their love and faith to endure the sufferings that marked this last stage of their earthly pilgrimage. Besides them and their physician only four servants were permitted to remain—the chambermaid Demidova, the footman Trupp, the chef Haritonov, and the boy Leonid Sednev, attendant and playmate of the sick Alexis. Chemodurov, the *tsar's* valet, was transferred to the town prison from the Ipatiev house three weeks after his arrival. He survived, but his mind was affected.

This building stands at the corner of Vosnesensky *prospekt* and Vosnesensky *pereulok* (lane) facing a large square in which stands the church of the Ascension (*Vosnesenia*), a prominent landmark in the city and suburbs. It is a two-storey stone building with a garden and outhouses behind, to which access is obtained through a gateway into the square. As the lane descends steeply from the square, the lower storey is a semi-basement in front, gradually clearing the surface of the street on the lane side. The lower floor was occupied by the guard; the prisoners lived upstairs in the corner rooms away from the stairs and entrance, which were on the gate side. Nicholas, Alexandra, and Alexis shared one room facing the square; the adjoining chamber, overlooking the lane, was occupied by the grand duchesses. The family could not leave these two rooms except for meals, which were taken in the adjoining dining-room. Another room, divided into two halves by an arch, accommodated Dr. Botkin and Chemodurov on one side and the servants on the other. From the dining-room a door led to a terrace, overlooking the garden.

Around the house, a wooden hoarding reached up to the windows of the upper floor. Soon after the prisoners arrived, another hoarding was put up, completely screening the whole house up to the eaves, and enclosing also the front entrance and gateway. There were double windows, as usual in Russian houses. Both panes were covered with whitewash, rendering it utterly impossible for the prisoners to see anything outside— even a crow flying.

Sentries paced between the hoardings, inside the garden, and were stationed at the stairs, beside the lavatory, and on the terrace. Here, and at other convenient points, machine-guns were posted. The prisoners were in a trap from which there was no escape. The awful thing about it was the constant surveillance, by day and night. There was no privacy, not even for the girls—no consideration for decency or modesty. The Ekaterinburg period was one long martyrdom for the Romanovs, growing worse—with one short interval—as the hour of their death approached. Their guards, at first, were Russians, who, brutal as they were, never attained the fiendish ingenuity in tormenting their helpless captives that came to be displayed by the alien guards and executioners of the final week.

There had been no provision for guarding the house—another proof that the prisoners had not been intended for Ekaterinburg. After the first few days, a regular guard was organised from workmen employed at the local mills and iron works. Alexander Avdeiev received the style of "*Commandant* of the Special Purpose House"—such was the name of the imperial prison. His assistants were Alexander Moshkin and Pavel Medvedev, both workmen and Russians. Avdeiev and his particular friends among the guards lived upstairs in the ante room and another chamber facing the square. They were, consequently, in immediate proximity to the prisoners. No pen can describe what this meant.

The men were coarse, drunken, criminal types, such as a revolution brings to the surface. They entered the prisoners' rooms whenever they thought fit, at all hours, prying with drunken, leering eyes into everything that they might be doing. Their mere presence was an offence; but picture the torments of the captives to have to put up with their loathsome familiarities! They would sit down at the table when the prisoners ate, put their dirty hands into the plates, spit, jostle and reach in front of the prisoners. Their greasy elbows would be thrust, by accident or design, into the ex-*tsar's* face. Alexandra was, of course, a special object of attention. They would crowd round her chair, lolling in such a manner that any movement on her part brought her in contact with their evil smelling bodies.

Prison fare of the poorest kind was provided. Breakfast comprised stale black bread from the day before, with tea—no sugar. For dinner they had thin soup and meat, the latter of doubtful quality. The ex-empress could eat nothing except macaroni.

The table cover was a greasy oil-cloth. There were not knives or forks or even plates enough to go round. All ate with wooden spoons out of one common dish. By the emperor's wish the servants sat at table with the family.

The guards sang revolutionary songs devised to hurt and shock the feelings of the prisoners, containing foul words such as no man should dare to utter in the presence of innocent girls, but the revolutionary warriors delighted in wounding the modesty of the grand duchesses in this and in other still more repulsive ways, by filthy scribbling and drawings on the walls and by crowding round the lavatory—there was only one for the prisoners and the warders. They went reeling about the house, smoking cigarettes, unkempt, dishevelled, shameless, inspiring terror and loathing. They did not scruple to help themselves liberally to the clothes and other property of the prisoners whenever anything came within their reach.

Only a quarter of an hour was allowed to the prisoners in the open air. No physical work was permitted. The ex-*tsar* felt this privation very much. Alexandra suffered terribly. Her son remained an invalid, unable to walk. The family seemed to be overwhelmed by grief. But their faith in God and their love for each other illuminated the gloom of this awful prison. Above the ribald songs of their tormentors might be heard the chanting of the Song of Cherubim, the Russian hymn of praise.

Now we come to the final phase that preceded the murder. It is full of significance. Every step taken by the occult powers of the Ekaterinburg *chrezvychaika*, which, it must be remembered, did nothing without orders from the central institutions in Moscow—Sverdlov being in direct communication with Goloshchekin—falls into its natural appointed place as part of the cruel fate reserved for the Romanov family.

The monsters who had been placed in charge of the prisoners—as if on purpose to torment them through the agency of Russians—did not fulfil their mission to the end. Even they became humanised by the spectacle of the sufferings and the patience and humility of their former sovereigns—not all of them, of course, but certainly a majority, including their *commandant*, Avdeiev.

One of these men afterwards related how the change came over him. He had begun with hatred in his heart. The *Tsar* was the head of the capitalistic system, the greatest capitalist of them all. To destroy him was to destroy capitalism itself—the Social-Democratic programme had made it all so plain to him. He watched the crowned enemy of mankind, the "drinker of the people's blood," as he walked about the garden, and listened to him exchanging simple, homely words with the other warders. His notions began to waver. This was not a bad man; he was so human, so kindly, just a man like other men, and even better. Then the idea occurred to him that it was wrong to desire his death. What harm could he do? Why not let him escape! Yes, it would be much better if he went away, and the children, too, they had done no harm, and the *tsaritsa* also. She was proud. Not simple and homely, like the *tsar*, but let her also go. If she had done harm, she had also suffered.

This man repented of the evil he and his fellows were doing. He would sing no more lewd songs, and tried to dissuade the others. Rapidly the whole of the guard—workmen from the Lokalov and Syssert companies' plants—were becoming disaffected.

Towards the end of June a secret emissary of one of the Monarchist organisations called upon the Bishop of Ekaterinburg and tried to get into communication with the Imperial prisoners through the clergy; but this proved to be impossible. He then proposed that, at all events, sane food and comforts should be sent to the prison-house. Dr. Derevenko, who had been permitted to remain in the city, gave his assistance at this juncture. By some means he was in touch with the warders. Avdeiev agreed to take in milk and other provisions if they reached the house without attracting notice.

The nuns of the monastery thereupon sent two novices, dressed in lay garments, to the house, with all manner of dairy produce. Avdeiev received them himself. These journeys became frequent. The poor captives felt comforted, morally and physically. They had not been forgotten, and the men who had been so terrible were so much kinder. Hope once more blossomed. The Grand Duchesses looked bright and cheerful, "as if ready to smile," says a person who saw them at this time. The nuns, emboldened by Avdeiev's attitude, brought even some tobacco for the ex-*tsar*. Avdeiev referred to him as "The Emperor."

In the beginning of July some suspicions must have arisen among the Jewish camarilla, or perhaps Moscow had received "information." As the time was getting ripe for "action," no doubt steps had been taken to verify the arrangements, and the discovery of disaffection among the Russian guards followed. Avdeiev was at once dismissed, the Russian guards moved out of the house into premises on the opposite side of the lane, and, with one exception, were forbidden to come into the house. This exception was Pavel Medvedev. He retained: his post as chief warder. The Russian guard continued to provide sentries for the outside posts only. They could do no harm there, and served to throw dust in the eyes of the public.

All these changes were carried out by the new *commandant*, a person with whom the reader is already acquainted, namely, Yankel Yurovsky, the son of a Jew convict, himself a mystery man, having obtained money in Germany for unexplained "services," and presently one of the chiefs of the local *chrezvychaika*. Yankel brought with him a squad of ten "Letts"—as the Russians called them—to mount guard inside the prison-house and take charge of the machine-gun posts. These men were the hired assassins of the red *okhrana*. They were not Letts but Magyars, some of them really Magyarised Germans. It must be remembered that Siberia was Sovietised from the east, not by Russians in the first place, but by the soldiers of Wilhelm and his Austrian henchmen, who acted under orders from the two *Kaisers*. These so-called Letts had entered the service of the *chrezvyckaika* after helping to carry out the German design to undermine Russia.

Innumerable evidences prove that the newcomers are correctly classified. The Russian guards could tell by their speech that they were foreigners. To designate them as Letts was quite natural because the Letts formed the backbone and bulk of the foreign mercenaries of Sovietdom and therefore any non-Russian Red-guard became a "Lett." But, as a matter of fact, the Magyars resemble Letts in their appearance and accent. Yurovsky spoke to them in a foreign language. Besides Russian and Yiddish he knew only German. Among the papers found afterwards in the prison-house was an unfinished letter to his "*Tereschen*" from one of the "Letts." It was in Magyar, but, according to the findings of experts, the writer was evidently a German. He used capital letters for substantives, often employed Gothic characters and made glaring blunders in grammar, such as no Magyar would make.

Another of the "Letts" left a still more eloquent evidence of his nationality. This man had stood on guard on the terrace communicating with the dining-room and overlooking the garden—a very important post with a machine-gun capable of sweeping the interior of the house and all the approaches from the garden side. On the very day before the murder, this man wrote in pencil on the wall of the house a record of his service as follows:—

András Verhás
Orsegen   1918 VII/15

Alongside this inscription he had tried to write the Russian equivalent, but could not spell out the word *"karaul"* (guard duty), in Magyar *örsegen.* Scraps of paper on which other "Letts" had practised writing Russian words were also found.

We are able to fix the date approximately when the German-Magyar guard and Yurovsky took possession. The lay sisters bringing their usual offerings met with a strange reception on or about July 10th— about a week before the murder. Avdeiev did not come out to them. Some of the Russian guards, whom they knew, were standing near the door, looking very much confused, and at first not disposed to take charge of the gifts. Finally, however, they did so. The sisters then walked away. Presently the soldiers came running after them. "Please will you come back," they said. The nuns returned. An individual whom they afterwards identified as Yurovsky, inquired by whose authority they had brought the provisions. "Avdeiev and Derevenko," was the truthful reply. "O, they are both in it, are they," he remarked ominously. He nevertheless permitted them to come again, "but with milk only."

This last week of their life must have been the most dreadful one of all for the Romanovs. Brutal and bestial as the Russians had been in the early part of their wardenship, they were preferable, even at their worst, to the silent relentless torture applied by Yurovsky, who also was a drunkard. He and his band watched them literally like a cat watches a mouse. He was polite to the *tsar* and spoke softly to Alexis; he even permitted a priest to come and say prayers, which comforted Alexandra and the poor captives unspeakably; yet there is evidence that never had they looked so utterly, hopelessly wretched as under the tutelage of the Jew. This man's brothers and sisters describe him as a "cruel tyrant who would not hesitate at anything to attain his ends."

The man and his executioners only waited for the signal that was to come from Yankel Sverdlov. Everything was ready for the murder. The victims had been adequately tortured. Goloshchekin, the Jew Sadist, licked his lips in pleasurable anticipation.

CHAPTER 9

Calvary

Yankel Yurovsky left the prison-house on several occasions. Each absence lasted many hours. He was surveying the environs of the city for a convenient place to dispose of the bodies of his victims. His escort consisted of one or two of the "Letts" mounted on horseback. Several witnesses deposed to meeting him and his bodyguard in the woods during the week that preceded the murder. They were seen near the very spot where the remains were afterwards destroyed.

Whenever he had to absent himself, Yurovsky placed Medvedev in charge. Besides the latter, there was another non "Lett" in the house, a certain Nikulin, respecting whom it is known that he came with Yurovsky from the *chrezvychaika*. He enjoyed Yurovsky's entire confidence, and was probably there to keep an eye on Medvedev.

On Monday, July 15th, the lay sisters came as usual in the morning with milk for the Imperial family. Yankel took it himself, and graciously informed them that on the morrow they might bring half-a-hundred eggs. This they did gladly, thinking that the poor captives would enjoy hearty meal, all unsuspicious of the cynical intention that had prompted Yurovsky's generosity. (These eggs were boiled by Haritonov, but they were eaten, not in Ipatiev's house, but in the woods.)

On the Tuesday morning, a whole nine days before the arrival of the Czechs, Yurovsky made his final arrangements for the murder of the family. The boy Leonid Sednev was removed early in the day to Popov's house across the lane, whither the Russian guards had been transferred. There he was seen sitting on the window-sill and crying bitterly, whether because he was dull without his play-fellow or had some inkling of his fate is not known. The boy disappeared, never to be seen again. Later this gave rise to rumours that Yurovsky had been told to reserve him for future use, perhaps to impersonate his little friend the *tsarevitch*—in short, to act the part of a False Dmitri.

Two important visitors came to the prison-house during the day—namely, the arch-inquisitor, Isai Goloshchekin, and his humble servant, the Russian workman Beloborodov, president of the regional Soviet. They took Yurovsky away in their automobile to some place unspecified, presumably to a meeting of the Soviet Presidium (Board). Yurovsky returned some hours later, towards evening.

At seven p.m. Yurovsky gave orders to Medvedev to collect all the revolvers of the outer guard. Medvedev complied. He brought twelve Nagans (the Nagan is the Russian service revolver) to the *commandant's* room and handed them to Yurovsky. The latter then confided to him the plan to shoot the whole "*Tsarian* family" that night. He (Medvedev) would have to warn the Russian guards "later," when he got word to do so. Meanwhile he must be silent. At nightfall (about 10:30 p.m. in these latitudes in summer time) Medvedev "told the Russians." The murderers were to be the "Letts."

There is no record of any open protests on the part of these men, who had been "disgraced" only a few days ago for their "friendliness" to the "arch-capitalist" and "drinker of blood." There is nothing to be surprised at. Beloborodov had been rendered "amenable," because he had "stolen;" here the crimes laid to these men's charge was not only pilfering but "counter-revolution." They knew—and we may be sure they were made to feel—that the *chrezvychaika* would know how to deal with them if they showed truculence. Having "warned" the Russians, Medvedev returned to the *commandant*.

Two other strangers now made their appearance. One of them was Peter Ermakov, "military *komisar*" of the Verkh-Isetsk iron-works; the other, his assistant, a sailor named Vaganov. Both these men had distinguished themselves by their ferocity. They were professional assassins, "working" for the Red inquisition out of sheer blood-lust. But there was another reason for inviting these butchers to the approaching feast of blood. They were both to play a leading part in the "disposal" of the bodies. Both were friends of Yurovsky. With him they had already, some days earlier, studied and arranged the whole grisly performance.

When midnight by solar time had gone some minutes, Yurovsky went to the Imperial chambers. The family slept. He woke them up, and told them that there were urgent reasons why they should be at once removed; that there was trouble in the city which might endanger their lives, and that they must dress quickly and come downstairs.

191

All rose, washed, and dressed themselves, the grand duchesses donning their jewel-stuffed garments. Each member of the family and their followers put on his or her going-out clothes and headgear. The empress wore her overcoat. Some of the prisoners even took their pillows—for comfort's sake or because they had precious possessions secreted within.

Yurovsky led the way downstairs; the family and suite followed. Alexis could not walk. His father carried him in his arms. Dr. Eugene Sergeievich Botkin came directly after the family, and after him came the chamber-maid Demidova, the cook Haritonov, and the footman Trupp.

The procession descended by the backstairs leading from the upper to the ground floor. The door from the lower landing (by the kitchen) to the rooms of the ground floor had been boarded up to prevent direct communication between their former occupants—the Russian guards—and the prisoners. One had to go into the yard and then enter the lower floor by a separate doorway. This was the route followed by Yurovsky and his victims. The motor-lorry that had come for the bodies waited outside the gate of this very courtyard, and in the dim light of the northern midnight the prisoners could probably see the vehicle and must have felt reassured, even if any suspicion of their imminent end had assailed their minds.

Still following Yurovsky, they traversed all the rooms of the lower floor, now tenanted only by "Letts," and came at last to the small lobby adjoining the front entrance on the lane (*pereulok*) side. This lobby was lighted by a small window, heavily grated, looking into the garden. Outside stood a sentry with a machine-gun. He could see everything that went on inside, especially when the interior was lit up for the execution. This man's account played an important part in assembling and corroborating the various depositions dealing with the murder. Opposite the window, a door leads into a small chamber (18 x 16 ft.) with a heavily grilled double window facing the lane. Here also stood sentries outside, able to see what was going on within. This chamber is partly basement. The guards had used it as a dormitory. A locked door led into a basement chamber situated immediately under the tsar's prison-room. This corner basement was a store-room where some of the Imperial belongings had been deposited—and pilfered. There was no escape in that direction. Besides, there were double barriers outside, intercepting sight and sound.

The family and their followers were ushered into the semi-base-

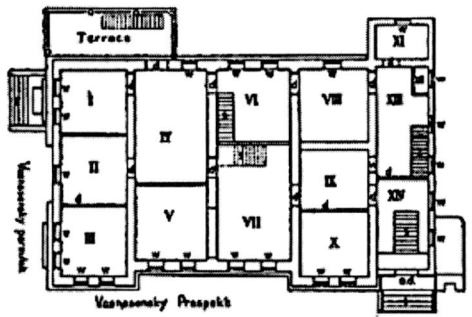

Plan of the Upper Floor

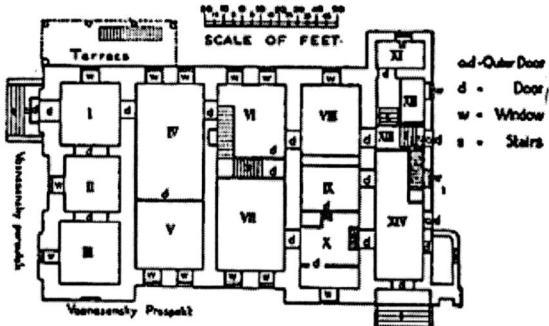

SCALE OF FEET·

od -Outer Door
d = Door
w = Window
s = Stairs

Plan of the Lower Floor

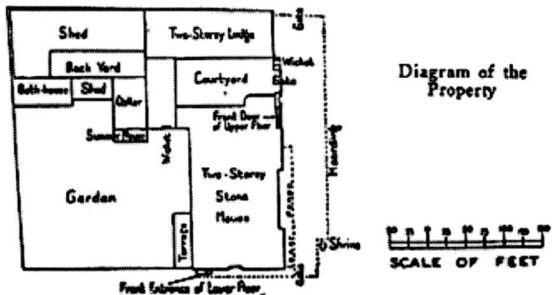

Diagram of the Property

SCALE OF FEET

PLAN OF IPATIEV'S HOUSE

ment chamber and told to wait. They were not suspicious. It did not occur to them that they were in a trap. As the room was bare of furniture, the *tsar* asked to have some chairs brought. He wished the suffering empress to rest and the sick boy to sit down. Three chairs were brought in. One was passed to Alexandra, who had been leaning against the wall facing the lobby. Nicholas seated Alexis where he had been standing, in the middle of the room, and sat down beside him. A pillow was placed behind Alexandra. Two other pillows remained in Demidova's arms. The *tsar* and the *tsarevich* kept their caps on, as if expecting any moment to go out. They thought the vehicles that were to convey them away had not arrived, the lorry being there to take the luggage. On the empress's right stood three of her daughters, on her left the other daughter and Demidova.

Almost immediately, the door into the lobby was obstructed by Yurovsky, his friends and the "Letts." There were Nikulin, Ermakov, Vaganov, Medvedev and seven "Letts"—the remaining three being on guard duty. There were twelve murderers. Each carried a revolver. The rifles of the "Lett" guard were stacked in the adjoining room (where they lived).

Yurovsky advanced into the death-chamber and addressed the *Tsar*. There are many versions of this utterance. According to the most trustworthy one he said: "Your relatives have tried to save you. But it could not be managed by them, and so we ourselves are compelled to shoot you."

The twelve revolvers volleyed instantly, and all the prisoners fell to the ground. Death had been instantaneous in the case of the parents and three of the children, and of Dr. Botkin and two servants. Alexis remained alive in spite of his wounds, and moaned and struggled in his agony. Yurovsky finished him with his Colt. One of the girls— presumably the youngest grand duchess, Anastasia—rolled about and screamed, and, when one of the murderers approached, fought desperately with him till he killed her. It seems as if the murderers had not been able to aim straight at the boy and the girl. Even their callous hearts had wavered. The maid-servant lived the longest. Perhaps the pillows were in the way. She was not touched by the first volley, and ran about screaming till some of the "Letts," seizing their rifles, bayoneted her to death. She was covered with stabs. Poor Demidova died the victim of a misunderstanding; the Reds thought that she was a maid-of-honour and therefore a *bourgeoise*, whereas she was a simple peasant girl.

Within a few minutes of their entering the room, all was over. No time was to be lost in removing traces of the crime. The floors and walls had to be washed quickly and the bodies sent away. Daylight would soon appear. There was a long way to go through the city. Hardened and ruthless, secure in the impunity of murder under the Soviet system, Yurovsky and his associates were none the less hurrying desperately. They knew that the arrangements for "executing" the Romanovs could not be regarded as a trial, nor would the people approve the deed. And so like common murderers, they were desperately anxious to get rid of the corpses. Here Ermakov and Vaganov became invaluable.

The evidence of three eyewitnesses is given below, namely of Medvedev, one of the actual murderers, of Yakimov, who was present at the shooting, and of a Red Guard named Proskuriakov, who helped to remove traces of the murder. The necessary comments of the investigating magistrate accompany the depositions so that the reader is able to study them in their true perspective.

Medvedev told his wife all about it directly after the murder. He did not conceal the fact that he himself had fired his revolver at the Romanovs. He even emphasised his active complicity, boasting that he was the only Russian "workman" who had taken part in the shooting, and that all the others, besides Yurovsky and his assistants, were "not ours"—*i.e.*, foreigners. Medvedev was caught at Perm while trying to blow up the bridge over the Kama to cover the retreat of the Red Army. He confirmed all the statements that he had made to his wife except in one particular: he denied having stated that he had himself done the shooting. It is a customary reservation in the case of all who take part in a joint and prearranged murder. The witness testifies to the fact of the murder and names the actual murderers, but persists in declaring that he himself did not do the killing, although he admitted to holding a revolver in his hand at the time of the shooting. To divert the evidence from himself he had to invent an *alibi*. Hear what he says in his signed deposition:—

"Yurovsky sent me out, saying, 'Go into the street; see if there is anyone about and if the shots can be heard.' I went out into the yard surrounded by the big fence" (he means the space between the outside wall and the hoardings), "and, before I had time to reach the street, heard the sound of the firing. I returned at once inside the house— only two or three minutes had passed—and, entering the room where the shooting had been carried out, I saw that all the members of the *tsar's* family—the *tsar*, the *tsaritsa*, the four daughters, and the *naslednik* (heir), were already lying on the floor with numerous wounds on their bodies, and the blood was flowing in torrents. The doctor, maid, and two menservants had also been killed. When I appeared the *naslednik* was still alive, groaning. Yurovsky went up to him and fired two or three times point-blank into him. The *naslednik* was still. The picture of the murder, the smell and sight of the blood, caused me to feel sick."

Anatoly Yakimov, the second witness, is the man who had become "converted" after remaining a few weeks with the *tsar*. He had been a sergeant of the Russian Guard, and remained so after the Russians had been relegated to the outer posts. It was his business to place the sentries and see that they remained at their posts. As the Russian sentries could see into the room where the murdering was to be done, it had not been possible to keep them in ignorance to the end, as explained above. Yakimov "sympathised" with the prisoners, but he did not dare to give effect to these feelings. There is good reason to believe that he was present at the murder. Possibly Yurovsky had insisted upon his being inside the house at the time, in order to implicate him in the deed. His *alibi* bears a family likeness to Medvedev's. Like him, he had a full, circumstantial knowledge of the killing that corroborates Medvedev in every essential point, and that could not have come to him unless he had been actually present. He explains that it was all told to him by the sentries—two men who stood outside the death-chamber window and two others who were in the courtyard when the bodies were removed.

He also unburdened himself to his family. According to his own account, he heard of the murder at four o'clock in the morning, after which he could not sleep, but "just sat and shivered," as he says. At eight o'clock he went to his sister, a woman of some education, who was married to Agafonov, an official of the Commissariat of Justice. Here is what his sister deposes:—"He came in without saying a word, looking dreadfully upset and exhausted. I noticed it at once and asked him: 'What is the matter with you?' He requested me to close the door, sat down and kept silent, his face convulsed with terror and his body trembling violently. I again asked him: 'What ails you?' I thought that some great misfortune had overtaken him. He still maintained an obstinate silence, although it evidently caused him suffering. The thought occurred to me: 'Maybe they have killed Nicholas.' I asked him if it was so. My brother answered something like: 'It is all over,'

and in reply to my further questions he said that all had been killed—
i.e., the *tsar* himself and all his family and all who had been with them
excepting their little scullion.

"I do not recall my asking him if he had taken part in the murder,
but I remember his saying that he had seen the spectacle of the murder with his own eyes. He related how this sight had so shaken him
that he could not hold out, and every now and then had gone out of
the house into the open air, adding that his comrades in the guard had
upbraided him for it, suspecting him of feeling repentance or pity. . . .
I then understood him to mean that he had been himself in the room
or so near that he could see the actual murder with his own eyes."

Here are two corroborative depositions of interest. When Yakimov
had left his sister, she immediately ran out to her husband's office. An
investigating magistrate named Tomashevsky was in the next room,
and saw her standing, weeping, and whispering to her husband. When
she had gone, Agafonov came and told this same story in confidence
to Tomashevsky. Agafonov saw Yakimov later in the day, and relates
what transpired:—

"Yakimov came to take leave. (He was going to the front.) I was
struck by his appearance: the face pinched, the pupils distended, the
lower lip quivering when he spoke. The mere sight of him convinced
me that all that my wife had said was true. Clearly, Anatoly had passed
through some terrible experience during the night. . . . I only asked
him: 'How are things?' He replied, 'It is all over'" (*vsi yóncheno*).

Philip Proskuriakov—a youngster, the type of the good-natured
peasant—deposed that he had entered the guard at Ipatiev's house
principally because he was curious to have a look at the *tsar*, not because he felt hostile to him; indeed, if he disliked anybody it was the
Jews. His narrative impressed the investigating magistrate by its evident
sincerity. He did not see the actual murder, having spent the evening
with some friends and taken copious draughts of "*denaturat*" (methyl-
ated spirits, which were in vogue since the prohibition of vodka) and
as a result of these libations, Medvedev had placed him under arrest.
He was locked up in the bath-house and sleeping off his "spree" when
Medvedev came to wake him and order him to go into the house.

The bodies had been taken out just before he reached the death-
chamber. Everything that happened in the house immediately afterwards came under his personal observation. He washed the blood
off the floor and the walls. That he positively admits. He discussed
the details of the murder with Andrei Strekotin, one of the guards,

who enjoyed Medvedev's friendship and had been selected by him to stand at the lower-floor machine-gun post during the "execution." This same Strekotin also related his observations to one of his brother-guards named Letemin, arrested later and found to be in possession of a whole collection of valuables belonging to the family and Alexis's spaniel Joy (afterwards brought to England). Letemin's version agreed with Proskuriakov's rendering of the Strekotin eyewitness account. What is still more important, Proskuriakov heard also Medvedev relate the story of the killing.

Medvedev told it to all the guards who with Proskuriakov were washing the floor:—

"Pasaka (Pavel—*i.e.*, Medvedev) himself related that he had loosed off two or three bullets at the *Gosukar* (the Lord—*i.e.*, the *tsar*) and at other persons. . . . I am telling the honest truth. He did not say anything at all about his not having fired himself on account of being sent outside to listen to the shots. . . . That is a lie!"

One pathetic incident escaped the notice of all these witnesses. The Grand Duchess Anastasia took with her a King Charles spaniel, carrying it in her arms into the death room. The corpse of little Jemmy was found above a heap of cinders—all that remained of the family that had loved her and shared with her their meagre fare. The murderers had knocked the faithful friend on the head and thrown the body down the iron-pit without troubling to burn it. Even in her death the little dog watched over them, and her mangled remains, still recognizable, brought final unmistakable proof of the end of the family.

CHAPTER 10

Without Trace

There has probably not been another instance in the whole history of crime of precautions to escape detection half so elaborate as in the Romanov murder case. All sorts of subterfuges have been tried by lesser criminals with more or less success. Here every ruse was combined. The murderers carried out the following comprehensive programme:—(1) They gave out a false announcement of the "execution"; (2) they destroyed the bodies; (3) they invented a mock funeral; and (4) they staged a mock trial. The thoroughness of their methods reminds one of their masters, the Germans. It is a case of "*spurlos*." However, in this, as in the other instance, detection followed. The criminal always gives himself away. The very complexity of the Soviet "precautions" proved their undoing.

In vain they drew innumerable herrings of their own colour over the trail, suborning false witnesses to give misleading information about the whereabouts of the bodies, announcing officially that the family had been removed to a "safe place," etc. Sokolov has run them into the open.

The murder accomplished, all the bodies were carried into the courtyard and placed on the waiting lorry. The corpses were not subjected to a thorough search—as we shall see—because Yurovsky was anxious to get away from the city before daybreak. They were rolled up in old coats and covered with mats to conceal the "cargo" from prying eyes. Yankel Yurovsky, Ermakov, and Vaganov went with them.

As soon as they had gone, Medvedev summoned the Russians to "wash up." They had not been trusted to do the other work, and Yankel had even deprived them of their revolvers—the "Letts" had their own—perhaps because he did not feel quite sure how they might behave during the murder. Even now, Medvedev, his henchman, called up the Syssert workmen—his own particular friends—to remove the tell-tale traces of the crime. They washed and swabbed the floor and the walls in the death-chamber and in the other rooms through which the bodies had been borne. (So much blood had flowed that the marks of the red-stained swab were distinctly visible a year later when I visited Ipatiev's house, and experts found unmistakable evidence of its being human blood.) The stones in the courtyard were also scoured.

Meanwhile the lorry, with its tragic burden, was making its way to the appointed place in the woods, a remote corner of some disused iron mines, once the property of Countess Nadezhda Alexeievna Stenbok-Fermor and now of the Verkh-Isetsky Works. This place is situated northeast of the Perm and Ural railway lines, about 11 miles out of the city, near the forest road leading to the village of Koptiaki.

Ermakov (military *komisar* for the district) placed a cordon of Red Guards all round the wood. During that and the two following days and nights all passage through it was stopped. As will be seen later, this "precaution" defeated its purpose.

Let us return for a few days to Ekaterinburg. Yankel Yurovsky had reappeared in the death-house in the morning of July 17th. None of the Russian guards knew where he had been. Medvedev had heard vaguely that he had "gone to the woods." At the same time there appeared the reprieved thief Beloborodov and his master, Isai Goloshchekin.

The movables belonging to the murdered family went to satisfy their rapacious instincts. Some of the witnesses describe tables laden with precious stones, jewellery, and all sorts of other articles scattered about the *commandant's* room. Everything had been ransacked, and what was not found to be worth keeping was thrown away or destroyed in the fireplaces, which were blazing despite the summer heat.

Yurovsky and Goloshchekin travelled by motor car to the woods on the 17th, 18th, and 19th, remaining for many hours—in fact whole days—at the iron pits. But all this time the sentries were on duty outside the death-house as if nothing had happened, so that the people should suspect nothing. They were removed only on the fourth day, when the cordon around the wood was also raised.

Only then (on July 20th) was the announcement made at Red meetings and in official proclamations that "Nicholas the Sanguinary" had been executed. The news was simultaneously transmitted by the wireless stations of the Bolshevist Government, and appeared in *The*

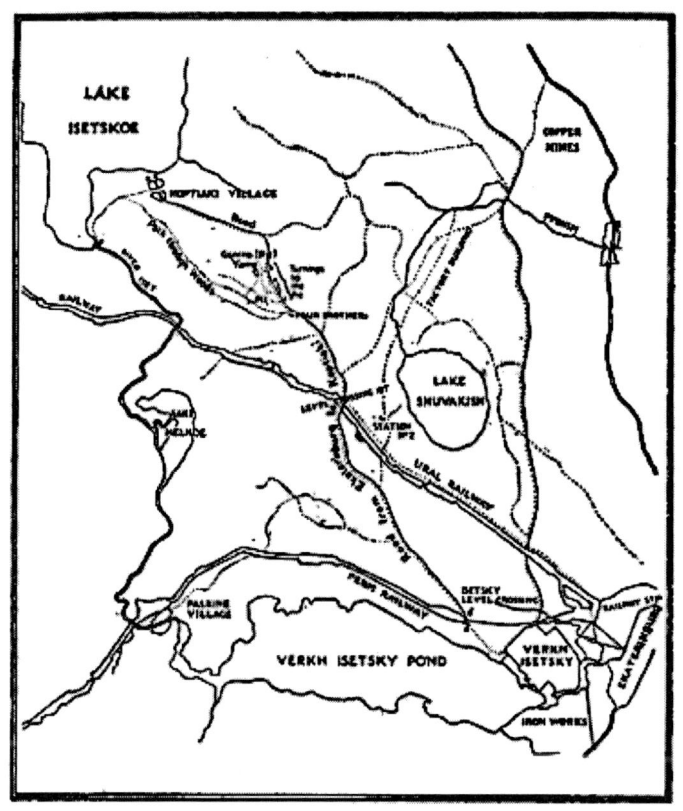

NEW ENVIRONS OF EKATERINBURG

SHOWING ROAD BY WHICH THE BODIES OF MEMBERS OF THE IM-
PERIAL FAMILY WERE CARRIED, AND THE PIT WHERE THE ASHES
WERE BURIED.
DISTANCES: EKATERINBURG, 11 MILES, PIT TO KOPTIAKI, 3 MILES.

London Times of July 22, 1918, in the following form:—

> At the first session of the Central Executive Committee elected by the Fifth Congress of the Councils a message was made public, received by direct wire from the Ural Regional Council, concerning the shooting of the ex-*tsar*, Nicholas Romanov.
>
> Recently Ekaterinburg, the capital of the Red Ural, was seriously threatened by the approach of the Czecho-Slovak bands. At the same time a counter-revolutionary conspiracy was discovered, having for its object the wresting of the tyrant from the hands of the council's authority by armed force. In view of this fact, the Presidium of the Ural Regional Council decided to shoot the ex-*tsar*, Nicholas Romanov. This decision was carried out on July 16.
>
> The wife and son of Romanov have been sent to a place of security. Documents concerning the conspiracy which were discovered have been forwarded to Moscow by a special messenger.
>
> It had been recently decided to bring the ex-*tsar* before a tribunal, to be tried for his crimes against the people, and only later occurrences led to delay in adopting this course. The Presidency of the Central Executive Committee, after having discussed the circumstances which compelled the Ural Regional Council to take the decision to shoot Nicholas Romanov, decided as follows:—The Russian Central Executive Committee, in the persons of the Presidium, accept the decision of the Ural Regional Council as being regular.
>
> The Central Executive Committee has now at its disposal extremely important material concerning the Nicholas Romanov affair; his own diaries which he kept almost to the last days; the diaries of his wife and children; his correspondence, amongst which are letters by Gregory Razputin to Romanov and his family. All these materials will be examined and published in the near future.

Every word of this official statement is important, for every phrase contains a lie, and every lie shows up in more glaring colours the diabolical nature of the plot hatched and carried out by Yankel Sverdlov and his tools and accomplices. I take the falsehoods seriatim:—(1) The message made public at the *Tsik* as coming from the Ural *sovdep* was in reality concocted by Sverdlov; (2) the Czechs entered Ekaterinburg on the 25th, nine days after the "execution," and there was no armed plot; (3) the Presidium of the Ural *sovdep* did not "decide" to shoot the ex-*tsar*, for that "decision" was dictated from Moscow; (4) the "wife and son" were not sent to a "place of security," but were basely murdered; (5) no "later occurrences" supervened that could by any stress of the imagination be construed into a justification for not bringing the ex-*tsar* before a tribunal, even supposing there had ever been any real intention to do so (as a matter of fact, this story of a "tribunal" was invented; (6) the Imperial correspondence taken with other "loot" from the murdered family has *not* been published to this day.(See note following)

Note:—Up to date (August, 1920), the only information that that reached the world respecting the Imperial family's private papers, removed to Moscow after their death, is contained in three short telegrams published in *The London Times* of August 16, August 289 and September 28, 1918.

The first gives an extract of the *tsar's* diary for March 2/15, the day of his abdication at Pskov:—"General Ruzsky came this morning and read to me a long conversation which he had had on the telephone with Rodzianko, according to which the situation at Petrograd is such that a Cabinet of members of the *Duma* will be unable to do anything because against it are fighting the Socialist Parties in the shape of workmen's committees. My abdication is necessary. Ruzsky has transmitted this conversation to General Headquarters, and Alexeiev passed it on to all the commanders-in-chiefs.

At 12.30 came answers from all, the sense of which is that, to save Russia and keep the army at the front quiet, I must make up my mind to this step. I have consented. From G. H. Q. they have sent a draft of a manifesto. In the evening arrived from Petrograd Guchkov and Shulgin, with whom I had a long talk, and handed them the signed manifesto as agreed (*i.e.*, renouncing the *tsarevich's* rights as well—the *tsar's* own decision).At one o'clock in the morning left Pskov with a heavy feeling, due to all I have lived through. Am surrounded by treachery, cowardice, and deceit"

The second reproduces a letter dated January 14, 1916, from the Empress Maria to "Niki," complaining of Witte's delay in summoning the *Duma*, bids the *tsar* be strong, congratulating him on his "new spirit" On April 5 (at Tsarskoe) the *tsar* in his diary speaks of preparations to go to England, and says that news of that proposal was communicated to him by Prince Lvov and Kerensky.

The third merely enumerates the other documents seized by the Soviet:—"The diaries of the empress and her daughters, notes by the *tsarevich*, over 5,000 letters of the correspondence of the *tsar* with his wife, with the *Kaiser* and other sovereigns, with Razputin with divers official personages, also with his father Alexander III, between 1877 and 1894."

Lastly, the *Manchester Guardian* (of July 1, 1920) published from its Moscow correspondent a summary of Alexandra's letters to Nicholas II., copies of which (the originals having disappeared) had been secretly lent to him by a member of the Soviet Government. The extracts quoted by him do not shed any new light on her life and character.

Here is a translation of the official announcement as it was made to the people of Ekaterinburg:—

DECISION OF THE PRESIDIUM OF THE REGIONAL SOVIET OF
WORKMEN'S, PEASANTS' AND
REDGUARDS' DEPUTIES OF THE URAL.

In view of the fact that Czecho-Slovak bands are threatening the Red capital of the Urals, Ekaterinburg; in view also of the fact that the crowned hangman (*palách*) may escape the people's assizes (a Whiteguard plot to capture the whole Romanov family has been discovered), the *Presidium* of the Regional Soviet in fulfilment of the will of the revolution has decided (*postanovil*) that the former Tsar Nicholas Romanov, guilty before the people of innumerable sanguinary crimes, shall be shot.

On the night of the 16th to the 17th of July, the decision (*postanovlenie*) of the Regional Soviet was carried into execution.

The family of Romanov has been transferred from Ekaterinburg to another and safer place.

The Presidium of the Reg. Soviet of W., P., and R. Dep. of the Ural.

Decision of the Presidium of the All-Russian Centr. Ex. Com. of 18th July A.C.

The All-Russian Centr. Ex. Com. of Soviets of W., P., R. and Cossack Deputies in the person of its Presidium approves the action of the Presidium of the Reg. Sov, of the Ural.

The President of the Tsik, Y. Sverdlov.

★★★★★★

The discrepancies between the Moscow and the Ekaterinburg announcements are interesting and significant, but they need not be discussed at this stage. I would call attention only to the date of the *Tsik's* "decision" and to the fact that it was kept secret for two days after its ostensible issue. As a matter of fact the whole murder had been directed from Moscow, and even the text of the "announcement" had been previously approved by Sverdlov, so it is not surprising that Beloborodov disregarded dates. But the real reason was that the Red chieftains feared the people and, above all, sought to obscure the facts.

I now return to the woods. On the 17th, 18th, and 19th large quantities of petrol and sulphuric acid were taken from the city to the iron pits; at least 150 gallons of the former and eleven *pouds* (400 lb.) of the latter. Ekaterinburg being the centre of the platinum industry required large stocks of sulphuric acid to generate the intense heat necessary for melting this hardest of metals. The *komisar* of supplies was Voikov, ex-passenger in Lenin's German train. He it was who furnished the acid to Yurovsky as his friend Sverdlov's agent. (I remember I wanted to order a platinum ring at a local jeweller's during my stay in the city. He could not carry out the order because there was no sulphuric acid "since the previous year.")

There is not the shadow of a doubt as to what happened around the iron pit, as the reader will convince himself after reading the next chapter. Yurovsky's acolytes cut up the bodies, steeped them in petrol, and burned them. The sulphuric acid was used to dissolve the larger bones.

I have spoken of the mock funeral invented by the murderers to deceive public opinion in Russia and abroad. Here is the telegram that appeared in *The London Times* of September 23, 1918:—

Amsterdam, Sept. 22.—According to a telegram from Moscow, the *Izvestua* gives the following description of the obsequies of the ex-*tsar*, which, according to newspaper reports, were solemnly carried out by troops of the People's Army (*sic*) at Ekaterinburg.

The body of the ex-*tsar*, which had been buried in a wood at the place of execution, was exhumed, the grave having been found through information supplied by persons who were acquainted with the circumstances of the execution. The exhumation, says the Soviet journal, took, place in the presence of many representatives of the supreme ecclesiastical authorities in Western Siberia, the local clergy, and delegates from the People's Army, Cossacks, and Czecho-Slovaks. The body was placed in a zinc coffin, encased in a costly covering of Siberian cedar and the coffin was exposed in the cathedral at Ekaterinburg under a guard of honour composed of the chief commanders of the People's Army. The body will be temporarily buried in a special sarcophagus at Omsk.

Comment is superfluous. The fourth and last of the "precautions" against conviction followed a year later, perhaps under stress of circumstances, but certainly without any regard for the Soviet's own previous announcements:—

Here it is:—

On September 17, 1919, in the House of the Executive Committee of the Soviet at Perm, the Bolshevists brought to trial twenty-eight persons arrested on the accusation of having murdered the *tsar* and his family. The following report of the proceedings is taken from the Bolshevist paper *Pravda*:—

The Revolutionary Tribunal has considered the case of the murder of the late Tsar Nicholas Romanov, his wife, the Princess of Hesse, their daughters Olga, Tatiana, Maria and Anastasia, and their suite. In all eleven persons were assassinated. Of the twenty-eight persons accused three were members of the Ekaterinburg Soviet—Grusinov, Yakhontov, and Malutin; among the accused were also two women, Maria Apraksina and Elizaveta Mironova. The account of the murder as gathered from the material under the consideration of the Revolutionary Tribunal is as follows:—

The *tsar* and all the members of his *entourage* were shot—no mockery and no cruelties took place. Yakhontov admitted that he had organised the murder in order to throw the discredit of the crime on the Soviet authorities, whose adversary he became after having joined the Socialist revolutionaries of the Left Wing. The plan of murdering the *tsar* was conceived during the latter's stay at Tobolsk, but the *tsar* was too strictly watched. In Ekaterinburg, when the Czecho-Slovak troops were approaching the town, the Soviet authorities were panic-stricken to such a degree that it was easy for him to avail himself of his position as chairman of the Extraordinary Commission (for combating counter-revolution) and to give the order to murder the *tsar* and his family.

Yakhontov admitted that he personally participated in the murder, and that he took upon himself the responsibility for it. He, however, said that he was not responsible for the robbery of the belongings of the *tsar's* family. According to his deposition, Tsar Nicholas said before he died, "For the murder of the Tsar Russia will curse the Bolshevists." Grusinov and Malutin stated that they did not know anything about Yakhontov's plans, and only carried out his orders. Yakhontov was found guilty of the murder and sentenced to death. Grusinov, Malutin, Apraksina, and Mironova were found guilty of robbery committed on the murdered members of the *tsar's* family. They were sentenced to death too. The death sentence was carried out the following day.

Several objects belonging to the household of the *tsar* were discovered with a thief named Kiritshevsky, who stated that these things had been given to him by a man named Sorin, who was the chairman of the Local Extraordinary Commission. At the time of the murder Sorin was the commander of a revolutionary battalion. Sorin was a personal friend of Beloborodov, who also participated in the assassination of the emperor.—*Rossia* (Paris), No. 1, December 17, 1919.[1]

---

1. This document has been widely quoted by Jewish organizations to prove that the murder of the *Tsar* was not carried out by the Bolshevists, and to dispel the notion of a "racial vendetta." *A propos* of this document *the London Daily Telegraph* stated (August 18, 1920):—"In the interest of truth it must be here said that the Moscow Central Soviet Government has always disclaimed all participation (*sic*) in the murder, explaining that its intention was to judge Nicholas II. publicly, but not to do away with him secretly in a cellar."

I have carefully compared the names given above with the list of 164 persons mentioned in the *dossier* as being implicated or even suspected of having acted any part whatsoever in the tragedy; I have perused the *cognomens* of the twenty-four members of the Ekaterinburg Sovdep presidium. There is not one name in the mock trial that even resembles any of them (one cannot possibly identify Yakhontov with Yurovsky); the very charge is farcical if one compares this report with the text of the official announcement of the "execution." Alone Beloborodov's name is familiar. He was nominally president of the Ural *sovdep* at the time of the murders. I explained his real position—that of a mere *helot*, a thieving workman, kept in office to serve as a screen for the rulers of Sovietdom.

After the murders he was "promoted" to the *Tsik*, the highest honour of Sovdepia. But they do not stand on ceremony with Russian *komisars* in the land where Yankel Sverdlov rules, and we read of him in the *Pravda* as being stigmatised as (1) a thief, and (2) a party to the very murder for which he was promoted—the very same appalling crime that Sverdlov had ordained—the stain whereof haunts the chieftains of the Soviet like a Nemesis, so that they utter things without sense.

Besides, the Soviet of Moscow received a lion's share of the loot! Between July 20th and 22nd it was taken from Ipatiev's house and removed to the Red Metropolis. The Bolshevists were fleeing before the advance of the Siberian troops. Yankel Yurovsky, evidently in a hurry to leave Ekaterinburg, took farewell of the death-house on the night of the 19th. His driver thus describes the exodus. That night he had by Yurovsky's orders called at the *chrezvychaika*, and thence conveyed two young men, one of them a Jew, to Ipatiev's house, where Yankel was waiting. These youths went into the house and brought out seven pieces of baggage, among them being a black leather trunk covered with seals. When he had taken his seat in the vehicle, Yurovsky gave his orders to the young men:—"Set everything to rights. Leave twelve men on sentry duty and send the remainder to the station."

The guard at Ipatiev's house remained till the 23rd, but even after that, on the 24th and 25th, some of the Russian ex-warders still visited the house. The Whites entered Ekaterinburg on the 25th, and occupied the house on the following day.

CHAPTER 11

Damning Evidence

Having established, with the evidence of accomplices and of the death-house, the fact that a murder had been committed, the investigating magistrate had to find the bodies or to show conclusively what had become of them; otherwise the whole case remained in doubt. This proved to be a task of immense difficulty.

Suspicions of the truth were rife from the outset. It was known that five motor-lorries had been requisitioned; that all had been absent several days; that two had carried petrol, and that one had returned covered with mud and gore. Too many persons were involved to conceal the truth for long; the peasants who had to come by the forest road from Koptiaki village at once detected something amiss, and quickly drew their conclusions, which turned out to be correct. But "suspicions" are not proof.

Somewhere within the purview of the disused iron mine "proof was obtainable—on that point there seemed to be no doubt. We took up our residence in the wood—Sokolov, Diterichs, myself, and others—and remained there throughout the late spring and early summer of 1919. We descended the mine, found water and ice and a floor. We searched the ground and scoured the woods, living from day to day in alternate hope or despair of settling the gruesome mystery. Sometimes I felt as if we were seeking the proverbial needle. The woods were full of disused workings, each easily capable of concealing what we sought.

Day by day we discovered fresh relics around the pit where the bodies had, we knew, been destroyed. Sokolov tirelessly passed through his searching examination every likely witness; not a peasant, or *dachnik* (summer resident), or railway servant that had been anywhere near the place escaped him.

Slowly, but surely, the scope of possible error lessened. We had got well away from the versions carefully sown by agents of Yurovsky, who remained in the city, that the bodies had been buried in one place, then reburied in another.

One of the witnesses cited in the preliminary inquiry (before Sokolov took charge) had described overhearing a conversation between several Bolshevists about the bodies. The speakers were said to be: Ermakov (whom we know), Mlyshkin, Kostuzov, Partin, Krivtsov, and Levatnykh. They spoke cynically of feeling the corpses while they were still warm. Levatnykh boasted that he had felt the *Tsaritsa* and that he "could now die in peace." They also spoke of the "valuables sown in their clothes."

The presumable genuineness of these confidences misled the earlier investigator into believing their other statements or perhaps the additions made to them by the spy who may have been a Red agent—to wit, that the bodies had been buried in various places round the city. This was a "red" herring that unfortunately drew the investigator off a hot trail. He did not even go near the wood. Had he done so, he could not have helped discovering easily then what we had such difficulty in finding a year later. His excuse had been that the wood was "dangerous" on account of Red bands; but even if this were so, he could have deputed a less timorous person. A number of self-appointed "investigators" took this opportunity of "gleaning" relics—perhaps invaluable clues.

Extreme measures had to be taken, nothing less than the complete sifting of the ground within the area of destruction and emptying of the shafts down which any remains could have been thrown. This was a task outside the province of an investigating magistrate. Here we wanted miners with pumping machinery, woodsmen, and surveyors; above all we wanted money.

Thanks to Admiral Kolchak the wherewithal was forthcoming. Indeed, I render him bare justice in saying that without his stanch personal support the investigation would have been overwhelmed long ago by the constant intrigues of the Omsk Government. He gave the money out of his own funds because the grant legally authorised by him was "held up" by his ministers.

Under the orders and supervision of General Diterichs, a command of White Guards was formed to carry out the necessary operations. The men were all from the Urals—*i.e.,* miners and peasants versed in woodcraft. Several hundreds of them camped around the

210

Ganina Yama (ditch), situated near a bend in the road to Koptiaki, not a hundred paces from the mine. These men knew what they were working for and put their shoulder to the wheel in all earnestness.

But we had to leave before complete success had crowned their efforts. Diterichs received the summons to save the armies. I went with him. General Domontovich, a very gallant soldier, took command in his place. (He died of typhus during the retreat and was buried in Chita early this year. "*Tsárstvie nebésnoie.*")

Success came before we had to evacuate Ekaterinburg. The contents of the shaft, extracted with infinite trouble, set at rest for ever any lingering doubt as to the destruction of the bodies. Sokolov had his "proof."

Here is the narrative of the investigation. It is a good commentary on the homely saying, "Murder will out."

It will be remembered that Ermakov went with the bodies from the death-house. Now Ermakov lived at the Verkh-Issetsk ironworks, adjoining the city and situated along the route to Koptiaki—*i.e.,* north-east of Ekaterinburg. The Stenbok-Fermer Wood lies a few miles beyond. At the works Ermakov found a detachment of his Red Guards (he was military *komisar*) and a number of conveyances ready harnessed. The whole procession moved off along the Koptiaki road. There is, indeed, no other road in the vicinity practicable for a motor-lorry. Vaganov, the other regicide, mounted his horse and acted as armed escort for the lorry.

Shortly after three o'clock in the morning (solar time) they reached that place where several paths, long disused and grass-grown, turn off to the left towards Ganina Yama. Here they forced a way through the undergrowth, and at one place nearly upset the lorry into a ditch. The mark of the wheels was still visible a year later, and alongside lay the beam which had been brought from the disused mine to jack up the canted lorry.

Around the shafts in this particular place the grass then showed no trace of human passage. Koptiaki villagers did not come that way as a rule. The place had been well selected. But the murderers forgot the habits of the peasant, especially the haymakers and fisherfolk.

Nastasia Z. left the village at dawn with her son and daughter-in-law. They approached the gruesome procession just as it was turning off the road. Two horsemen rode up to them. One wore a sailor's uniform. Nastasia knew him—he was a Verkb-Issetsk resident—Vaganov. The latter yelled out: "Turn back!" and coming abreast of the peasant cart brandished a revolver at Nastasia's head. Frightened, the peasant woman pulled her horse round so sharply that the cart almost upset, Vaganov rode alongside, still pointing his weapon and shouting "Don't look around or I shoot. . . ." After chasing them about a mile towards the village, Vaganov rode back.

The peasant had not been able in the faint light to make out clearly what was behind Vaganov. "Something long and grey, like a heap," was all that they could distinguish. The *baba* (peasant woman) concluded that it was the Red Guard army marching to Koptiaki. Urging her horse onward, she immediately roused the whole village, informing the *muzhiks* that the "army" was coming "with transport and artillery." They listened in consternation, alarmed chiefly for their hay crop. An army coming meant fighting in the neighbourhood, and here it was just the time for mowing. The hay might all be lost.

They discussed the matter long and passionately, then some of the boldest among them, headed by an old soldier, set out to investigate.

On the road they encountered some Austrian war prisoners who were hay-making, and asked if they had seen the army. They replied that quite early, while they were working on the road, some Russian Cossacks had ridden up and driven them away. The villagers became all the more curious to know what it all meant.

Presently, as they came abreast of the mine, they heard horses neighing. Coming to one of the turnings, they saw that the grass had all been crushed and the saplings bent. They were on the point of following this strange trail, when out of the wood appeared a horseman armed with sword, revolver, rifle and hand-grenades and asked them what they were doing. The *muzhiks* put on a bold face, although badly frightened, and asked if the *tovarishch* (comrade) would kindly reassure them, because the whole village was in a state of excitement.

They were graciously informed that there was no cause for alarm. "Our front has been entered at several points. We are merely scouting and practising. Do not be afraid if you hear firing!" They had a friendly smoke together and then the *muzhiks* departed. They had scarcely gone when a report like the explosion of a hand grenade was heard, and then a short while afterwards another explosion. Soon after their return to the village the same horseman appeared "to tranquillise them all," as he explained.

They were reassured about the hay-making, but now arose another matter. Many of the villagers fished in the large Issetsk Lake which spreads its lovely waters in front of Koptiaki. They had obtained a good haul that night and must take it into the city—it was market day (Wednesday) and in the hot weather fish does not keep. But the "Russian Cossacks" were inexorable.

On the city side there was a crowd at the level crossing over the Ural line striving to get to Koptiaki, which being a pretty place attracted many summer residents. These unfortunates, thus "stranded," waited for hours and hours in vain. Some of the railway servants were accommodated with "*benzine*" from the casks of petrol waiting in reserve. The stream of fisher folk and the procession of *dachniks* coming and going enabled the investigation to define very precisely the exact limits of the cordon placed round the wood. It pointed in one direction—Ganina Yama. That was the locality that had to be kept from prying eyes.

The peasants were also the first to discover the place where the bodies were destroyed. Their evidence afforded immense, invaluable service to the investigation; in fact, without them the truth might never have been established owing to the earlier mistakes of the inquiry.

As soon as the cordon was raised, some of the Koptiaki men hastened to the spot where the horses had neighed and the detonations had been heard. They had thought that the Red guards were burying arms. The ashes around the pit suggested something else. They started to scrape; soon they found a cross belonging to the empress and the brass buckle of the *tsarevich's* belt. Some instinct prompted them to jump to the conclusion that it was "the *tsar's*," although they knew nothing of the murder.

There were eight of the *muzhiks* standing round the pit examining with awe the finds that they had made:—"Boys," said one, and he voiced the secret thought of all, "it is just this, they have been burning Nicholas here. That cross can belong only to him. And that buckle, I tell you, is the *tsarevich's*." They crossed themselves in prayer and silently came away. Needless to say, these honest souls promptly handed over the relics to the White authorities.

On my first visit to the burning-mound, I was attracted by an inscription carved on the giant birch that overhangs one pyre. It read:— "T. A. Fesenko" and the date "July 11, 1918," *i.e.,* six days before the murder. A young man sat beside the tree. He was a stranger to me. I took him to be one of Sokolov's agents, especially as outsiders were not encouraged to hover round the iron-pits. I was looking closely at the ground to note where the bodies had been burned and pick up any remaining clues.

The stranger exclaimed:—"You will have to look very hard!" I thought this was a strange remark; the singed and scorched appearance of the ground was, indeed, very noticeable still, although nearly a year had passed. But I encouraged the conversation, suspecting a surprise. The stranger proceeded to give in rather excited tones his conviction that the story of the bonfires and the burning of the bodies was all a myth. "See for yourself! How could they have destroyed all those bodies and left so few cinders!" he insisted.

Of course I did not enlighten him as to the petrol and sulphuric-acid—which so powerfully aided the work of cremation—or the probable scattering of the ashes around and down the pit. I went straight to Sokolov, who was not far away and told him what the young man had said. "That must be Fesenko," was his remark. We walked up to the place. The stranger had resumed his seat beside the birch and appeared to be suffering, Sokolov continued: "Yes, that's the man. He brought Yurovsky to this place. He is just a young fool of a Bolshevist Yurovsky took him because he was in charge of this wood, and he was so proud of escorting a *komisar* that he recorded the visit by carving his name and date on the tree.

"Why then is he at large?" I queried.

"Well, the fact is we hope he may give himself or some of the murderers away. We arrested him and let him go. He haunts this place, and is ever trying to prove that nothing could have happened here!"

I felt rather sorry for the poor wretch. Perhaps he had not suspected Yurovsky's purpose; Yurovsky did not confide such secrets. At all events I gave him the benefit of the doubt, feeling sure that there would be no peace for his tortured mind in this life.

But Sokolov dispelled my sympathy: "The fact is, he touches a sore point. Where are the cinders? That is the question. We have found too few. They must be hidden somewhere. Now Fesenko could not possibly have discovered this weak point in our armour himself. He has probably been put up to it by the murderers or their spies. That is why we let him wander about."

However, Fesenko did not give away himself or his associates.

Not a hundred paces away from the pyres I noticed a little clearing with a comfortable tree-stump. Here one could sit quietly, unseen by the people at the pit's mouth. A pleasant birch and pine grove stretched its fragrant, sonorous maze between this natural arbour and the scene of grisly horror. Here on this stump Yurovsky had sat while his henchmen performed the last act in the tragedy. Beside this seat we found (a year later) egg-shells—the remains of the fifty eggs ordered by Yurovsky from the nuns, ostensibly for the Romanovs. But this fare had not sufficed for the dainty *komisar.* There were also chicken-bones. There were also torn pages from a treatise on anatomy in German (Yurovsky was only a *feldsher,* he knew little about anatomy). And in order that there be no doubt as to the origin of these various clues, it so happened that Yurovsky left behind a newspaper published in German at the very period under discussion full of abuse of the Czechs, accusing them of servile subserviency to the Entente High Command, and treating the war as a slaughter arranged in the interest of capital.

Reference has been made in preceding chapters to the manner in which the Grand Duchesses had concealed their jewels. Two of their confidential servitors, Miles. Tutelberg and Ersberg, came to our camp in the woods to identify the relics. They had sewn up the bodices, buttons, hats, and other receptacles and knew precisely what jewels were on the persons of the victims when the murder took place, it being obvious that during their residence in Ipatiev's house none of the prisoners would venture to undo or change these receptacles, as they were under constant observation. The Grand Duchesses Olga, Tatiana, and Anastasia each wore double-quilted bodices stuffed with jewels weighing several pounds. Olga carried a satchel round her neck with some special gems and wore several ropes of pearls concealed across her shoulders. The manner in which the concealment had been effected misled the first superficial search of the bodies in the house.

We now trace the gruesome picture of the cutting up and destruction of the bodies. First of all the clothes were partly removed. The bodices at once aroused attention owing to their weight. The "ghouls" began to tear them apart. Their contents were spilled on to the ground, and some of the things rolled into the grass or were trodden into the soil of the mound.

But they did not trouble to denude the corpses completely, and began hacking them in pieces on the clay mound that surrounded the pit's mouth, smiting and severing at the same time some of the valuables that still remained. The large diamonds, which had been camouflaged as buttons, have disappeared with the exception of one. They may have been burned with the clothes of the grand duchesses or have been looted. One was found trampled into the clay beside the pyre. Here also was found the empress's emerald pectoral cross. Some of the bullets dropped out of the bodies during the chopping, others while the limbs were in the flames.

Two pyres were used—one near the shaft, the other near the birch tree. After the cremation had been completed the cinders of both pyres were collected and thrown down the shaft of the mine, which had been previously prepared. Ice remains throughout the summer in deep workings like this one. It had been tested by means of hand grenades, and had then been smashed in order that the cinders, etc., should sink to the bottom of the water. Over them a flooring had been adjusted and anchored.

Innumerable witnesses saw the coming and the going of the lorries. The "ghouls" remained in the wood till their task was done. Their shelters and camps were discovered. They were seen leaving—rolling about in the lorry, like men tired to death.

The flooring had deceived all search in the mine. Only when the operations that I have described above had brought all the core of the shaft to the surface everything was explained. The corpse of little Jemmy lay just under the false floor. It had been preserved by the ice. When good Domontovich made this discovery he immediately telegraphed to us. We all realized that the mystery of the bodies had been solved. . . .

There were literally hundreds of clues now available. Sokolov busied himself classifying and identifying them. It would be quite impossible to enumerate them all. Several volumes of the *dossier* are devoted to it. There are the *procès-verbaux* of each "find" and each identification. I give here a brief but accurate summary of the clues:—

(1) A large diamond of the finest water, identified as forming a pendant to a necklace belonging to the empress, valued at 20,000 gold *roubles*; slightly touched by fire.

(2) An emerald cross belonging to Alexandra, identified as a present from the Empress Marie, found by experts to be of high workmanship, valued at 2,000 gold *roubles*; broken and singed.

(3) A pearl earring untouched, having been thrown with some earth down the shaft, recognized as one of a pair always worn by the empress, declared to be of extremely fine workmanship, valued at 3,000 gold *roubles*.

(4) Four fragments of a large pearl and settings, declared to be a pair to (3).

(5) Two fragments of emerald declared by experts to have formed part of a large and very fine stone, severed by some hard and heavy object and trampled.

216

(6) Eleven fragments of emerald.

(7) Thirteen round pearls as of high quality, all belonging to one rope.

(8) Five fragments of pearl, belonging to one large gem of finest orient, severed by a heavy weight or trampling.

(9) Another broken pearl of high quality.

(10) Two fine brilliants declared to have formed part of an ornament of large size.

(11) Portion of a large diamond silver-mounted ornament bearing traces of heavy blows.

(12 to 21) Precious stones—diamonds, sapphires, rubies, almandine, and topazes—and settings, all bearing marks, as experts show, of having been crushed or severed by heavy or cutting objects.

(22 to 28) Articles and appurtenances of apparel, including pieces of cloth identified as parts of the empress's skirt, the *tsarevich's* military overcoat and Botkin's overcoat; six sets of corset steels—(the empress would not permit her daughters or the servants to go without corsets, neither would she herself; Demidova wore them also—that would make exactly six); metallic parts of corset suspenders and fragments of silk and elastic; the *tsarevich's* belt buckle; the *tsar's* belt buckle, both identified; three paste shoe buckles of first-class workmanship, one identified as the empress's, two as belonging to the grand duchesses; a large number of buttons, hooks and eyes, etc., some identified as belonging to the empress's dress, also military buttons corresponding with the uniforms and caps of the *tsar* and *tsarevich*, as made for them by the court tailor in Petrograd.

The appurtenances of female costume were such as the court dressmaker used for the family. There were also parts of apparel such as were used by the tailor who dressed the court servants. The footgear remnants showed strong action by fire. Experts were able, however, to note that they included cork and fine brass screws, both evidences of high-class articles. In their opinion the remnants might well represent seven pairs of boots.

(29 to 41) Exhibits of equal if not greater interest. Among them may be cited:—A pocket case in which the *tsar* always carried his wife's portrait; three small *ikons* worn by the grand duch-

esses, having in each case the face of the saint destroyed as if blows had been aimed at them; the empress's jubilee badge of her lancer regiment; the gold frame of Botkin's eye-glasses; a large spectacle glass such as the empress wore at Tobolsk; remnants of the *tsarevich's* haversack, in which he was accustomed to keep his treasures; several bottles as used for smelling salts, always carried by the grand duchesses, and finally a varied assortment of nails, tinfoil, copper coins, etc., which vastly puzzled Sokolov till somebody, I think Mr. Gibbes, reminded him that Alexis was fond of collecting odds and ends, being of a very saving disposition, like his father.

Then came a number of specially important relics. First, a series of Nagan bullets, some entire but bearing the marks of the rifling, some without the lead core, some in the shape of blobs of molten lead, still unmistakable. Secondly, in the shaft itself, a human finger, two pieces of human skin, and in the clay of the mound many fragments of chopped and sawed human bones, which could still be certified although they had been subjected to the action of fire and perhaps of acid. Experts found that the skin was from a human hand. The finger is described as belonging to a woman of middle age. It is long, slender and well-shaped, like the empress's hand.

Near the shaft was found a set of artificial teeth (upper jaw with plate), identified as Dr. Botkin's. The front teeth were deeply encrusted with mire, as if the body had been dragged face downwards and thereby the teeth, catching in the hard clay soil, had dragged the plate out of the dead man's mouth.

When the first inspection of the death house was made—ten days after the murder—it bore all the traces of having been plundered by people who had first slaughtered the owners. The reader will be able to picture it, but his imagination will not come up to the reality. Amidst this scene of pillage and confusion one felt that a careful hand had destroyed everything that could help the investigation; nevertheless highly important clues came to light, among them a full list of the Red guards who had acted as gaolers, the *tsar's* private cipher which he had hidden away—as if expecting to be able to reclaim it someday.

In the death chamber there was a curious inscription in German, written by a man of some culture—not Yurovsky, therefore, but perhaps one of the two men from the *chrezvychaika* whom he had left in charge of the house on his departure. It was an adaptation of Heine's lines on the fate of Belshazzar:—

Belsatzar ward in selbiger Nacht
Von seinen Knechten umgebracht.

He had omitted the conjunctive "*aber*" which comes in the poet's line after "ward"; and then, having first written "*selbigen*," had changed it to "*seinen*," feeling perhaps that these modifications were necessary to fit the occasion. Perhaps unconsciously he also converted Belsazar (as Heine spells the name) to Belsatzar. The writer was quoting a Jew whose poem expatiates on the overthrow of a Gentile sovereign who had offended Israel. The Book of Daniel is not so explicit. It says:— "*In that night was Belshazzar the King of the Chaldeans slain.*" (Dan. vi. 30.) But the author of the inscription wished to make it "plain" that "Belsatzar" was slain by his own people.

CHAPTER 12

All the Romanovs

The death of Nicholas II. and his family did not suffice for the Soviet plan of "government" with, or without, Germany. Nothing short of extermination of all the Romanovs could satisfy the enemies of "Belsatzar." Whenever the *Tsik* (Central Executive Committee) and the *ckrezvychaika* (inquisition) laid hands on any of the ex-*tsar's* relatives their fate was sealed. It did not matter where the unfortunate princes might be, or what local authority happened to be ostensibly involved—the *Tsik* and Yankel Sverdlov, Red Jewish Autocrat of All the Russias, directed the disposal of them.

It is quite useless for the apologists of Soviet rule to insinuate that local bodies may have committed excesses without the knowledge and approval of the centre; in these murders of grand dukes and a grand duchess—in all 11 persons of the blood Royal—the hand of the Central Government is clearly apparent. Moreover, they were all slain in cold blood, of deliberate purpose; not like the victims of the holocaust at Perm, because a reign of stark terror had been ordained from Moscow.

It is with mind and hand still atremble after reciting the horrors of the cellar and the woods of Ekaterinburg that I take up this tale of woe, all the more pitiful on account of the utter absence of any pretext for the crime—just sordid murder unrelieved by any shadow of political expediency or provocation.

First, I take the case of the Grand Duke Michael Alexandrovich; he "disappeared" before the others—about a month before the *Tsar*—and he was the ostensible heir although he had formally resigned his rights to the people. I have collected all the materials concerning his last days in Perm.

The *Tsar's* brother had remained at Gachina, his usual residence, during the early months of Bolshevist rule. There he was arrested in March, 1918, and sent into exile. His secretary, Nicholas Nikolaievich Johnson, and the former chief of the *gendarmerie* at Gachina, Colonel Znamerovsky, were arrested at the same time and transported together with him, guarded by Letts. Perm was their destination, and in that city they resided for the next two months.

Apart from being under surveillance, the exiles enjoyed comparative freedom. The grand duke took his walks with his secretary. Although suffering from a chronic complaint (gastric ulcers) which required constant exercise and a special diet, he had no cause to complain of his health while in Perm. The fact was many people sent him dainties, such as *sterlets* freshly caught out of the Kama, so that his rooms at the Korolevskie Nomera (King's Inn) were always full of provisions. He felt so well that he seldom had recourse to the medicine for stilling the terrible pains that he suffered during acute attacks of the malady.

Popularity has its drawbacks. The people of Perm did not realise that their attentions to the exile might arouse suspicion among his Red enemies. When things came to such a pass that the *Tsar's* brother found himself running the gauntlet of popular ovations, it became necessary to avoid too frequent appearances in the streets. Znamerovsky warned the grand duke that the Reds at the suburban Motoviliha arsenal were beginning to grow restive and openly agitating against the liberty allowed to the exiles. So thereafter the familiar figure of Michael Alexandrovich in his shabby grey suit and top boots was seen no more, and he took his exercise under the cover of darkness.

The grand duke had left his wife and children at Gachina. Countess Brasova (his morganatic spouse) came to visit her husband in the middle of May. Madame Znamerovskaia had also arrived in Perm. It was a rash step. Countess Brasova had much difficulty in getting away; in fact it was only managed by a stratagem. The *komisars* were told that if they interfered the matter would be referred to Moscow. This frightened them.

Reaching Moscow on the 22nd or 23rd of May Countess Brasova decided to take a still bolder step to save her husband. Conscious of his complete aloofness from politics, she imagined that personal intercession with the Red chieftains would move them to let him go. Of course it was an illusion excusable only in a distracted wife. I mention it because Lenin himself intervened in the matter. It was the lofty idealist of Sovietdom that absolutely refused to permit the departure of

Michael, and thereby assumed responsibility for what happened. Madame Znamerovskaia did not leave Perm. She was there when her husband was shot and later shared his fate. But I am anticipating. Unbeknown to any member of the family or even to N. N. Jackson, Colonel Znamerovsky had conceived a plan of escape which he intended to put into practice, fearing that the Motoviliha workmen might be goaded into violence. I am in possession of the details of this plan, and I can state most positively—in the light of subsequent events—that it was not carried out, nor even attempted.

On the 13th June a telegram reached Gachina from Perm, announcing that "our general favourite and Johnny had been removed by whom and whither unknown." This message was supposed to have come from Znamerovsky—it could have come only from him. The first feeling was one of unmixed joy; then doubts began to arise, and no small anxiety as to the probable repression that would at once fall upon the household at Gachina. Surely enough soon afterwards Countess Brasova was arrested by Uritsky, the bloodstained Komisar of Petrograd, who himself was assassinated two months later by another Jew. After innumerable tribulations, she managed to escape with her children out of Russia.

What had happened in Perm? A despatch from Mr. Alston, the British Acting High Commissioner, reported from Vladivostok, February 13, 1919:—

> Mr. T. has just arrived here. . . . When at Perm he says he lived in the same hotel with Grand Duke Michael and Mr. Johnson, his secretary, who was a Russian. At two a. m. on or about the 16th June he saw four of the Perm *militzia* or police take them off, and he is convinced that they were killed.

Later, it became possible to obtain the evidence of eyewitnesses, which corroborated and amplified Mr. Alston's despatch. The grand duke had two servants with him in Perm, Borunov and Chelyshev. They lived in an adjoining room. Mr. Johnson lived upstairs. Chelyshev escaped and gave the following version:—

At about the date above mentioned (12th to 16th June—he was hazy on this point) he was asleep one night when three men in soldiers' dress, fully armed, entered his room, woke him up and roughly ordered him to lead them to Michael Romanov. In vain he protested that the grand duke was asleep. They threatened him with the Chrezvychaika. He had to comply. He first woke Mr. Johnson. Then he led the way to the grand duke's room. He was asleep. Chelyshev roused him and explained the reason. The grand duke looked at the armed men.

One of them said: "We have orders to take you—orders from the Sovdep."

The grand duke replied: "I shall not come unless you show me a paper."

One of the men then stepped forward and, laying his hand roughly on the grand duke's shoulder, exclaimed: "Oh! these Romanovs! We are fed up with you all!"

Realising that resistance was futile, the grand duke rose and dressed himself. Mr. Johnson had also meanwhile made himself ready, and insisted that the men should take him away as well. After some argument they agreed. Chelyshev declares that he also asked to be taken, but that the men refused.

As the soldiers and their prisoners were going out of the room, Chelyshev remembered about the medicine, and, grasping the bottle, followed, calling out: "Please your Highness, take it with you." He knew that without his medicine the grand duke might be subjected to great and needless suffering. The soldiers roughly pushed him aside and, making some brutal remark about the Imperial family, led the prisoners away. From that moment they were lost to view. Many stories of Michael's escape and of his having been seen at Omsk, at Semipalatinsk, at Chita, at Harbin, etc., have been successively disproved.

Against the version of an escape there are the strongest evidences:— The grand duke would never have been a party to any attempt to evade his gaolers, knowing full well that both the *tsar*—for whom his loyalty and affection were proverbial—and his own family would suffer for him. It may be objected that he was removed against his will by friends in disguise; but this theory cannot explain away their refusal to allow him to take with him a remedy necessary to his health and perhaps to his life. There had been plots to procure his escape—so I have reason to believe; but in every case the plans had been betrayed. Colonel Znamerovsky knew this. He would trust nobody with his plan, but obviously it miscarried, for he was himself to go with Michael, and we know that instead of that he was murdered. The shooting of Znamerovsky followed close upon the grand duke's disappearance.

Chelyshev afterwards professed confidence in his master's escape, but at the time he had no such illusion. In fact, he was convinced then that the grand duke had been trapped, for when he had had time to recover from his surprise, he went to the local Soviet and complained that the grand duke had been kidnapped. He relates that no attention was paid to him at first but that later some semblance of a search was made and quickly dropped.

Regarding the ultimate disposal of the two prisoners, stories circulate just as numerous and varied as the stories of their escape. I need not cite them. It suffices that the Grand Duke Michael, gentlest of men, to whom all thought of power and even of ambition was repugnant, disappeared to be seen no more.

Perm and its vicinity was destined to witness other tragedies full of horror. Many other members of the Romanov family had been interned there including (1) the Grand Duchess Elizabeth, sainted sister of the empress, venerated by grateful Muscovites while Alexandra was disliked; (2) the Grand Duke Sergius Mikhailovich former Master of the Ordnance, and quite remote from politics; (3) Prince Igor; (4) Prince Ioan; (5) Prince Constantine, all three brilliant young men, the sons of the late Grand Duke Constantine Constantinovich, none of them concerned with political matters; and (6) Prince Vladimir Pavlovich Palei son of the Grand Duke Paul and stepbrother of the Grand Duke Dmitri Pavlovich. This youth of seventeen had given promise of being one of the world's greatest poets.

Prince Ioan was married to Princess Elena of Serbia, who had come to the Urals to share her husband's exile. She had been persuaded to go to her country, the Bolshevists hesitating to incarcerate her, and she was at Ekaterinburg when, towards the end of June, she heard that Prince Ioan and the other captives had been put on starvation rations. She decided, come what might, not to leave him behind. Thereupon the Bolshevists arrested her. She was in the prison at Ekaterinburg when the *Tsar* and his family were murdered. In the same prison were some people who had followed the Imperial household into captivity; young Countess Anastasia Hendrykova, Mile. Schneider, the emperor's valet Volkov. (Prince Dolgoruky and General Tatishchev had "disappeared" earlier.) Of course none of them knew anything about the awful happenings in Ipatiev's house.

When the Jewish murderers and their accomplices, the German-Magyar "Letts," had taken wing before the advance of the Whites these prisoners were sent to Perm for future disposal, while they themselves had hurried westward, having helped to accomplish the hellish design of the Jew fiend, Yankel Sverdlov—to exterminate "all the Romanovs." Orders had already preceded them to Perm and the design had been fully accomplished there. The murder of the Romanovs of Perm took place exactly twenty-four hours after the murder of the family in Ekaterinburg.

Here are the bare facts of this new butchery.

The six Romanov prisoners above-mentioned with the grand duchess's companion, the nun Varvara, and S. M. Remes, manager for the princes, were interned in the village school of Alapaevsk, a place in the environs of Penn.

On the night of July 17 (1918) their warders came to tell them the story that Yurovsky had retailed to the *tsar:* that there was danger for them, that the enemy (*i.e.*, the Czecho-Slovaks) were approaching, and that in the interest of their personal safety they would be removed. It was even confided to them whither they were going, namely to the Siniachkhin Works. All unsuspicious, they at once complied. The programme of the murder was here somewhat different. It was not convenient to carry it out on the premises. The party took their seats in the native *korobs* (a small *tarantass*) and were driven north.

When twelve *versts* (eight miles) out the caravan halted in a wood which contained a number of disused iron-ore mines—one sees the similarity of detail in the murderers' plan—and here the unfortunates were slain and their bodies thrown down the shafts.

It was a much cruder performance than that of Ekaterinburg. The actual murderers here were simply Russian criminals, escaped convicts who "worked" for the *chrezvychaika*, the Red Inquisition. They just slaughtered the victims and got rid of the bodies without so much as rifling their pockets.

Meanwhile at the school certain "precautions" were being taken. A pretended "escape" was staged. The school building and its approaches were "faked" to show evidence of combat between the Red Guards and pretended White Guards, and to give verisimilitude to the performance they took a peasant who happened to be locked up in the local gaol, murdered him and placed his dead body in the school to represent the White "bandits."

Mr. Preston, the Consul, telegraphed from Ekaterinburg, October 28, 1918, that on the retaking of Alapaevsk by the White troops on September 28, the corpses of the Romanov princes, the grand duchess and their attendants were found sufficiently preserved to be recognised, and that they were buried in the presence of a great concourse of people.

The discovery had been made, thanks to the resource of a local police agent, whose name I do not give for special reasons. *Post mortem* examination showed that the victims had been bludgeoned to death but must have undergone a prolonged agony before they died. The Grand Duke Sergius was shot through the head, perhaps to put him out of his misery; for the murderers were just butchers who did not seek to torture their victims. There was no refinement of cruelty about them. They were only Russians. It is not true that they threw their victims down the shaft before life was extinct. The autopsy has dispelled that legend. The murderers even exploded hand grenades down the shaft, probably to make assurance doubly sure.

The investigation has clearly established the authorship of these murders. The orders came from Moscow through the same channels that had been used in the murder of the *tsar*—namely, from the Jew Sverdlov to the Jew Goloshchekin, and, as usual, the Russian workman Belodorodov acted as the dummy president of the Ekaterinburg Soviet board—the channel through which Moscow acted in the Urals. These orders were carried out by the leading *komisars* of Perm, among them being the Komisar of Justice Soloviev.

As in the case of the murder at Ekaterinburg, the Bolshevists at Perm followed up their traitorous crime by announcing that there had been a conspiracy. The world was told that the princes had been kidnapped by bands of White Guards. (When the Whites had to evacuate Perm, General Diterichs arranged to have the bodies of the martyred princes removed eastward. They rest in a place of safety—at the Russian Cathedral in Peking).

More than half a year later a crime equally abominable was perpetrated at Petrograd. The victims were the Grand Dukes Paul Alexandrovich, Dmitri Constantinovich, Nicholas Mikhailovich (the historian), and George Mikhailovich. They had been imprisoned for some time without any charge being preferred against them. On January 29, 1919, they were removed to the Fortress of SS. Peter and Paul, and there on the same day without any investigation or form of trial they were "killed by Red Guards with revolvers"—such is the trite information that is available. But the crime of Ekaterinburg and the slaughter of Alapaevsk give a clue as to the authorship of this atrocity. The last of the Romanovs within the power of the Jew-ruled Soviet had passed away. Perhaps, some day, N. A. Sokolov will be able to investigate the crime of Petrograd.

We now approach the end of this long martyrology. The members of whom I am about to speak form part of the Red Terror ordained by the Soviet to avenge the murder of Uritsky and the attempt on Lenin, which took place about a month after the crime of Ekaterinburg.

I referred above to the transfer of certain prisoners from that city to Perm. Volkov, the *tsar's* valet, has deposed that altogether thirty-six persons travelled in the prison train. Among them were Countess Hendrykova, Mile. Schneider, and Princess Elena. They all found themselves interned in the same prison in Perm. Here Volkov met Chelyshev, who had also been locked up, and from him heard the account of the abduction of the Grand Duke Michael. They saw the princess leave. After great difficulty the Siberian Government had managed to rescue her. She did not, of course, know that her husband had been murdered. She thought he had escaped, and went away willingly enough this time.

The Terror had been proclaimed on September 1, 1918. The official *Izvestiya* declared that the "proletariat (*sic*) will reply . . . in a manner that will make the whole *bourgeoisie* shudder with horror." The *Krasnaia* (Red) *Gazeta* announced:—"We will kill our enemies in scores of hundreds. . . . Let them drown themselves in their own blood."[1]

I am quoting Volkov:

> On the night of September 3rd, we were led out of the prison, eight of us. There were Countess Hendrykova, Mile. Schneider, and Mme. Znamerovskaia, myself, and four others. We were surrounded by twenty-two armed guards, part Letts, part Mag-

---

1. "The *chrezvychaika* of Petrograd, presided over by the Jew Peters, proclaimed that "the criminal hand of the Socialist-Revolutionary Party, directed by the Anglo-French, has dared to fire at the leader of the working classes. . . . This crime will be answered by mass terror . . . representatives of capital will be sent to forced labour . counter-revolutionaries will be exterminated. . . .'" Petrovsky, Komisar for Interior, telegraphed all local Soviets, reproving them for "the extraordinarily insignificant number of serious repressions (the hate-laden Jew could not abide the innate kindliness of the Russians) and mass shootings of White Guards and *bourgeoisie*" Petrovsky denounced these "grandmotherly" methods (—). He ordained "all Right Socialist-Revolutionaries must be immediately arrested. Considerable numbers of hostages must be taken from *bourgeoisie* and former officers. At the slightest attempt at resistance, or the slightest movement in White Guard circles, mass shootings of hostages must be immediately employed. Indecisive and irresolute action in this matter on the part of local Soviets will be severely dealt with." Early in September (1918), Zinoviev (Apfelbaum), one of the "cultured" leaders of Sovietdom, publicly declared: "We must win over to our side 90 millions of the 100 millions of population of Soviet Russia. As for the rest, we have nothing to say to them, they must be annihilated." Bolshevism, White Book.

yars.

We had been told that we were to be transferred to another prison; we carried our small possessions. When we saw that they were leading us out of the town, we realised that our last hour had come. It was terribly hard on the ladies. They dragged themselves along with difficulty in the heavy mud. After several miles, we came to a corduroy road with swamps on either side. (It was a sewage farm.) Some of our guards suddenly began offering to carry our bags. I knew that meant that they were going to shoot us directly, so each one wanted to secure his booty beforehand. It was now or never. While they were wrangling over the spoils I made a dash for it.

Volkov leapt the ditch and was scuttling across the slimy waste when the Magyaro-Letts opened fire. He fell just as the first shot rang out and remained lying. They thought he was dead and moved on. He then made another dash and finally got away. After wandering about for forty-three days, he came into the White zone and was saved.

The frightfully mangled remains of Countess Hendrykova and Mlle. Schneider were discovered by us in the summer of last year and committed to the grave in Perm, in full view of the prison windows where they had been fellow captives of Princess Elena.

"Comrade" Petrovsky's accusations were undeserved in Perm. The Red Terror ran a full stream of blood in that region. The peasants, being regarded by Bolshevists as the worst kind of *bourgeoisie*, provided the bulk of the "scores of hundreds" of victims. For details of these horrors I would refer the reader to the White Book on Bolshevism issued in April, 1919.

Respecting Count Tatishchev and Prince Dolgoruky, nothing is known as to the manner of their death. According to Volkov, who was in prison with him in Ekaterinburg, Tatishchev was summoned to the office on or about June 8th, and was there informed that, by order of the Soviet, he was to be deported to the province of Ufa. He was thereupon taken away from the prison and seen no more.

Although secret-service investigation among the Reds strengthens the belief that Michael was murdered, it is a fact that no trace of his dead body has been discovered; and it is, therefore, conceivable that he survived. There are many records of wonderful escapes from Red Guard shooting squads. Volkov is an instance. Chelyshev, the other servant, was twice led out to execution, yet in the end reappeared. If the grand duke was taken away by Russians, the chances of his escape would be naturally greater. But even admitting this happy contingency, the murderous intention of the Soviet rulers remains unaffected.

Prince Dolgoruky remained sometime in the Ekaterinburg House of Detention. He was frequently in communication with the worthy Mr. Preston, trying to relieve the sufferings of the captives in Ipatiev's house. Probably this hastened his end. We know that the British Consul was threatened with death if he "interfered" any more. Dolgoruky disappeared like his senior, the count. Their memories, like the memories of Hendrykova and Schneider, will live through the ages as of those who have been "faithful unto death."

CHAPTER 13

The Jackals

Around the tigers of the Soviet and their feasts of blood hovered the jackals, singly, in twos and threes, and in packs, waiting to snatch some morsel.

It would be impossible to mention all the sorry scavengers that thronged around the Romanovs before and after their martyrdom. I refer only to such of them that affected, one way or another, the course of the tragedy and its investigation.

Chronologically I record the name of Soloviev first, because he figures in the *dossier* as an actor while the family was still at Tobolsk. The depositions of numerous witnesses, substantiated by Soloviev himself, show that he was receiving a salary of *Rs.*40,000 (nominally £4,000) from a banker named X. (well known in Petrograd and reputed to be a Jew), who acted as the chief of the German secret service during the war, having the disbursement of secret funds from Berlin in his hands.

Having married a daughter of Razputin, named Matrena, after the "saint's" death, and formed a connection with Anna Vyrubova, then at liberty in the Red capital, and with other friends of Grishka, this young man, an ex-officer in the Russian Army and former A.D.C. to Guchkov, started on a "mission" to Siberia. Ostensibly he went to his wife's home. His own explanation is that he was interested in the fisheries of the Ob; also that he took money and comforts to Tobolsk to the Imperial family from their friends in Petrograd. He deposes that he handed the money to the priest Vasiliev, also the presents. He accuses the priest of appropriating the one and the other. The priest makes counter accusations.

There appears to be reason to believe that the empress knew of this "mission," and, retaining to the very end all her illusions regarding

Grishka and Anna, gave her confidence to Soloviev as his son-in- law and the associate of Vyrubova. How he repaid this confidence will be seen.

The agent of X. naturally kept him and the Germans informed as to all the happenings at Tobolsk, but one may be quite sure that he did not stop there. Information given to the Germans meant, of course, its communication, when Berlin so desired, to the Bolshevists, its servants. Is it surprising in these circumstances that each of the four separate and independent organizations formed to release the Imperial exiles was betrayed before anything could be attempted?—for the Solovievs were many and the tentacles of X. were far-reaching.

It could not be a coincidence that officers who met Soloviev in Tiumen were arrested by the Reds and "disappeared." Two such cases are recorded in the *dossier*. It is certainly more than a coincidence that before and after the fall of the Kolchak Government he was in mysterious association with persons who were strongly suspected of being German agents, and could give no satisfactory account of the source of his income since he had been cut off from the supplies of X.

N. A. Sokolov found him and Matrena at Chita, enjoying the confidence and support of Maria Mihailovna, the so-called "Queen of Diamonds," who presided over the destinies of the Ataman's household and had a decided finger in the Traas-Baikalian pie. The "Queen" bore a striking likeness to a certain Jewess who had spied on the Russian South Western front in the days of the war. She came in person to release the Solovievs from the House of Detention to which they had been relegated by Sokolov's legal order. Sokolov himself had to flee from Chita to avoid worse consequences.

The priest Vasiliev was of another stamp. His antecedents should have dispensed him from ecclesiastical office. He had killed the sexton of the church where he had previously served. The plea of accident, of which he availed himself to secure a nominal punishment of "penitence," could not engender a proper recognition of his responsibilities. The man was a self-seeker; he saw in the captivity of the Romanovs an opportunity to advance his own and his son's interests. He indulged in all manner of demonstrations of "loyalty"—bell-ringing and prayers—without regard to their effect upon the captives and their gaolers. As a matter of fact, they did much harm to the family.

The accusation brought against him by Soloviev appears to be borne out in part by the discovery of a certain quantity of articles belonging to the Imperial family in his (Vasiliev's) house.

The Czech pharmacist Gaida, commanding their rearguard when they were stopped by orders from Berlin and Moscow, who afterwards entered the service of the Omsk Government, played a sorry part in the investigation of the *tsar's* murder. Immediately after the occupation of Ekaterinburg by the Whites, Gaida requisitioned Ipatiev's house for his personal use and took for himself the room in which the *Tsar* and his wife had lived. The judiciary begged him not to do so, explaining that it was most necessary that the house should not be disturbed, in the interests of justice. They were brushed aside. Gaida threatened violence if they did not leave him alone. They drew up a *process-verbal* on the matter. It is in the *dossier*.

In the light of this incident, it is rather strange to read the Red proclamations denouncing the Czecho-Slovaks as the agents of the counter-revolution who were coming to deliver Nicholas Romanov. Gaida's complete indifference to the Romanovs and their fate was shared by his countrymen, and it is extremely doubtful if they would have behaved better towards the Romanovs than they did afterwards to Kolchak.[1]

Among the spies and officers employed by Gaida, some are known to have been Bolshevist agents. One of the officials of his intelligence branch proved to be the Nikolsky who had behaved so brutally to the exiles at Tobolsk and was afterwards president of the local Soviet. When the Russian officers at Ekaterinburg heard of his previous exploits they killed him, without giving the investigation an opportunity to obtain his deposition.

Another hostile Czech was a certain Zaiêek, a former Austrian officer, who was in charge of an important section of the Intelligence Department. When the former Extraordinary Komisar Yakovlev, .repenting of the part he had played in the removal of the *Tsar* from Tobolsk, came over to the Whites and applied to General Shenik for service, he happened to come into the hands of Zaiêek, who, being a traitor and a spy, took measures to have Yakovlev sent away, perhaps knowing that he had been in the confidence of Mirbach and might give the whole German show away.

The Omsk Government, largely composed of Socialist-Revolu-

---

1. "Admiral Kolchak was surrendered by the Czechs to the Reds at Irkutsk while he was travelling eastward in February, 1920, under the protection of the Allied flags. The order to surrender him was countersigned by the Czech "commander-in-chief," General Janin. Admiral Kolchak was shot soon afterward in a peculiarly cruel manner.

tionaries, gave little encouragement to the investigation. To them the murder of the ex-*tsar* appeared to be a matter of quite inferior interest. The investigating magistrate, being in straits for money, applied to the Governor-General of the Ural, a mining engineer named P——, for a sum of 100 *roubles* (then worth about £1) to provide the monthly stipend of a typist. Being a member of the S.R. party, this high official refused, explaining that in his opinion no inquiry was needed, as it was clearly "a simple case of the shooting of hostages," too common to worry about.

When, at a later stage, this person was making his way eastward in a *luxurious* car stuffed with "loot," the officers of Ataman Semenov searched it, found several millions of Romanov *roubles* (the currency of the old régime, worth even now about 250 to the £) besides gold and platinum, and shot him on the spot as a "speculator."

The investigating magistrate was able to discover the whereabouts of a noted Bolshevist named Ilmer, who had come to Siberia secretly with an important mission from Moscow. He communicated with the Secret Service at Omsk, requesting that an officer should be sent to apprehend Ilmer. But Ilmer did not turn up. It was ascertained that the Secret Service instead of sending the officer had sent a telegram, with the result that Ilmer escaped.

Perhaps the worst enemies of the investigation were in the Ministry of Justice. It being a cardinal maxim of the Kolchak Government that it yielded supreme authority over the Russian dominions pending the convocation of a constituent assembly, the blessed formula consecrated by advanced politicians and adopted as a *sine qua non* by the powers of the *entente*, the Minister of Justice had to be a Socialist-Revolutionary. M. Starynkevich, a lawyer who had been exiled by the former *régime*, fulfilled the necessary requirements.

He persistently and deliberately declined to treat the *tsar's* murder as anything more than an ordinary penal offence and would not appoint a special investigator. The inquiry was therefore conducted casually. A member of the Tribunal of Ekaterinburg without special training in criminal investigation had the case in hand. (Curiously enough he was of Jewish extraction.) The blunders or worse then committed are directly ascribable to Starynkevich.

It was only by, direct and categorical orders from the supreme ruler (Admiral Kolchak) that the appointment of a special investigator (N. A. Sokolov) was assured. But realising that renewed and constant attempts would be made to upset the investigation, Kolchak gave

Sokolov a special warrant of appointment and otherwise supported him in his work. It was very necessary, for all that Omsk would allow him for expenses was Rs.4.50 *per diem* (about 6d.), and when he arrived in Ekaterinburg he had exactly 165 Siberian *roubles* (then about £2) in his possession for all outlays.

Bad enough, this was nothing to what came after. The investigation was frequently embarrassed by the excessive zeal of amateur Sherlocks or Pushfuls. In some cases their thirst for information could not be ignored, as they claimed to make their demands from a high personage friendly to the Omsk Government. In February of last year Sokolov prepared a confidential report for transmission abroad, and handed it to Admiral Kolchak. The next morning it appeared in full in the local organ of the Socialist-Revolutionary Party. The paper was suppressed a few hours later, but, of course, the mischief had been done. The murderers knew exactly how the investigation stood. All the names of the accused and witnesses were printed in full for the whole world to read, and there also was the name of the investigator (Sokolov), whose appointment had been so distasteful to Starynkevich, practically inviting anybody to come and kill him. (A summary of the disclosed information was published in *The London Times* of February 18, 1919.)

This same Starynkevich, now an ex-minister, has lately come out in another "disclosure." He has informed the representatives of Jewry that not a single Jew was concerned in the murder of the Imperial family. It seems almost incredible, but here is the document. It is a letter from the Secretary of the Joint Foreign Committee of the Jewish Board of Deputies and the Anglo-Jewish Association, giving details of an interview with M. Starynkevich. It says:

The minister, in a statement given to me written down with his own hand, and herewith literally translated, declares that:—
On the strength of the data of the preliminary inquiry, the course of which was reported to me every week by the attorney-general, I can certify that, among the number of persons proved by the data of the preliminary inquiry to have been guilty of the assassination of the late emperor Nicholas II. and of his family, there was not any person of Jewish descent.
I put to him the question as to how he explains the fact of General Knox having sent to the British War Office a report to the contrary. M. Starynkevich . . . said that the Russian military circles had vehemently asserted from the very outset that the

assassination of the *tsar's* family was the handiwork of the Jews, and that this point must be established by the inquiry. They started an investigation of their own, and insisted on the whole course of their inquiry being left to themselves. The Minister of Justice had to contend with great difficulties before he obtained that the inquiry should be carried out by the regular organs of his department. Even the impartial investigation did not cease to be hampered by the interference of the military.

Thus, when the First Examining Magistrate, Sergeiev, had failed to discover any trace of Jewish participation in the crime, these military circles vociferously protested against him and insinuated that M. Sergeiev was a Jew himself. This campaign was so violent and persistent that the Minister of Justice had to discharge M. Sergeiev from the case and to entrust the further proceedings to another examining magistrate. His successor (*i.e.,* Sokolov) was likewise unable to discover any trace of Jewish participation in the murder of the *tsar's* family."

I have given this "statement" in full to prevent any subsequent "misapprehensions." M. Starynkevich's record is known to the reader. He shows himself in his written "denial" to be a quibbler. The degree of "guilt" of the implicated persons had not been fully established in the initial stages of the inquiry, but they were known to be implicated and known to be Jews. The names of Yurovsky, Goloshchekin, Safarov, Voikov are in Sergeiev's own *procès-verbaux*, and they were perfectly known by him to be Jews.

It was only natural that the maintenance of Sergeiev, reputed to be of Jewish descent, at the head of the investigation alarmed all who were concerned with the establishment of the truth, but M. Starynkevich carefully conceals another, still more important, reason for their anxiety. Sergeiev was a judge, not an investigating magistrate. He had been deputed to take over the conduct of the investigation from the first magistrate (Nametkin) in the early days of August, 1918, and, contrary to law and to the rules of criminal investigation in Russia as well as in other countries, had continued to conduct the inquiry after the formation of the government at Omsk and despite the fact that fully qualified investigating magistrates were available.

The persistent refusal of the minister to relieve Sergeiev could be understood only in one sense. Not till February of the following year did Starynkevich at last comply with the law, but even then it was not by his own initiative. Soon afterwards he himself had to leave. Hence his complete ignorance of the subsequent course of the investigation. His slurs upon the military are beneath contempt. But on this and on any other points, Sokolov and the *dossier* are here to answer him, if necessary.

CHAPTER 14

By Order of the "Tsik"

The murderers of the Romanovs have been unmasked in the preceding chapters, but not all of them. The parts played by Yurovsky and Goloshchekin are apparent. They were confidential agents of Yankel Sverdlov, the Red Tsar. Other very important personages remained in the background; they were the Komisars Safarov, Voikov and Syromolotov.

I give here a complete list of the names or *cognomens* of the so-called "judges": (1) Beloborodov, (2) Goloshchekin, (3) Sakovich, (4) Voikov, (5) Bykov, (6) Syromolotov, (7) Safarov, (8) Ukraintsev, (9) Kiselev, (10) Vainer, (11) Hotimsky, (12) Vorobiev, (13) Andronokov, (14) Andreiev, (15) Simashko, (16) Avdeiev, (17) Kariakin, (18) Zhilinsky, (19) Chufarov, (20) Yurovsky, (21) Efremov, (22) Anuchin. The above formed the Oblastnoy Sovdep (Regional Council of Deputies), *i.e.*, the representatives for the whole of the Ural region. The board was composed of five members, Beloborodov, the Russian "dummy," as President, and Goloshchekin, Safarov, Voikov and Syromolotov, all four Jews, as members. The "*chrezvychaika*" (inquisition) was "run" by Goloshchekin, Yurovsky, Efremov, Chustkevich and three other Jews.

These "inner circles" are the men who "tried" the *tsar* and condemned him to death, in other words, assumed the duty of carrying out Sverdlov's orders. They sent "compromising" documents to Moscow afterwards: letters alleged to have been surreptitiously exchanged between the *tsar* and officers outside. They are rank forgeries. One of them alludes to "five windows" facing the square, whereas the *tsar's* quarters comprised only two windows on that side, and if the alleged plotters had succeeded in penetrating the double barriers, scaling the house and entering as directed, they would have jumped into a veritable hornet's nest. Besides, how could they hope to escape the

237

machine-gunner on the roof?

This mockery of a trial has been perpetuated by the "fakes" of sensation-seekers and imaginative writers. One enterprising foreigner cabled thousands of words from Ekaterinburg not long after the murder, describing the aeroplanes that hovered over the city—presumably to carry off the *tsar*—and the dropping of bombs, etc., all of which was, of course, rank nonsense; but he also gave a wonderful account by "the *tsar's* faithful servant," whose name had never been heard of, who told with a wealth of detail how the *tsar* was fetched away "for trial" and how he came back and took an affecting leave of his wife and children before being shot all alone. . . . There are pages and pages of this stuff, and it is all absolute twaddle, but none the less mischievous.

There was no trial of any sort whatsoever. The person named Sakovich in the above list was found in Ekaterinburg afterwards. He admits that he was in the room when Goloshchekin and his friends were talking to Yurovsky just before the murder, but he did not even pay attention to what they said, as the conversation was of such a banal charaacter.

No trial—therefore no verdicts, judgments or other such like formulae, and no reading of any papers to the *tsar* before the family was sent to its last account. This so-called "paper" is an invention inspired by the murderers, to fit in with the Moscow story of an intended trial. The only "paper" concocted by the murderers was the "Decision" as to the "execution." At the Soviet headquarters in Ekaterinburg numerous drafts of this document were afterwards discovered and figure in the *dossier*. They show how troubled the murderers were to invent an appropriate lie for approval by Moscow.

Why was the *tsar* moved from Tobolsk and why was he not brought to Moscow, as Yakovlev had been instructed? It is absurd on the face of it to hint that the Ural Regional Sovdep was over-riding the decisions of Moscow. We have just seen that the virtual rulers of the Ural were Yankel Sverdlov's fellow-Jews and associates, even subordinates.

An answer is offered by the Soviet organ, of the 4th May, 1918. It explains that it was "owing to alleged indications of efforts being made by local peasants and by Monarchist groups to promote escape." We trace here the handiwork of Soloviev and Vasiliev. And it adds: "The regional Soviet of the Urals are charged with surveillance over the Imperial family" (*The London Times*, May 6, 1918).

But while this answer goes a certain way, and definitely involves the responsibility of the Moscow government for all that happened in the

Urals, it by no means tells the whole truth. The inside history of Yakovlev's mission has been explained. Yakovlev was the agent of Sverdlov. But Sverdlov as president of the *Tsik* [2] was over the foreign as well as the domestic affairs of Sovietdom, being in fact Prime Minister. Now Sverdlov had been a paid agent of Germany and was still in the closest touch and relationship with Mirbach. The *tsar's* own definition of Yakovlev's mission was unquestionably right, in substance, if not in detail: to obtain his endorsement of the Treaty of Brest-Litovsk.

The Soviet organs published long accounts of Yakovlev's journey. In these he is falsely described as the representative of the Sovnarkom, *i.e.*, of Lenin's parliament. That was merely to cover up the tracks. Yakovlev is quoted as speaking of Nicholas Romanov as a pleasant enough person, but of "extraordinarily limited intellect." He was not clever enough to realise the advantages that were offered to him.

The Germans, of course, were extremely displeased by this *contretemps*, more especially as it came in conjunction with the failure of their plan to nobble the Russian *intelligentzia* and with their aid to set up the "new government" that Ludendorff craved. One of Mirbach's chief assistants, a Dr. Ritzier, then remarked to one of these Russians that "the Bolsheviks were still necessary." A few months later the Red terror avenged the slight inflicted upon the German associates of Sverdlov.

Voikov, the Jew, boasted to his "lady" friends in Ekaterinburg after the murder that "the world will never know what we did with the bodies." It was his accomplices that suggested to the remorse-stricken Fesenko that the "cinders were not there." The insolent confidence in the superiority of their "precautions" displayed by Voikov is characteristic of his race.

The murderers invented another story in Perm, of which I have not yet spoken. Their agents gave information that one of the grand duchesses had been seen in the city and that she had been shot during the Terror some months after the "execution" at Ekaterinburg. They were quite positive about it.

They even pointed out the place where "Anastasia" had been buried. The bodies—there were many—were exhumed; the only one that was a young woman's was unmistakably identified by the local police

---

2. Even this high body (the Red Cabinet of Ministers) was, like all Soviet institutions, ruled by an Inner Ring (Presidium or Executive Committee) which was (and is—at time of first publication) invariably composed of Jews, with one or two Russians as lay figures.

239

"FAITHFUL UNTO DEATH"

The above group was taken at Tobolsk during the captivity. All except M. Pierre Gilliard, the French tutor (in the centre), died for their loyalty to the Imperial family. Countess Hendrikova is seated on the right with Mlle. Schneider by her side. Their mangled bodies were found outside Perm. Count Tatishchev (left) and Prince Dolgoruky (right) "disappeared" at Ekaterinburg. Two bodies, supposed to be theirs, were found outside the city, one bearing documents of "citizen Dolgorukov."

THE FAULTS OF THE EARLIER INQUIRY

N. A. Sokolov, pointing to the wall of Ipatiev's house, calls attention to a serious omission made by his predecessor. General Diterichs (seated) listens. The other auditor is M. Magnitsky, Prokuror (Public Prosecutor) of the Ekaterinburg Court. Photograph taken in the garden, beside the terrace.

AT THE GANINA MINE

On the left, Mr. Sydney Gibbes, the Tsarevich's tutor; on the right, looking down the shaft, Mr. Robert Wilton, "The London Times" Special Correspondent. At the bottom of this shaft was a false floor beneath which the ashes of the victims were cunningly concealed. The bodies had been cut up near the shaft and burned on two pyres, one next to this spot.

THE PYRE AT THE BIRCH TREE

N. A. Sokolov, General Domontovich and his A. D. C. pose at the limits of the larger pyre, where most of the bodies and clothing were cremated. Alongside stands the tree with the tell-tale inscription.

МОСКВА

Председателю ЦИК Свердлову
для ГОЛОЩЕКИНА.

Сыромолотов какраз поехал для организации дела согласно указаний
Центра опасения напрасны точка Авдеев сменен его помощник Мошкин
арестован вместо Авдеева Юровский внутренний караул весь сменен
заменяется другими точка.- 4558
Белобородов

4/VII

as that of "Nastia Vorovka" (the thief Nastia)—a well-known criminal.

The Komisar Safarov, afterwards editor of the official *Izvestiya*, wrote an article on the "execution" which figures in the *dossier* as an interesting sidelight on the motives of the crime and its methods. It is only fair that the accused should speak for themselves. I here give a plain, unvarnished rendering of this "defence."

> In the places seized by the Czecho-Slovaks and bands of White-guards in Siberia and the Southern Ural, authority has fallen into the hands of Black-hundred pogromists composed of purest Monarchists by profession. The real intentions of the White-guards of the Quadruple Entente are made plain by the mere fact that at the head of them all, as supreme war-lord, stands the *Tsar's* general Alexeiev, the most devoted servant of Nicholas the Sanguinary, himself a convinced blood-shedder (*palách*). . . . Around Nicholas all the time was spread an artful network of conspiracies. One of them was discovered during the transit from Tobolsk to Ekaterinburg.

(Safarov here suggests that Yakovlev was a traitor, and passes over in silence the whole history of the interrupted journey. This compels the inference, which is borne out by scores of direct evidences that the *Tsik*, *i.e.*, Sverdlov, deliberately sent the Romanovs into a death-trap.) Safarov continues:

> Another plot was discovered just before the execution of Nicholas. The participants in the last conspiracy to deliver the murderer of workmen and peasants out of a peasant-workman's prison clearly identified their hopes with the hope that the Red capital of the Ural would be occupied by Czecho-Slovak-Whiteguard pogomists.
> General Alexeiev wanted to bring over into his Stavka (G.H.Q.)

his own *tsar*." (The general had long been dead when Safarov wrote this article.) "His calculations have not been justified. The people's assizes (*narodny sud*) have judged the All-Russian murderer and anticipated the plans of the counter-revolution. The will of the Revolution has been accomplished although many of the formal aspects of *bourgeois* legal procedure were infringed, and the traditional, historical ceremonial of the execution of 'crowned personages' was not observed. The peasant-workingman's authority here also expressed itself in a form of extreme democratism; [3] it made no difference for the All-Russian murderer and had him shot just like an ordinary robber (*razboinik*). Nicholas the Sanguinary is no more, and the workmen and peasants may with full right say to their enemies: You played your stake on the Imperial crown. You have lost. Take your change—an empty crowned head.

The Russian peasants at Ekaterinburg looked at the matter differently. They caught Vaganov, one of the regicides, and killed him on the spot. It was very distressful to the Investigating Magistrate, but he could not prosecute the peasants: there were too many of them, and they would not have understood. It had appeared to them the right thing to do, to slay the Russian who had laid hands upon the *tsar*.

But Safarov eludes issues he himself raises. Why not have sent the *Tsar* for trial to the capital, to Moscow? Surely, that was the place where the "will of the Revolution" could have been properly displayed! All these wonderful conspiracies of which he speaks made it all the more necessary to send him there and save the Ural Soviet from all responsibility. The approach of the Whites should have caused the local chieftains not to delay one single day. Why not? Because Sverdlov

3. "Here is the way "Democratism" was applied. I cite Bolshevist writers: The "instruction" issued by the All-Russian Extraordinary Commission to all Provincial Extraordinary Commissions (*Chrezvychaiki*) says:—"The All-Russian Extraordinary Commission is perfectly independent in its work, carrying out house searches, arrests, executions, which it afterwards reports to the Council of the People's Commissaries (Sovnarkom) and to the Central Executive Council (*Tsik*). The Provincial and District Extraordinary Commissions are independent to their activities and when called upon by the local Executive Council (Ispolkom) present a report of their work." In so far as house searches and arrests are concerned, a report made afterwards may result in putting right irregularities committed owing to lack of restrains. The same cannot be said of executions. . . .. It can also be seen from the "instruction" that personal safety is to a certain extent guaranteed only to members of the government, of the Central Executive Council (*Tsik*) and of the local Executive Committees (Ispolkom). With the exception of these few persons all members of the local committees of the (Bolshevik) party, of the Control Committees and of the Executive Committee of the party may be shot at any time by the decision of any Extraordinary Commission of a small district town if they happen to be on its territory, and a report of that made afterwards. (From an article by M. Alminsky, *Pravda*, October 8, 1918.)
"Comrade" Bokiv gave details of the work of the Petrograd District Commission since the evacuation of the All-Russian Extraordinary Commission to Moscow. The total number of arrested persons was 6,220. 800 were shot (During about six months.) (From a report of a meeting of the Conference of the Extraordinary Commission, *Izvestia*, October 19, 1918. No. 228.)

had already sent for Syromolotov to arrange the murder...

The cynical references to "*bourgeois* legal procedure" and to "historical ceremonial" will, it is to be hoped, put an end for ever to the legend of a "trial."

Yankel Sverdlov conversed with his agents in Ekaterinburg over the direct wire before and after the murder, giving directions when necessary. They forgot to destroy all evidence of these conversations. When the investigation was confided to experienced and fearless hands, one of the first measures taken was to thoroughly overhaul the records of the Telegraph Office. It yielded astonishing results. I give some of the documents in this and the following chapters.

Here is the record of a conversation between the Red Tsar and, apparently, Beloborodov, the former in Moscow, the latter in Ekaterinburg. This record was written in pencil on the backs of telegram blanks. There are six such blanks. The writing is evidently of one and the same person. It consists of questions asked by Sverdlov and answers thereto. The record was made obviously on the 20th July, three days after the murder. Here it is, textually translated:—

What is heard with you?

The position on the front is somewhat better than it appeared yesterday. It is ascertained that the opponent has denuded all fronts and flung all his forces on Ekaterinburg. Can we hold Ekaterinburg long? It is difficult to say. We are taking all measures to hold it. Everything superfluous has been evacuated from Ekaterinburg. Yesterday a courier left with the documents that interest you. Communicate the decision of the *Tsik*, and may we acquaint the population by means of the text that you know?

At a meeting of the *Tsik* presidium on the 18th it was decided (*postanovleno*) to recognise the decision of the Ur. Reg. Sovdep as regular (*pravilnym*). You may publish your own text. With us yesterday, in all the newspapers was inserted a corresponding announcement. I have this instant sent for the exact text and will communicate it to you (*tebié, i.e.*, to thee. Sverdlov is speaking to an inferior).

This moment I shall hand over the exact text of our publication. . . .

I do not reproduce it. There is no need. The "wireless" printed in *The London Times* of July 22, 1918, is the exact and accurate transla-

246

tion of the text given in this conversation recorded in Ekaterinburg two days previously. (The Moscow and the Ekaterinburg texts are given in Chapter 10.) What better evidence could be found of the genuineness of the above record? It stops there. But it tells us volumes. It is the language of conspirators, of accomplices in a crime, and of a superior whose orders and whose initiative alone count. Yankel Sverdlov assumes his true proportions. He and the Bolshevist Government in which he was omnipotent as president of the Central Executive Committee (*Tsik*) and virtually chief also of the Red Inquisition are forever identified with the murders that have been described in this work. The courier referred to is Yurovsky. We know that he left on the 19th with the plunder and, it is believed, the "'heads." The Whites were beginning to concentrate their forces. That was four days after the "execution."

But why all these precautions? If the people are so anxious to try and to punish their late ruler, why resort to all manner of subterfuges, both in committing the "execution" and in acquainting the people of the death of their "oppressor"? The answer is a simple one: Sverdlov and his associates were not sure of the people. The reason of that is equally simple: they were not Russians; they were Jews. They were "internationalists," repudiating all nationality, yet disguised under Russian names. The Russians in their midst were dupes or dummies. Krassin might come to clear the ground, but Apfelbaum-Kamenev appeared for the serious work. What happened in London in 1920 is comparable in a modest way with the Red mechanism in Russia itself.

Taken according to numbers of population, the Jews represented one in ten; among the *komisars* that rule Bolshevist Russia they are nine in ten—if anything, the proportion of Jews is still greater.

There has been no intention here to ascribe the murder of the Romanovs to a race vendetta: it is the Jewish organisations in this and other countries that have emphasised this aspect of the Soviet crimes by their persistent attempts to prove that no Jews took part in them. Why do they not follow the example of the bold *rabbi* who excommunicated Laiba Braunstein, alias Leo Trotsky, for the abominable crimes that Jew had committed against humanity and against civilisation? Why are they trying to screen the sinister Red Tsar Yankel Sverdlov and his host of Jewish assassins—the Isai Goloshchekins, the Yankel Yurovskys?

They feared the Russian people, they feared the Romanovs because they were Russians, they feared Nicholas Romanov because he had been a Russian Tsar and when he refused to be seduced from his loyalty to his people and to the Allies they resolved that he should die—he and all the Romanovs. This resolve was carried out when the advance of anti-Bolshevist forces gave a reasonable hope of sophisticating the crime and avoiding a just punishment.

And so definite was Jew-ruled Moscow on the necessity of the ex-*tsar's* death that a whole month before the murder, the report persisted that Nicholas II. was dead. On the 21st June the Komisar of the Press, named Stark, telegraphed to the Presidium of the Sovdep at Ekaterinburg: "Urgently inform regarding authenticity reports Nicholas Romanov killed"; on the 23rd, Bonch-Bruevich, the secretary of the Sovnarkom (Council of people's Commissaries of which Lenin is president), telegraphed to the President of the Ekaterinburg Sovdep (*i.e.,* Beloborodov): "Information circulating Moscow alleging former Emperor Nicholas the Second killed. Send any available information." A certain Boyard arrived in Ekaterinburg on the 9th July and telegraphed to the French Consul in Moscow: "Am staying meanwhile at British Consulate. Reports about Romanov false."

The Germans knew what they were doing when they sent Lenin's pack of Jews into Russia. They chose them as agents of destruction. Why? Because the Jews were not Russians and to them the destruction of Russia was all in the way of business, revolutionary or financial. The whole record of Bolshevism in Russia is indelibly impressed with the stamp of alien invasion. The murder of the *tsar*, deliberately planned by the Jew Sverdlov (who came to Russia as a paid agent of Germany) and carried out by the Jews, Goloshchekin, Syromolotov, Safarov, Voikov and Yurovsky, is the act not of the Russian people but of this hostile invader.

The Jewish domination in Russia is supported by certain Russians: the "*burgess*" Ulianov *alias* Lenin, the "noble" Chicherin, the "dissenter" Bonch-Bruevich. They are all mere screens or dummies behind which the Sverdlovs and the thousand and one Jews of Sovdepia continue their work of destruction; having wrecked and plundered Russia by appealing to the ignorance of the working folk, they are now using their dupes to set up a new tyranny worse than any that the world has known.

Sovietdom has consecrated three heroes to whom monuments have been erected: to Karl Marx, to Judas Iscariot, and to Leo Tolstoi, the three names that are associated with Revolution, Apostacy and Anarchism; two of them Jews.

When the Jew Kanegisser assassinated the Jew Uritsky, the Soviets ordained a Terror throughout the land. Rivers of Russian blood had to wipe away the stain caused by a Jew who dared to oppose the Jewish rulers of unhappy Russia.

CHAPTER 15

The Red Kaiser

When Yakovlev failed to remove the *tsarevich* from Tobolsk and to "convert" the *tsar*, he disappointed Mirbach more than he disappointed Sverdlov.

The Jews feared the Russians, but the Germans wanted to use them. The Red Tsar planned to exterminate the Romanovs, but the Red Kaiser proposed to reinstate Nicholas.

For a time their respective schemes assumed divergent courses; in the end, Wilhelm's agents realised that they could not dissociate themselves from the Red Tsar, and it was the latter's plan that prevailed. But, morally as well as practically, the German hand which had brought the Jew murderers into Russia controlled and directed the assassins' work. Only when Berlin realised that the Romanovs were irrevocably on the side of the *entente* did they release the hands of the murderers.

The proposal that Yakovlev brought to Tobolsk was much more insidious than the *tsar* understood it to be. Nicholas was not only to endorse the peace concluded at Brest; he was to seize the reins of power with the help of German bayonets and to give his only son to be a lawful *tsar* under German tutelage.

This meant the intervention of Russia in the war again, but on the German side. The Red Kaiser and his staff did not trust their Red agents any more.

While Yakovlev went to Tobolsk as envoy extraordinary of the *Tsik* (but in reality of the German G.H.Q.) the official representative of Germany to the Soviet Government, with which she was in treaty and in virtual alliance, was summoning a secret conference of Anti-Soviet Russians to arrange for the advent of the "new government" desired by Ludendorff.

It was a very pretty scheme, quite on German lines. But it failed at every point. The Germans once more had shown a total incapacity to under-stand human nature. Nicholas scorned the base overtures; the Russian *intelligentsia* displayed, on this occasion, a sound understanding of their duties and interests.[1] The illness of Alexis was another obstacle, though in itself it made no difference.

Sverdlov was not disturbed by Yakovlev's failure to bring Nicholas and Alexis to Moscow. He had his agents everywhere. While Soloviev acted as watch-dog over the captives of Tobolsk so that no stranger to German plans should spirit them away, innumerable Red Solovievs hemmed the captives in. The common herd of the Soviets knew nothing, of course. The strings were cunningly, discreetly pulled from Moscow according to the best methods of Potsdam and the Wilhelmstrasse.

No sooner had Yakovlev started on the terrible rush of 160 miles over bogs and rivers running deep water over breaking ice to Tiumen than the Jewish conclave in Ekaterinburg received its orders—to stop the travellers at all costs. Omsk was at once "stampeded" by the false statement that Yakovlev was trying to arrange a rescue. Yakovlev was really seeking to escape the North Ural net by taking the south Ural route. He did not have to go through Omsk at all, but to change from the Perm on to the Samara line. There was no escaping out of the country by that route then. It could lead only to Moscow. Nevertheless, the train was turned back to Ekaterinburg. Sverdlov did not really want the Romanovs to go further. He could not afford to quarrel openly with his former paymasters, but he was probably shrewd enough and sufficiently well informed to suspect their secret designs.

The talk of a trial in Moscow did not been till much later, when Moscow rumour reported the *tsar* as already defunct, and solely as an antidote to those rumours, as they threatened to upset the plan of murder.

Sakovich, formerly surgeon in a hussar regiment and ex-ultra-monarchist, appertained to the Ural Regional Sovdep as Komisar of Health. He deposed afterwards that he had overheard Goloshchekin, Safarov and Voikov discussing with Beloborodov the alternative of wrecking the train with Nicholas Romanov or of "arranging" an accident. In the former case, the responsibility would be placed on "counter-revolutionaries" trying to effect a rescue. He did not listen to all the details as it did not concern his department. But the Jews did not have to carry out the plan then. The Germans were still in favour

1. See footnote, Chapter 7.

of the survival of Nicholas. The idea was utilised some months later at Alapaevsk. I have a copy of the message sent afterwards to Moscow and Petrograd in which the murderers seriously describe the "rescue" staged by them after the murder as having been the cause of the grand ducal "disappearance."

The Romanovs were suffered to live. A German mission (ostensibly Red Cross) came to Ekaterinburg at the end of May to ascertain all about the life of the "residents of Ipatiev's house," as the Imperial prisoners were officially styled. These spies went straight to Berlin with their report. The Red Kaiser knew full well what torments were being endured by those whom he had professed to cherish, who after all were his kith and kin. He could have saved them at any time. But . . . they would not be saved by him, . . .

Mirbach's death did not, perhaps, introduce any modification of the plan of slaughter. He was assassinated one week before the event. The Bolsheviks declared that his death was an act of provocation committed by their Socialist opponents and gravely resolved that they must not quarrel with Germany, because that would only be playing into the hands of the assassins. This solemn farce had a deeper meaning.

During the summer of that year the Siberian anti-Bolshevist units began to grow in numbers and strength. The Germans had themselves foolishly promoted this reaction by arresting the departure of the Czechs and compelling them to fight. A Siberian Army was quickly springing into existence. It might drive the Red Tsar out of Moscow and thus, instead of an ally or agent there, the Red Kaiser would find himself confronted by a hostile Russia. The war was slowly dragging to its fateful end; every battalion counted. The *entente* knew what the assistance of Russia meant, so the *entente* went to the aid of the Czechs and Siberians.

Ludendorff does justice to this tragic dilemma in his book of *War Memories*.

> The *entente*, realising that they could not work with a government which looked for support to Germany, took action against Bolshevism, and instead of sending these troops (the Czechs) to France, held them up along the Siberian railway on the frontier between Russia and Siberia, in order to fight the government in Moscow. In addition to this, by garrisoning the railway, the *entente* prevented the return of our prisoners of war from Siberia. This was unquestionably a serious loss to us. (Vol. II.)

The holding up of the Czechs was Ludendorff's own work. He is ashamed to admit it, and puts the cart before the horse in pleading that the *entente* displayed such far-sighted activity. Moreover, it was precisely the German-Magyar prisoners of war who, rallying to the appeal of their Kaisers, stopped the departure of the Czechs. Ludendorff is too modest. But his statement makes one point crystal-clear: that in the German view the plan to get rid of the played-out Red Tsar, to put a subservient White Tsar in his place, had to be dropped. The Red Tsar might be useful yet. As Dr. Ritzier had remarked: "The Bolsheviks are still necessary."

The usefulness of the Bolsheviks was to be two-fold: (1) to defend the German front in Russia; (2) to prevent the White Tsar from joining the Russian forces of the *Entente*,

This being the story of the *Tsar's* murder, we are concerned chiefly with the second part of Yankel Sverdlov's German programme. How was it to be carried out, so that there should be no possible mistake? Obviously, there was only one way—through death's dark portals. To bring the *tsar* or the *tsarevich* to Moscow would involve risks. The Jews were in a fright; telegrams discovered in Ekaterinburg show that they trusted none of the Russians in their employ. That is why the Romanovs remained in Ekaterinburg.

Four days before Mirbach's assassination, consequently while the Red Tsar had his daily audiences with the representative of the Red Kaiser, Goloshchekin was already in Moscow, had discussed the murder with Sverdlov, and had telegraphed to Beloborodov to send another member of the Conclave to Moscow.

The Germans approved the murder; there can be no doubt on this point. The position held by Mirbach in Moscow, his daily reports from the members of the Red Inquisition, which naturally had the closest connection with the arrangements for the murder, such as the sending to Ekaterinburg of the ten Magyar-German "Letts" as executioners, are conclusive evidences. The Red Tsar and the Red Kaiser were in accord.

But it was absolutely essential that no Russians should be left inside the house where the Romanovs were to die. Whether the Germans assented to the wholesale slaughter that took place remains in doubt. By that time Mirbach had gone to his last account, and the bloodthirstiness of the Jewish murderers perhaps exceeded the German design, and therein may be found a good reason for the report of the "safety" of the family, but the Red Kaiser cannot escape responsibility for the whole crime, any more than can the Red Tsar who planned it and the Soviet *régime* that rendered such a crime possible.

Here is a translation of the original typewritten telegram found in the archives of the Telegraph Office in Ekaterinburg and included in the *dossier*:

Moscow,

To the President of Tsik Sverdlov for Goloshchekin. Syromolotov has just gone for organisation of affair in accordance with directions of Centre. Apprehensions unfounded stop Avdeiev superseded, his assistant Moshkin arrested. Yurovsky replaces Avdeiev. Interior guard all relieved replaced by others, stop. 4558.

Beloborodov.

Below the text in black ink is marked the date: "4/VII" and further, in ink of the same colour: "Telegram received," after which in black pencil is the signature: "Komisar To . . ." (the rest of the name illegible), this representative of the Soviet being in charge of the telegraph office and endorsing all official messages as they were handed in for transmission.

This message needs no explanation. It is a full and crushing confirmation of all that has preceded: Fear of the Russians; preparation of the murder; direction of the plan from Moscow; and eagerness of the local Jews to anticipate the signal for the butchery. The horrible servility of the dummy president Beloborodov is disclosed in all its nakedness. He hastens to assure his Jewish masters that their "apprehensions" are "unfounded." The German-Magyars who had done their best to carry out the Red Kaiser's behest to capture Siberia and to crush any hope of Russia's military revival, they were now called in to consummate the Red Kaiser's plan by murdering the *tsar*.

For all that has been stated in these chapters there is unimpeachable authority. There is the *dossier*. And there is the overwhelming corroboration of the horrible realities that have converted a large part of Europe into a charnel, Russia into a pest-house and the rest of the world into a hot-bed of unrest.

And pre-eminent among the Doers of Evil, murderers and despoilers, has been the Red Kaiser.

When, in 1915, he wrote to the *tsar*, asking him to recall the days when they were friends, and Nicholas, mindful of the bitter lessons that friendship had entailed, replied that those days must forever be forgotten, Wilhelm of Hohenzollern started the machinery that was to sweep out of existence the *Tsardom* and Russia, and the hapless Romanovs.

In the autumn of 1915 there assembled in Vienna the representatives of the German and Austrian General-Staffs to discuss a plan for the promotion of a revolutionary movement in Russia. It was then that all the outlines of the "Russian" revolution were laid down; it was at this meeting that the leading actors in the Red tragedy were chosen: the Lenins and the Sverdlovs and the host of Jewish wreckers, who spent the interval between their engagement and their appearance on the Russian stage in the calm of Swiss resorts, studying and rehearsing their parts.

The money that financed the "Russian" revolution was German money, and—I say it on the strongest evidence which can be corroborated in the German secret archives—*Yankel Sverdlov received a salary from the Germans till November 7, 1917,* when, becoming Red Tsar of All the Russias, he had at his disposal loot unimaginable.

And thus it came to pass that the Germans who slew the *Tsar* and the Jews who organised, aided and abetted the murder each left his mark upon the walls of Ipatiev's house.

CHAPTER 16

Epilogue

Many hundreds of relics were collected in and around Ekaterinburg by the law, and more particularly by the military, officers of the White government. The larger number had no value as clues. They were personal belongings—jewellery, clothing, linen—that had been stolen before and after the murder. By Admiral Kolchak's orders, this property was taken to Vladivostok by General Diterichs in February, 1919, and sent to the *Tsar's* sister the Grand Duchess Xenia as next-of-kin.

Those of the Romanovs who had not been in the power of the Soviets and had succeeded in leaving the country were destitute. The total fortune belonging to the *Tsar* in England amounted to £500.

Two days after the murder, the Soviet government issued a decree declaring all the property and possessions of the Romanovs forfeited to them. This act had a double purpose: to afford any banks holding funds to the credit of the family a pretext for non-payment; to "legitimise" the robbery of the corpses in the wood and the appropriation of the valuables left in Ekaterinburg. The ropes of pearls and the matchless pearl necklaces snatched from the bodies have been the objects of barter on the Continental and London markets. Red missions smuggled in a huge quantity of jewels belonging to the Crown and to the Romanovs personally as well as to other individuals—all "forfeited" in the same manner. Among the relics was a private code that was found in the ventilator of the Ipatiev lavatory. It bore the following inscription in the empress's hand:

For my own beloved Nicky, dear, to use when he is absent from his '*spitzbu*.' Fr. his lovingly, Alice. Osborne, July, 1894.

The German word had been erased and rewritten in Russian! The owner of this little book had evidently prized it above everything else and fearing that it might be taken away from him had hidden it—hoping, no doubt, to claim it someday.

Also among the mementoes from her funeral pyre came a ruby that belonged to the murdered empress. It was identified by her maid who told the following story:

> The emperor gave Her Majesty a ruby ring when she was only fifteen. They fell in love even then. It was at the wedding of her sister the Grand Duchess Elizabeth. After that they thought about each other for eight years. The empress always wore the ruby ring hanging on a chain on her breast.

The spaniel Joy also came to England. Both the dogs that were most highly prized by the Imperial family were of English breeds. Jemmy, who died with his masters, was a diminutive black-and-tan King Charles, so small that he could not mount the Ipatiev stairs unaided.

The sufferings of the Romanovs in Ipatiev's house were so terrible that it is not seemly to misrepresent them, as some writers have done, in sordid fashion. I have the inventory of the house and its contents, signed by Ipatiev and the *komisars*; I have the *process-verbal* of Sergeiev's inspection, made within a fortnight of the murder; lastly, I have the evidence of my own eyes. The house itself contained every comfort and convenience: electric light, excellent stoves, a well appointed bath-room and lavatory, electric bells everywhere, plenty of good and even luxurious furniture. The bath was in working order and, when Sergeiev visited it contained: firewood for the heater, sheets bearing the Imperial monogram and a cake of soap on the rack, besides numerous other signs of frequent usage. The brutal guards, being used to the Russian steam bath, were not interested in this "outlandish" contrivance, and except for their prying and offensive habits did not apparently stand in the way of personal cleanliness.

The story of girlish locks shorn because of the impossibility of other methods of combating dirt and its consequences is not borne out by the evidence. "Combings" of hair of four different hues were found; also some short hair in the bathroom. One would expect to find them. It is stated in the *dossier* that a barber visited the house to attend the *tsar* and the *tsarevich*.

Each member of the family had his or her bed. There were sheets, pillows and blankets. There was a wash-house in the courtyard.

For some reason the house was deficient in crockery and plate and table linen, hence quite needless discomfort was inflicted upon the family at mealtimes. The peasant-guards, inoculated with the anti-*bourgeois* theories, saw no particular hardship in their feeding out of one dish, as they themselves are accustomed to do in the villages.

The torment that was endured by the captives was far worse than any merely physical privations. But one such privation did affect them very grievously: the utter impossibility of seeing anything at all beyond the painted glass of their windows. The youngest Grand Duchess (Anastasia) one day could not brook this privation any longer and managed to open a window in the girls' room. She almost paid for this act with her life. The sentry in the inner hoarding immediately fired, just missing her. The bullet lodged in the window frame. Anastasia gained nothing except a fright. She saw nothing except the hoarding of the sentry, and did not wait for a second shot.

In the room where the Imperial couple and Alexis lived and slept—next to the chamber in which their four daughters were crowded—Alexandra placed a good-luck sign. It was so unobtrusive that Gaida, the Czech commander who forcibly installed himself in this room, probably did not notice it. In pencil she formed the mystic sign of

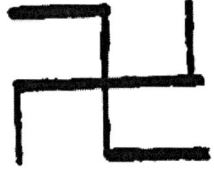

ALEXANDRA'S GOOD LUCK SIGN

swastika and inscribed the date "17/30 April," the day of her arrival in the house.

In the death-chamber in addition to the "Belsatzar" inscription was one that has yet, (at time of original publication), to be deciphered.

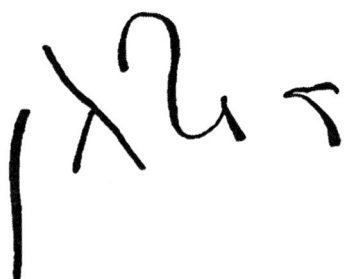

THE MYSTERIOUS INSCRIPTIONS
IN THE DEATH-CHAMBER.

It is in thick black ink, written with an expert hand, and just below, on the window-sill are three groups of figures that may or may not have a meaning.

Some of the persons with whom the reader has become familiar have gone to their last account.

The Russian regicide Medvedev died in prison of typhus early last year. His accomplice Yakimov died in prison of inflammation of the lungs at the end of last year. Their death and burial certificates are both in the *dossier*.

Yurovsky wrote a letter to a certain Dr. A. before he fled from Ekaterinburg imploring him to protect his old mother "who does not share my views but who may suffer simply because I am her son." It is at once an avowal of guilt and a proof that even the most bloodthirsty wretch has some good in him. This man had coolly tortured, murdered and cut up innocent children, and was not able to remove his old mother because he had to take the proofs of his crime to Moscow, yet he does not forget her. . . . Before the Kolchak armies left Ekaterinburg we heard that Yurovsky had been seen in the city. Had he come at great risk to look for his mother? Sokolov had had her removed to Irkutsk. She feared and loathed her son.

Yankel Sverdlov, the Red Tsar, died in Moscow early in 1919. He was knocked on the head by the workmen at one of the Morozov mills, and succumbed to concussion of the brain. Sovietdom was in an uproar. It was officially announced that this "valiant defender of the people's rights" had come to a natural end, by inflammation of the lungs. Nevertheless, the *chrezvychaika* could not allow the Red Tsar to be so dishonoured. Yankel was followed to the outer bourne by thousands of innocent victims offered up in holocaust to his memory.

The mortal remains of the bloodstained agent and associate of the Red Kaiser were exposed to the public gaze and given a pompous Red funeral, and the Theatre Square which faces the building where Yankel had spun his web of blood received a new name, the accursed name of Sverdlov.

None of the Red Jews dared to wear the mantle of Yankel Sverdlov openly. His office was delegated to Kalinin, a "dummy" of the Beloborodov variety, who provided the needful Russian screen to cloak their villainies. For there was no change in the spirit of the Red Jew government of Russia, only an adaptation of methods, a variation of victims—first the *bourgeois*, then the *proletaire*.

The Russians who fought and bled for their country are almost extinct. One of the last who died in the sacred cause was Nicholas II. and the other Romanov victims of the Red invaders, German and Jewish. A remnant persisted to the end. To them the Red Usurpers of Moscow could never be anything except an alien domination.

I recall the night before we left Ekaterinburg. The Reds were approaching, but Sokolov went into the darkness and the rain to obtain the evidence of important peasant witnesses. He told them who he was and the object of his call. They could have locked him up in a cellar and given him up to the Reds. It was to their advantage to do so. By giving him information they incurred great risk. He explained it all to them. "And now, what will you do?" he asked. "Will you help justice? Will you remember that he who is dead was your *Tsar*?" They did not hesitate one instant. They chose the path of honour, of self-sacrifice. They gave their evidence and brought Sokolov on his way.

It is the peasant that will bring Russia back to new life. Alexandra's vision may yet come true, and Nicholas and the Romanovs may not have died in vain.

PART 3

1

The Members of the Imperial Family at the Outbreak of the Revolution

1. Nicholas II, Alexandrovich, Emperor of Russia, oldest son of the Emperor Alexander III, born in Gachino (near Petersburg) on May 6, 1867. Ascended to the throne on October 20, 1894. Married Princess Alice of Hesse on November 14, 1894. At the outbreak of the Revolution was forty-nine years of age.

2. Empress Alexandra (Princess Alice) Feodorovna, wife of the Emperor Nicholas II, born Princess of Hesse, on May 25, 1872. At the outbreak of the Revolution was forty-four years of age.

3. Grand Duchess Olga Nikolaievna, the emperor's oldest daughter, born on November 3. 1895.

4. Grand Duchess Tatiana Nikolaievna, the emperor's second daughter, born on May 29, 1897.

5. Grand Duchess Maria Nikolaievna, the emperor's third daughter, born June 14, 1899.

6. Grand Duchess Anastasia Nikolaievna, the emperor's youngest daughter, born on June 5, 1901.

7. Grand Duke Alexis Nikolaievich, the emperor's only son and heir to the crown, born July 30, 1904.

8. Grand Duke Michael Alexandrovich, the emperor's brother; considered to be the heir to the throne before the birth of Alexis Nikolaievich. born November 22, 1872.

2

Chronology of the Documents

1917

1. March 2/15—Emperor Nicholas II signed in Pskov the act of his abdication, assigning the throne to the Grand Duke Michael Alexandrovich.

2. March 3/16—Grand Duke Michael Alexandrovich refused to ascend the throne before the decision of the Constituent Assembly was made.

3. March 4/17—Arrival of the deposed emperor at the general headquarters at the front.

4. March 7/20— General Kornilov, fulfilling the order of the Council of Ministers, arrested the empress in the palace of Tsarskoe-Selo. All the children had the measles.

5. March 8/21—The arrest of the emperor by a *commissar* of the provisional government.

6. March 9/22—Arrival of the arrested emperor at Tsarskoe-Selo.

7. July 31-August 13—The departure of the imperial family for Tobolsk, according to the orders of the provisional government, under the supervision of the members of the Petrograd soviet of workmen and soldiers' deputies.

8. *August 6/19—Arrival of the tsar* and the imperial family at Tobolsk. The night was spent on board the steamer, before the family moved to the house of the governor.

9. December 29-January 11, 1918—Uprising of soldiers in Tobolsk because of a prayer made by the deacon during the church service for the prolongation of the days of the imperial family.

1918

10. February 12/25—Arrival of an order from Moscow cutting down the allowances of the imperial family to the limits of a soldier's ration. Beginning of the life of privation.

11. March 30-April 12—Arrival of an order from Moscow to increase the severity of the supervision of the imperial family.

12. April 13/26—Departure of the emperor, the empress and Grand Duchess Maria Nikolaievna to Ekaterinburg. The other daughters and the *tsarevich* remained in Tobolsk.

13. April 17/30—Arrival of the emperor and the persons with him at Ekaterinburg. A search of the emperor's belongings.

14. April 18-May 1—Dismissal of all persons attached to the imperial family, with the exception of the physician.

15. May 7/20— The *tsarevich* and grand duchesses left Tobolsk for Ekaterinburg.

16. May 10/23—Arrival of the *tsarevich* and grand duchesses at Ekaterinburg.

17. July 4/17—The last day of the life of the imperial family, and the last walk in the garden.

18. July 5/ 18—At daybreak the emperor, his wife and children were killed in the basement of the Ipatiev house. The bodies were searched.

19. The same day the bodies were taken out of the house and burned.

3

Explanation of Russian Names
Mentioned in the Documents

C. E. C.—Central Executive Committee of the All Russian Congress of Workmen, Soldiers and Peasants' Deputies, the most important institution in the Soviet Republic.

Chrezvychaika—Extraordinary Commission of Inquiry—an institution of secret political police, of the Soviet Republic, which exists in every district town. Through this institution, according to the scheme of the Bolsheviki, the reign of terror is carried out.

Kresty—A jail in Petrograd where political prisoners were confined.

Motoviliha Works—Situated on the River Kama, three miles from Perm. Large production of war material.

Sisserts Mining Works—Fifty *versts* from Ekaterinburg, producing cast-iron, iron, marble, and gold.

Tobolsk—Town on the right bank of the River Irtysh, near the mouth of the river Tobol, formerly a very important town. After the trans-Siberian railroad was constructed it lost its importance being too far from the railroad.

Verkh-Issetsk Iron Works—Situated half a mile from Ekaterinburg.

Znamensky—Ikon of the Holy Virgin— A very ancient holy image given to the Tsar Alexis Mikaielovich (the second *czar* of the Romanoff dynasty) by the Patriarch of Antioch. To the memory of this image the Empress Elizabeth Petrovna built a church in Tsarskoe-Selo.

4

Alphabetical Index of Names

Avdeiev, Alexander, formerly a locksmith. Was *commissar* to the imperial house at Ekaterinburg from May till June, 1918,

Aksiuta, Captain, in command of the First Rifles Regiment in Tsarskoe-Selo, was commanding the detachment of the guards of the imperial family in Tobolsk.

Apraksin, Count. At the outbreak of the revolution was attached, to the empress, being in charge of her affairs.

Benckendorf, Count. Cavalry general. Was grand marshal of the imperial court.

Botkin, Eugene Sergeievich, physician. Stayed permanently with the imperial family from the moment of their arrest till the time they were murdered. Was shot with the imperial family.

Buxhoevden, Sophie, Baroness. Personal maid of honour to the empress. Accompanied her to Tobolsk.

Beloborodov, Alexander. Chairman of the Ural provincial soviet of the workmen's and soldiers' deputies. Following his orders the imperial family were assassinated.

Chemodurov, Terenty Ivanovich; servant to the emperor; arrived with the imperial family at Tobolsk; stayed with the emperor up till the time the imperial family was moved to Ekaterinburg. He died shortly after.

Chkeidze, Member of the *duma*; one of the leaders of the Petrograd soviet of workmen's deputies during the first months of the revolution.

Dmitriev, High *Commissar*, commissioned to Tobolsk by the Omsk soviet of workmen's deputies.

Demidova, Anna, favourite maid of the empress. Stayed permanently with her in Tsarskoe-Selo, Tobolsk and Ekaterinburg. Was shot with the imperial family.

Dehn, Julia, Mme. Wife of first officer on emperor's yacht *Standart*. An intimate friend of the empress.

Derevenko, Vladimir Nikolaievich, physician. Stayed with the imperial family in Tobolsk.

Dolgoruky, Alexander Vasilievich, prince, marshal of the imperial court. Stayed with the imperial family in Tobolsk.

Domodzianz, Ensign, Armenian origin. Was elected by the Tsarskoe-Selo soviet of workmen's deputies to assist Colonel Kobylinsky.

Dutzman, *Commissar* to the imperial family. Commissioned from Omsk by the Siberian soviet of workmen's deputies.

Erzberg, Elizabeth. The grand duchesses' maid. Parted from the imperial family on the way to Ekaterinburg.

Gibbes, Sidney. An English teacher to the grand duchesses and *Tsarevich*. Joined the imperial family in Tobolsk and stayed with them until their arrival in Ekaterinburg.

Gilliard, French teacher to the grand duchesses and the *Tsarevich*. Stayed with the imperial family in Tobolsk and accompanied the *Tsarevich* to Ekaterinburg, where he was dismissed from the imperial family's service.

Haritonov, Ivan. The chef to the imperial family. Was shot with the imperial family.

Hendrykova, Anastasia Vasilievna, Countess. Personal maid of honour to the empress. Came with her to Tobolsk.

Hitrovo, Margaret. Maid of honour to the grand duchesses. Arrived at Tobolsk and was arrested.

Hlynoff, Priest in Tobolsk who replaced the priest Vasiliev.

Hohriakov, a graduate of an ecclesiastical seminary; chairman of the Tobolsk soviet of workmen's and soldiers' deputies; became *commissar* to the imperial family after the resignation of Yakovlev.

Kerensky, Alexander Feodorovich, minister of justice, formerly prime minister of the provisional government.

Kobylinsky, Eugene Stefanovich, Colonel; was appointed commander of the garrison in Tsarskoe-Selo. Later was *commandant* of the palace. Brought the imperial family to Tobolsk, and was in command of the guards until the time the imperial family moved to Ekaterinburg.

Kornilov, Lavr Georgevich, famous Russian general and patriot. A prominent name in the history of the Russian revolution. During the first days of the revolution was made commanding officer of the forces of the Petrograd military district. Was the executor of the order of the provisional government for the arrest of the imperial family.

Korovichenko, Paul, Colonel, military jurist; was made commandant of the Tsarskoe-Selo palace after Kotsebue.

Kotsebue, Captain of Uhlans, commandant of the Tsarskoe-Selo palace. Was dismissed and succeeded by Korovichenko.

Kuzmin, Ensign; was in command of the military forces of the Petrograd district after Kornilov and Polovtzov.

Lvov, George Evgenevich, prime minister of the provisional government during the first three months of the revolution. Was imprisoned in Ekaterinburg at the time the imperial family was kept in Ipatiev's house.

Makarov, Engineer; was attached to the imperial family during their journey to Tobolsk.

Medvedev, Pavel; aged thirty-one; senior guard of the imperial family in Ekaterinburg. Took part in the murder of the imperial family.

Moshkin, Alexander; formerly locksmith; was assistant to Commissar Avdeiev in Ekaterinburg. Was discharged for drunkenness and theft of the emperor's belongings.

Mrachkovsky, Serge; Military *Commissar* in the Red Army. Collected the men for the guard of the imperial family in Ekaterinburg.

Nagorny, Clement Gregorievich; a servant of the *Tsarevich*; stayed with them permanently. After the time the imperial family moved to Ekaterinburg, was dismissed, put in prison and shot.

Naryshkina, Lady of honour to the empress.

Nikiforov, Alexis; senior guard of the imperial family in Tobolsk.

Nikolsky, Alexander; Ensign, member of the Social Revolutionary party. Was assistant to Commissar Pankratov in Tobolsk.

Nikulin, Assistant to Commissar Yurovsky in Ekaterinburg.

Pankratov, Basil Semenovich; was appointed in September, 1917, as *commissar* to the imperial family and was dismissed by the soldiers after the Bolshevik revolution.

Pereverzeff, Paul Nikolaievich; lawyer, replaced Kerensky in the post of minister of justice and resided on account of trouble he had with the Petrograd Bolsheviki. Made the search of the emperor's papers at Tsarskoe-Selo.

Pignatti, District *Commissar* in Tobolsk; occupied this position from the first days of the revolution till the time of the downfall of Admiral Kolchak's government.

Polovtzov, General; took General Kornilov's position as commander of the military forces of the Petrograd district.

Proskuriakov, Philip; aged seventeen, workman; was amongst the guards of the imperial family in Ekaterinburg.

Razputin, Gregory; half monk and half adventurer; was killed a month before the revolution.

Rodionov, Commander of the Letts detachment in Tobolsk; escorted the *tsarevich* and the grand duchesses from Tobolsk to Ekaterinburg.

Sednev, Ivan; servant of the grand duchesses.

Schneider, Katherine, court lecturer; was separated from the imperial family in Ekaterinburg.

Sverdlov, a prominent Bolshevik, chairman of the central executive committee of the All-Russian congress of Soviets of workmen's, soldiers' and peasants' deputies.

Tatishcheff, Ilia Leonidovich, Count, general A. D. C. to the emperor; stayed with the imperial family in Tobolsk; discharged on their arrival at Ekaterinburg; shot.

Tegleva, Alexandra, nurse of the *tsarevich* and grand duchesses; stayed with the imperial family up to the time of their arrival in Ekaterinburg.

Trupp, Alexis; servant of the imperial family; Stayed with them and was shot with the imperial family.

Tutelberg, Mary, maid to the empress; was separated from the imperial family on the way to Ekaterinburg.

Vasiliev, Clergyman of the Blagoveschensky church in Tobolsk; officiated at divine service in the imperial family's house.

Vershinin, Member of the *duma*, accompanied the imperial family to Tobolsk as *commissar* of the provisional government.

Volkov, Alexis; servant to the empress, discharged and arrested on the arrival of the imperial family at Ekaterinburg.

Vyrubova, personal maid of honour and a friend of the empress.

Yakimov, Anataly; workman who was a senior guard of the imperial family in Ekaterinburg.

Yakovlev, Bolshevik *commissar* to the imperial family. Replaced Pankratov on April 9, 1918. Came from Moscow to Tobolsk and went back on account of trouble he had with the Ekaterinburg Bolsheviki, who seized the imperial family.

Yurovsky, *Commandant*, jailer and executioner of the imperial family.

Lightning Source UK Ltd.
Milton Keynes UK
UKOW04n0856021214

242507UK00007B/47/P